The Oppressive Present

The Oppressive Present

Literature and Social Consciousness in Colonial India

Sudhir Chandra

LONDON NEW YORK NEW DELHI

This edition published 2014 in India
by Routledge
912 Tolstoy House, 15–17 Tolstoy Marg, Connaught Place, New Delhi 110 001

Simultaneously published in the UK
by Routledge
2 Park Square, Milton Park, Abingdon, Oxfordshire OX14 4RN

First issued in paperback 2015

Routledge is an imprint of the Taylor & Francis Group, an informa business

© 2014 Sudhir Chandra

Typeset by
Solution Graphics
A–14, Indira Puri, Loni Road
Ghaziabad, Uttar Pradesh 201 102

All rights reserved. No part of this book may be reproduced or utilized in any form or by any electronic, mechanical or other means, now known or hereafter invented, including photocopying and recording, or in any information storage and retrieval system without permission in writing from the publishers.

British Library Cataloguing-in-Publication Data
A catalogue record of this book is available from the British Library

ISBN 13: 978-1-138-66017-5 (pbk)
ISBN 13: 978-0-415-71731-1 (hbk)

For

Shonu

Contents

Prologue to this Edition	ix
Acknowledgements	xxiii
Introduction	1
1. Crushed by English Poetry	18
2. Tradition: Orthodox and Heretical	79
3. Defining the Nation	129
Conclusion	173
Notes	179
About the Author	206
Index	207

Prologue to this Edition

The Oppressive Present Today

♠

> You are he who writes and is written.
> Edmond Jabes

The Oppressive Present seeks to understand the nature of social consciousness in colonial India through contemporary literature. Ostensibly, it covers a short span of roughly the last forty years of the nineteenth century. But the book is informed by a belief that it offers an outline of the consciousness of, at least, the educated in modern India down to the present day.

This is a work of history — social science — which is also an autobiography, a personal and collective autobiography. Readers may sense throughout the text a repressed desire to break into the personal pronoun which, finally, asserts itself in the last five pages, signalling the fusion of the author's present into his colonized forebears' present. That makes it a work of history without a past as its subject of study.

That is not, though, how the book was conceived. It was, indeed, designed to study a past. As it progressed, however, the study began to discover a defining feature of that past. It was a past inhabited by generations of Indians who lived with the cheerless thought that, for all their patriotic pains, they would die as they had been born: in subjection. Moreover, this discovery brought with it slowly the realization that the past was not yet past; that the oppressive present of those subjugated generations was also the present of their freed descendants, who continue to be swayed by what, as a shorthand, is described in the book as hegemonic western discourse.

It is this interweaving of autobiography and history that I wish to highlight in this 'Prologue'.

All institutionalized modes of knowing produce their peculiar protocols of enunciation. So does history. Its protocol is deeply suspicious of the enquiring self. From the selection by individual historians of a particular subject for study to their modes of selecting and reading — constituting — their evidence, it forever worries, as historiography, about what it sees as the vitiating intrusion of the conscious and unconscious of the enquiring self. Little appears of the concerned historian's self during the actual act of history-writing. But that remains part of the operation — it cannot be otherwise — a near absent presence.

The Oppressive Present was published twenty years ago. Why the urge, today, to recall and lay bare its subterranean interweaving of autobiography and history? It stems from a feeling that the exercise will serve to open up the book, especially the continuing contemporaneity of the oppressive present presaged in the title. Should it also serve to valorize the enquiring self's existential experience, the historian's craft will have gained something.

My life as a researcher has been one of captivity to the nineteenth century. The captivity began, unbeknown to me, fifty years ago with my doctoral research which later appeared as *Dependence and Disillusionment: Emergence of National Consciousness in Later 19th Century India* (1975, new edition 2011). That became the prelude to *The Oppressive Present*, which in turn led to *Enslaved Daughters: Colonialism, Law and Women's Rights* (1998, revised edition 2010). The three books were not designed as a trilogy; they are joined nonetheless by a common impulse to probe the same phenomenon and seek a coherent understanding of it. Revealing, in hindsight, the unfolding of a pattern of personal historiographical development, they show that ambivalence was always already the kernel of that understanding.

The Oppressive Present marks a decisive moment in the evolution of that understanding. It breaks away from binary categories and proposes ambivalence categorically as the key constituent of that consciousness. Some unease with binary categories had already appeared in *Dependence and Disillusionment* following its discovery of mutually irreconcilable traits within the emerging national consciousness. What, however, was seen in that irreconcilability was varying mixes of binary categories, not their negation. The unease with binary categories was not conscious enough to pursue the logic of its own discovery. But it survived the euphoria of a maiden publication, to be pursued in further research.

It was a difficult struggle, requiring freedom from habitual obedience to received modes of thinking. It was greatly facilitated by the decision to focus on literature. Reading the literary texts that form the corpus of *The Oppressive Present*, I often found them pointing, simultaneously, in different directions. How was I to understand the resultant equivocations, ambiguities and paradoxes? Even as they suggested the ineffectuality of the either-or language of social science and its modes of binary thinking, it was not easy to be rid of habitual cognitive reflexes. And, to further complicate things, whatever sense I could make of that polyvalence, it had to be articulated in the self-same either-or language.

Through this struggle was the revelatory power of ambivalence finally made evident. It was further corroborated in my *Enslaved Daughters,* which is a very different kind of work. It concentrates on a single concentrate event — a *cause célèbre* occasioned by a young woman's refusal to cohabit with a husband she disliked. Played out within a mere three years, the event sharpened social antagonisms, inflamed public passions, and inclined people to side with either the wife or the husband. Such a study seemed unlikely to provide evidence for ambivalence. But it did. Further, belying the initial assumption that this would be an examination of a moment in colonial Indian history, *Enslaved Daughters* revealed that the moment is still with us. For all the evidence of dramatic changes, post-1947 India has remained essentially the same.

To return to the writing of *The Oppressive Present*, the decision to focus that research on literature was apparently serendipitous. At the same time, there was also dissatisfaction with the archival material and journalistic writings used for *Dependence and Disillusionment*. To that extent, there was something deliberate as well about looking beyond the historians' conventional resources, and something uncanny about relying on literature.

Just when literature was pointing towards a new understanding of history — indeed a new epistemological shift — pure chance conspired to bring about an event without which *The Oppressive Present* would have either not been written or been a different book. The single most emancipatory — indeed subversive — event in my intellectual life, this was a meeting with Jacques Derrida in October 1983. I was in my office at Maison des Sciences de l'Homme (MSH), in

Paris, when Maurice Aymard, Director Adjoint of MSH, came in and said: 'Sudhir, you have to see Foucault and Derrida.' I thanked him, but said that I was not intellectually ready to meet either of them. Aymard smiled and said: 'Well, Foucault can wait, but Derrida you have to meet.' On my persisting that I was not in Paris to have *darshan* of iconic French scholars, he said: 'But Derrida wants to meet you. You cannot disappoint him?' Derrida, Aymard explained, was interested in India, and that was the reason why I must see him. The following day I was told the time — it was in the evening — and the place — Ecole Normale Superieur (ENS) — of my rendezvous with the great man.

The day of the meeting happened to be the day the clocks had been turned back by an hour to usher in the winter time. This caused some confusion and I got late for the meeting. Worrying that I should make Derrida wait, and also that any delay might mean less time with him, I jumped into a taxi to reach the ENS. Just as I was frantically looking at the board in the ENS hallway to check where Derrida's office was, a handsome man rushed in and asked me in English: 'Are you looking for me?' It was, obviously, Derrida, but some mischievous impulse made me say: 'Monsieur Derrida?' He said: 'Oui!' His identity confirmed — my mischief was apparently not lost upon the philosopher — I said: 'Oh yes, I am looking for you!'

Giving me a warm hand-shake and apologizing for being late — citing the confusion caused by the clocks — Derrida walked me courteously to his office on the first floor. After we were comfortably settled and had gathered our breath, he began: 'Monsieur Aymard must have told you that I am interested in your country, but know nothing about it. So I am really grateful that you agreed to see me. I want to know what kind of work you are doing. Please tell me.'

He sat back, indicating that he was ready to listen, and in no hurry. And, indeed, he turned out to be the most attentive listener I have ever met. I spoke for around half an hour, explaining that I was trying to understand the kind of social consciousness that had emerged in India as a result of the colonial connection. I had already written a book in which my focus had been on national consciousness and its public articulation. During that work I had realized that what I called national consciousness was part of a more general social consciousness. Also, that this required me to move beyond well-thought-out expressions of people's ideas, attitudes, beliefs, etc., and, *a fortiori*, look for that which was not so neat, rational and premeditated. Studying social consciousness would also involve understanding, so far as possible, the confusions, uncertainties, irrationalities — indeed the unconscious — of that consciousness. With this end in view, I had decided to go to Indian literature of that period. The little I had done had persuaded me that the attempt was worth making. But I had run into a serious methodological, perhaps epistemological, problem. I was trying to understand history through literature. These were different modes of discourse, and I was unable to resolve the problem of transference from one mode of discourse to another.

A slight change appeared here in Derrida's expression. He was ready to speak. I stopped.

The very embodiment of lucidity, he began: 'Monsieur, I must again say that I know nothing about your country. But I think I have understood what you are doing. I want to ask you one question. You are trying to understand the social consciousness that developed in colonial India by studying contemporary Indian literature. Are you sure that there is some such thing as Indian literature? I must tell you why I am asking this question. Actually I am presently grappling with a similar question at a different level. My question is: Is there some such thing as literature?' (Those interested in Derrida's articulation of this question may like to see his interview — given less than six years later, in April 1989, and aptly titled 'This Strange Institution Called Literature' — with Derek Attridge.[1])

After explaining what he was trying to do, Derrida gave the *mantra* he had prepared me for. He said: 'You say you are concerned about the methodological or epistemological problem of inter-modal transference. As Lacan would put it, each mode of discourse rests on an underlying fiction. Remove that fiction, and the discourse collapses. Where, then, is the problem?'

That done, he passed me a slip of paper on which to spell my name, took out three of his four books that had by then been translated into English — *Of Grammatology*, *Dissemination* and *Writing and Difference* — and presented them to me, each with a gracious inscription. He could not, he apologized, present me the fourth book — *Speech and Phenomenon* — because he was left with only one copy of it.

When, hesitatingly, I asked if he could lend it for me to photocopy, he readily obliged.

A mantra may not always come like a revelation. But even when it does, as it did to me that October evening, it unfolds gradually within the recipient's awareness. My mind, when I walked out of Derrida's office, had learnt that nothing is axiomatic. *The Oppressive Present* was made possible by the mantra about the ultimate fictionality of disciplinary distinctions. It also, though, bears witness to the inadequacy of the internalization of the mantra. The entire text seems constrained, despite the absence of archival material, by the kind of fidelity to evidential veracity that characterizes history-writing. It does not permit itself the imaginative leap that enables literature to aspire to *vraisemblance* instead of being tied to resemblance.

Still literature helps history, as a discipline, move towards *vraisemblance*. Walter Benjamin, in his *Illuminations*, distinguishes between a critique and a commentary to tell those seeking to understand a work of art something which those seeking to understand society may ponder also. He says:

> Critique is concerned with the truth of a work of art, the commentary with its subject matter. The relationship between the two is determined by the basic law of literature according to which the work's truth content is the more relevant the more inconspicuously and intimately it is bound up with its subject matter.... If, to use a simile, one views the growing work as a funeral pyre, its commentator can be likened to the chemist, its critic to an alchemist. While the former is left with wood and ashes as the sole objects of his analysis, the latter is concerned only with the enigma of the flame itself; the enigma of being alive.[2]

If outward events and other manifestations are the wood and the ashes, and social consciousness the enigmatic flame, *The Oppressive Present* has, while grappling with the former, sought to get a sense of the enigma.

I

The serendipitous turn to literature and the fortuitous meeting with Derrida were followed by an extraneous event which also, foregrounded the question of understanding of history. This was the eruption of anti-Sikh violence following Indira Gandhi's assassination on 31 October 1984. Two days into the violence, an exhortation appeared overnight on Delhi's walls. It commanded:

Hindu–Muslim bhai bhai,
Sikhon ki ab karo safai.

In plain English, conveying little of the ominous lilt of the Hindi original, the exhortation read:

Hindus and Muslims are brothers,
Liquidate the Sikhs now.

Unsettling as the sudden eruption of violence against the Sikhs was, looking at the writing on the walls was like having history enter my bones. I was no longer asking questions. I was feeling them. The existential, in that moment, became one with the intellectual. Could the conception of a Hindu–Muslim fraternity — one designed to liquidate the Sikhs — possibly have preceded the actuality of anti-Sikh violence? Even if the idea had been thought of earlier, could it have been publicly stated? Would it not have been dismissed as wild and absurd?

Although related, these questions were different from those that arose in response to the actual eruption of violence. These were: How could the act of assassination catalyze a divide so sharp between two communities that had, despite long years of Sikh militancy, betrayed no signs of drifting apart? What deep antagonism had lain hidden for so long? How reliable, then, was a description of the harmonious relationship between the two communities when that description hid within it a radically different possibility as well? What function could descriptions like 'sudden' or 'unexpected' exercise, apart from veiling and misleading?

It was difficult now to trust even the most unequivocal evidence, and not suspect in it also diametrically opposite latencies. Real-life experience was duplicating the refusal of the world of literature to answer to the binary categories employed to make sense of human reality. Personal experience was pressing for formal incorporation into history-writing, instead of being dismissed as a vitiating presence.

Yet, *The Oppressive Present* remained silent on the subject. Even when, towards its very end, the text broke into the first person singular, it did no more than mention an earlier *auto-critique* of my writing on the issue of 'communalism'. The silence seems the more significant because the entrenched Indian binary of 'communalism' and 'nationalism', along with its twin-like binary of communalism and secularism, has been for me the most difficult to escape. Whatever literature may have done to facilitate freedom from these binaries, I doubt if it would have come without the revelatory force of the existential. Fear of appearing solipsistic and anecdotal, however, prevented any discussion in the book of the interplay between the existential and the intellectual.

It took me another 10 years to be able to trace openly my experience of that interplay. In 2002, when a selection of my writings was published, I wrote an introductory essay called 'The Self and the Work'.[3] Without covering that ground all over again, I should like to recall here one particular experience that highlights the interweaving of autobiography and history as well as the continuance of the book's oppressive present. The experience occurred in Surat a few months after the publication of *The Oppressive Present*. The city was gripped by anti-Muslim violence in the immediate wake of the demolition of the Babri mosque on 6 December 1992. I was at a friend's place when a middle-aged woman, a neighbour, rushed in to announce that a train had been stopped at the city's outskirts and some women passengers raped. That done, the neighbour ran out. Even as my friend was suggesting that this must be a rumour, I caught myself wondering if the violated ones were *Hindu* women.

This happened in a flash, and just at that moment came a guilty disbelief that such a thought should have struck me. From conscious self-shaping to the external shaping of my mental make-up, just about everything had schooled my reflexes into a humane liberal mould. Born in a nationalist family, I had grown up, from as far back as memory goes, in a syncretic milieu. As a young college student, I had lived for a whole year with a noble Muslim couple and been treated like a son. I was further privileged, courtesy two distinguished scholars — Mohammed Mujeeb and Irfan Habib — to be on the faculty of two eminent 'minority' universities, the Jamia Millia Islamia and the Aligarh Muslim University. Could I even in my most self-flagellating moments have imagined the latency of such a thought within my consciousness? What kind of consciousness was mine?

From the moment violence broke out against the Muslims in Surat, I was among those who were doing whatever little could be done in the city's charged atmosphere. Of the kind of things we saw and the tales we heard, I shall briefly mention one. There was this dazed little girl in a relief camp. Frail and barely in her teens, she was standing mute beside an elderly woman. The woman was shouting hoarse, cursing the *haivans* (inhuman creatures) who had done *bura kam* (literally, bad deed) with her little one.

It was when I had been overwhelmed by experiences so overpowering that the thought, if the violated ones were Hindu women, had occurred to me.

Sudden surfacings, like the writing on the walls of Delhi and the flash from my dark depths, are not aberrations. They are reminders that, in the unpredictable structuration of consciousness, non-visibility is not a sign of non-existence. Indeed, the rarer and more unexpected a surfacing, the greater the reason to examine what it could possibly portend.

II

The Oppressive Present was written in an intellectual–political climate that, treating modernity and tradition as dichotomous, valorized the former. Those were also the years of 'globalization' and 'liberalization' which, having begun under duress as part of the IMF-dictated 'structural adjustment', soon became triumphant. Words like poverty and social justice disappeared from the country's dominant political discourse. Gandhi, it seemed during those years, was unlikely to be heard of except for the ritual remembrance on the days of his birth and assassination.

The intellectual–political climate has changed with a rapidity that could hardly have been anticipated then. An unending avalanche of crises and exposes has shaken faith in the triumphal claims of the emerging global regime. India has had more than its share of the resultant suffering and disenchantment. Gandhi is back, albeit more as a comforting escape than a serious civilizational alternative.

Tradition is the subject of scholarly engagement like it has never been in a century.

Yet, the world has remained essentially the same. For all the suffering and disenchantment of the last decade and a half, there is little chance of real alternatives gaining ground. Part of the reason lies in the near impossibility of displacing the existing world-system and its underpinning hegemonic western discourse. Shaken by some catastrophe for a while, people may long for radical alternatives like Gandhi, but the basic faith in the prevailing system remains intact. (This is but a reflection of the universally noticed tendency of human beings to go into temporary detachment immediately upon the death of someone near and dear. Indians have for centuries known the phenomenon as *shmashan vairagya*.)

People in their thousands, to give a random example, may come out on the streets to protest against the 1 per cent in the name of the 99 per cent. Or, diktats of 'structural adjustment', forcing financial austerity on countries in the 'developed' world, may force people in Spain or Greece or Portugal to stage mammoth demonstrations. In doing so the 99 per cent dream of being like the 1 per cent, and the Spaniards, Greek or the Portuguese wish to be like their better-off counterparts in Germany and France. Their demonstrations are not for an alternative world. They are protesting at the glaring inequality of wealth within their own society, not the unsustainability of the prevailing global system.

Whatever be the questions and concerns about it, the system persists. The recent Fukushima Daiichi nuclear disaster is the latest manifestation of the system's imperviousness to subversion. Even as news of the disaster was coming in, experts had started explaining that the affected nuclear plant had been designed to withstand one natural disaster at a time. Unfortunately, two disasters — an earthquake and a tsunami and both enormous — occurred simultaneously. There were also some noises about the obsolescence of the plant, followed by accusations that the rigorous norms prescribed for its maintenance had been disregarded and certain snags reported by experts wilfully ignored. And then, within less than two weeks of the disaster, experts claiming that the latest generation of reactors had already been so designed as to be capable of automatic meltdown in the event of a mishap.

Lay people may, in specific instances, distrust the experts' claim to have a solution. But, except for a hard core of environmentalists and the like, that does not weaken technology's overall claim to be always already in possession of the capacity to solve the problems it has caused. Whatever its scale, every anxiety dissolves sooner or later. Life assumes normalcy. The Japanese elect a right-wing nationalist, Shinzo Abe, as their prime minister in the wake of the Fukushima disaster, and the Indian government sanctions new nuclear reactors.

In the case of India, whose predicament is the focus of *The Oppressive Present*, the impregnability of faith in the existing system, despite discontent with it, is best illustrated by the irony of Gandhi's resurrection. The resurrection rests on an erasure that neutralizes the very reason for remembering him. It erases that irreducible minimum in Gandhi's thought without which he ceases to be an alternative to today's world. A most finished summation of that irreducible comes in a letter from Gandhi to Nehru which is discussed in the 'Introduction'. Gandhi appears there to prefigure the *denouement* of the book. Showing the rejection of his dream in the very moment of freedom, the 'Introduction presages how the vanquished would have their dreams fashioned by the victors. But it does not emphasize that absolute minimum in Gandhi which alone makes him a civilizational alternative. The fact of the rejection of Gandhi's alternative in the moment of the country's freedom was crucial to the book's narrative. Yet, for all the poignancy of the tale, the book and its introduction were being written in a climate in which one could hardly have ventured more than plead for an open-minded consideration of Gandhi.

Things have changed since. Given the way violence, in its myriad forms, has seized control of human lives, it is impossible not to long for non-violence, and to ignore the man who had demonstrated the possibility of delinking war from violence. But it is no longer possible to remember that man only for his non-violence. Even when he was leading that historic non-violent fight against the mighty British Empire, he had warned that non-violence was not possible within factory civilization. The ruthlessness of the factory civilization that lay at the heart of his warning has since become infinitely more anonymous and monstrous. The opponents to be fought are hard to identify. There are no hearts for the non-violent resister to change through suffering and self-denial. It is futile in the face of this monstrous anonymity to remember Gandhi's non-violence and forget the irreducible minimum he prescribed. I must, therefore, reproduce in this 'Prologue' Gandhi's own perfect summation of that minimum:

> ... if India is to attain true freedom, and through India the world as well, then sooner or later we will have to live in villages — in huts, not in palaces. A few billion people can never live happily and peaceably in cities and palaces, or by killing one another, that is, by violence, or through untruth. I have not the slightest doubt that except for this pair (meaning truth and non-violence) the human species is doomed to destruction. We can see that truth and non-violence only in the simplicity of villages. That simplicity depends on the spinning wheel and on the essence contained in the spinning wheel ... The villager in this imagined countryside will not be apathetic. He will embody pure consciousness. He will not lead the life of an animal in a squalid dark room. Men and women will live freely and be ready to face the entire world. The village will not know cholera, plague or smallpox. No one will live indolently, or luxuriously. Everyone will have to do manual labour.[4]

The prescription, except for stray small-scale experiments, today seems even less feasible than it did at the time of its peremptory rejection by the very people who had accepted Gandhi's leadership. At the same time, ironically, it is now most alluring, and no longer seems as absurd and outlandish as it did earlier. Yet, Gandhi's vision does not seem a practical possibility. He tantalizes as an impossible possibility.[5] Meanwhile, the world moves along its ruinous course.

It is difficult to resist thinking of the many today, in India, and the world, for whom the present is as oppressive as it was for the subject generations that this book is about.

III

The Oppressive Present was shaped by the questioning of the ontological distinction between history and other social science disciplines and literature. But it continued to see itself as belonging within the discipline of history. It felt constrained, as a book of history, to justify what it was setting out to attempt, and opened with a justification that sounds more like a defence, if not an apology. A sufficient sense of freedom had not yet developed to overcome concerns about its disciplinary status. Unaware of the irony that the publisher would list it as a work of sociology, the book was at pains to discuss the issue of diachrony and synchrony in order to explain that history, too, could in certain situations be concerned with continuity rather than change.

Looking back, it seems surprising that an explanation needed to be provided at all. Fernand Braudel had already demonstrated the indivisibility of time by showing the inseparability of what he chose to call the *long duree, conjuncture* and *evenement* (event). No matter how a historian decides to study a particular theme, every historical moment must be recognized as encapsulating different times within it. Disciplinary insularity and arbitrariness appear in the meanwhile to have declined, and new disciplinary — even inter-disciplinary and multi-disciplinary — protocols have emerged, creating a rather euphoric sense of openness and freedom. Yet, faith in the reality of the diachrony–synchrony dyad still persists.

In the context of the continuum of the abiding and the changing, it is significant that *The Oppressive Present* sees an epochal change in the wake of the colonial mediation. It assumes the loss of a pre-colonial self and sets out to delineate the reconfiguration of a new, colonized self. But it does not see in that loss a rupture. It charts the growing loss by the new self of the language — the world — of the old self. Alongside of that, however, the new self continues to be tantalized by the vestigial presence of the lost self. That being the case, it is difficult to resist the conclusion that the book is insufficiently critical in its assumption of that pivotal loss. Even while lamenting the *near* impossibility of retrieving that lost world in its own terms, the book should have attempted to pursue that 'near' to get a sense of what the Indian pre-colonial world was like.

A final admission. I have, like the others, learnt much from osmosis, forgetting and misreading. *The Oppressive Present* opens with a chapter which owes its title, and underlying insight, to a misreading. Called 'Crushed by English Poetry', the chapter uses English poetry as a synecdoche for the ensemble of influences that contributed to the colonization of the Indian *imaginaire*. The insight came from a misreading which mistook the Marathi word *kaava* — deception — for *kavya* — poetry. Some careful Marathi-knowing readers were quick to point out the error. They are right. But I will not forego the vivid revelation that probably no other source could have brought me. There may be other misreadings, perhaps no less insightful, waiting to be discovered. This new edition could provide an occasion for that, and for a more critical engagement.

Acknowledgements

♠

As I write, a feeling of dissociation from this work overtakes me: the work is no longer with me and seems no longer mine. The moment of severance brings back to me the pleasure of growing with this project over the years. Despite all the difficulties, anxieties and inadequacies, I was never made anything but happy by it.

This happiness was not merely on account of my relationship with the work. It was also made possible by the generosity of several institutions and individuals. As a project it suggested itself, almost subliminally, during the two and a half years I spent at the Indian Institute of Advanced Study (IIAS). In present shape it began to emerge when I worked at the Centre for the Study of Developing Societies (CSDS) as Senior Fellow of the Indian Council of Social Science Research (ICSSR), and later when a fellowship from the Nehru Memorial Museum and Library (NMML) enabled me to pursue this project further. Ravinder Kumar, Director of the NMML, initially provided me with much needed self-confidence, and later warned me against the risk of running into a *cul-de-sac*, especially with regard to what he and others saw as my excessive reliance on 'ambivalence'.

Then I joined the Centre for Social Studies (CSS), where the sylvan surroundings were motivation enough to carry the work forward; more so after Ghanshyam Shah, then the Director and now a friend, had suggested that the thrust areas of the Centre should be enlarged to accommodate my kind of research. But for these institutions and individuals I could not have ventured on, and 'completed' this work in the limited sense of that word in such a context. My heartfelt gratitude to each one of them.

My exposure to European society and scholars, especially during my trips to France and Germany in 1983 and 1985, enriched my understanding of society in ways that may not always be visible in the text that follows. For supporting these trips I thank the ICSSR, the Maison des Sciences de l'Homme (MSH), and the German Academic Exchange Service. My special thanks to M. Clemens Heller and Professor Maurice Aymard of MSH for assuring me that I could look upon that excellent institution as my own. Also to the South Asia Institute of the Heidelberg University for inviting me over twice. The joy of working in the glorious autumn of Heidelberg was enhanced by the hospitality extended by Professors Dietmar Rothermund, Jurgen Lutt — also Barbara Lutt — and Lothar Lutze, a hospitality that was both warm and lavish.

I filled some of the gaps in the sources that constitute the staple of this monograph, and got a feel of English society and people, when the Charles Wallace India Trust and the Indian Council of Historical Research provided me grants to visit England. I thank both these organizations, and Mr R. E. Cavaliero of the Charles Wallace Trust.

This work has taken me to many libraries, public as well as private, particularly the following: Hindi Sahitya Sammelan, Bharati Bhavan and Hindi Academy in Allahabad; Nehru Memorial Museum and Library, Sahitya Akademi, Central Secretariat Library, especially its Tulasi Sadan Branch, and Marwari Pustakalaya in Delhi; Kashi Nagari Pracharini Sabha; and the India Office Library in London. I recall with gratitude the prompt and courteous service of the staff of these libraries. There is one person whom I must single out for special mention: Manibhai Prajapati, who befriended me at Tulasi Sadan and never spared any effort to meet my demands, not all of which were convenient.

Pandit Shrinarayan Chaturvedi disregarded his old age and showed me, day after day, nineteenth-century Hindi magazines, of which his collection is perhaps the single richest. There was never a day when this grand old man, alas no longer among us, forgot to get me my afternoon tea. Though he has been the subject of some criticism in my monograph, my reverence for him remains undiminished. I gratefully recall, also, the kindness of Pandit Advait Charan Goswami in permitting me access to the private collection of his grandfather, Radhacharan Goswami.

I have benefited immensely from the comments, criticisms and advice of a large number of friends and scholars. It gives me great pleasure to express my sincere appreciation of their contribution to the making of this monograph. Suresh Sharma, Geeta Kapur, Giridhar Rathi, Raju, late Satish Saberwal, D. L. Sheth, Kamlesh, Pradip Kumar Bose, Tanika Sarkar, Shahid Amin, A. N. Pandey, Kumkum Sangari, Kapil Kumar and Bhupen Khakhar readily come to my mind. So does the memory of the late Suresh Joshi, the great Gujarati writer, who explained to me, in spite of his frail health and as only he could, the meaning of Narmad's 'Aryotkarsha'. There are others, like the scholars whose writings have educated me, whom I cannot mention individually. To them my gratitude is no less sincere.

My colleagues from the academic, administrative and support staff at the CSS have provided an ideal atmosphere for academic pursuits. I must mention particularly the friendly patience shown by K. M. Bhavsar, Dayanandan, Chandrasekhar, Nita Desai and Harish Jariwala; they encouraged me to keep changing my draft without fear of exasperating them as they typed its different versions. I cannot thank them too much.

Three friends edited the text in their own characteristic ways and offered many useful suggestions: Alok Bhalla, Gyan Pandey and Basudev Chatterji (Robi). The final draft was edited by Rukun Advani. I profusely thank these co-authors. The faults and deficiencies which remain are mine.

Geetanjali is, in a very special sense, responsible for the making of this monograph.

I wonder what happiness I would have seen at the appearance of this work on the beautiful face of my friend Hetram Chaturvedi — Panditji — had cancer not snatched him away from our midst.

In this edition, I acknowledge some more special debts. The quiet as also the intellectual stimulation that the Nantes Institute of Advanced Studies provides its Fellows have facilitated the writing of the 'Prologue'. Gulammohammed Sheikh has at very short notice chosen from among his large corpus a work to grace the book's cover. Alok Bhalla and David Page have taken the trouble to edit and help improve the 'Prologue'. Finally, at a time when the balance between the book and the market is tilting fast towards the latter, Routledge have risked adopting this book; and their staff have shown exemplary efficiency, patience and courtesy. I feel obliged to them all.

Nantes   S. C.
11 June 2013

♣

Introduction

♠

Historiography tends to highlight change, for it is drawn by the logic of conventional conceptions to those aspects of humans-in-society that reflect movement. Being concerned, by the same logic, with the particular as against the general, historians tend to stress variety and contrast more than uniformity and similarity. However, underlying processes of change and the existence of variety there exist various dimensions of the same social reality that represent continuity and uniformity. Depending upon the questions one asks and the vantage point one chooses, one may discern, within any segment of social reality, apparently contradictory indices of change and continuity, or similarity and variety; apparently contradictory because, inasmuch as they are aspects of the same entity, they are not mutually exclusive. They need to be ordered into one whole.

In seeking to understand the dominant structure of social consciousness in modern India, the present book traces the patterns of synchrony in the face of obvious diachrony. It concentrates on the later nineteenth century, when, following the colonial encounter, the dominant structure of social consciousness crystallized as part of the general shaping of modern Indian society. This structure neither presupposed nor effected an undifferentiated social consciousness that characterized all the dominant sections within Indian society. It consisted, rather, in an arrangement of the constitutive elements of this consciousness. While the relative value of the constitutive elements fluctuated and produced varying manifestations in terms of individual responses to a whole range of issues, I argue that the basic mode of these responses remained the same.

The concept of structure resonates with the idea of synchrony. But synchrony is not stasis. It does not negate temporality. Nor is a structure — a social structure — something eternal. Structures follow temporal courses and come about through a process.

While this more 'dynamic' view of structure informs my study, it does not deal primarily with change, dissimilarity and contrast.

Assuming the existence of such features, and occasionally referring to these explicitly, I delineate the making of a structure of social consciousness that, initially, characterized the literati, and in course of time influenced the rest of Indian society.

The justification for this selective stress constitutes the very *raison d'etre* of this enquiry. Change and variety have been the centre of concern within historical and sociological works on modern India. This has generated some widely accepted stereotypes on the nature of society in colonial and independent India. These stereotypes often appear as a series of binary pairs, in terms of which the whole society is seen as divided. Individuals, groups and movements are, accordingly, categorized as progressive or revivalist, reformist or reactionary, secular or communal, nationalist or communalist, and so on. These pairs are not treated as isolated dyads. They are assumed to be logically and empirically interconnected in such a way that qualities associated with the first category of any pair imply, in an individual or a group or a movement, the existence of qualities associated with the first categories of the other pairs. Thus, for example, those who are seen as progressive are presumed to have been reformist, secular and nationalist; and, in the same way, revivalism is presumed to have been accompanied by reactionary and communal tendencies.

In this normative-descriptive scheme the first categories are invested with positive properties while the counter-categories are charged with negative properties. This follows from the fact that the scheme is part of a larger explanatory dyad in which modernization is historically poised to get the better of tradition. Naturally enough, the first categories in the binary pairs are related to modernization and the counter-categories to tradition. The whole world, in this monolithic framework, is living through a teleology of which the end is not only inevitable but also desirable.

Even though it may often remain unstated, the normative bias of this framework is clear from the valorization of modernity at the expense of tradition. The acceptance of this framework may well demonstrate the predominance of a particular ethical choice in the world as it is today. It could, though, as well be the result of acquiescence in a situation seemingly permitting no viable alternative accounts to oppose the dominant theory. Be that as it may, individuals can be either resigned or enthusiastic vis-à-vis the underlying moral imperialism of the modernity–tradition polarity. But that is a matter of ideological freedom; one ought to ensure that people do actually exercise such a freedom, even if the exercise leads to the despairing realization that choice is only an illusion.

This, however, is more than just an ideological matter, for the modernity–tradition polarity introduces a serious perceptual limitation: the dichotomy is projected back to explain and categorize even those actions, attitudes, beliefs and values that did not rest on, or stem from, such a polarity. After all, people can — as it often happened in nineteenth-century India — view the phenomena separately designated as 'modernity' and 'tradition' without opposing them to each other; in such perceptions there may even be a reversing of the way in which these two constituent units figure in the explanatory framework of modernization. If change is not seen as external to tradition, a precedence is accorded to tradition over change. The word 'change' has not always been synonymous, or associated, with modernity; it has in the past been conjoined equally well with 'tradition'.

This is a mentality which, without being necessarily hostile to modernity, neither treats tradition as a counter-category nor eschews change per se. In fact, even when hostile to modernity, it is not necessarily opposed to change. Thus, tradition and change are not oppositional categories in such a world-view. Change, in this view, does not mean going back to an earlier 'purer' tradition,

Within the available modernity–tradition polarity framework, it is difficult to see this mentality in anything other than dichotomous terms. Ideologically, with its totalitarian moral presuppositions, those who see the world from this polarized perspective can only approve of a change that is in consonance with modernity; the only destiny they envisage for tradition is that it be 'modernized'. At the methodological plane, such a perspective presents in neat oppositional categories the forces that contribute to the coexistence of tradition and change.

There is admittedly some schematic simplification in this description of the modernity–tradition polarity. During its development, especially after it shed its earlier nomenclature of 'Westernization', the modernization approach has acquired the sophistication to recognize the complexity of actual human and social situations. It is, for example, willing to recognize the coexistence of change and persistence and realize that the same person, group of persons or movements may be both progressive and revivalist, reformist and reactionary, secular and communal, and so on. Nevertheless, its basic ideological and methodological blocks are untouched. With all its sophistication, the modernization approach continues to proceed along normatively inspired dichotomous divisions.

If the forces of change and persistence are conceived of as dichotomous, the coexistence of these dichotomies can be explained in terms of either a thematic or a chronological divide. The thematic divide suggests that with regard to certain issues one may be secular, progressive and reformist while in certain other respects the same person may be revivalist, reactionary and communal. The chronological divide explains the same phenomenon in terms of life stages: a person who displays, up to a certain point in life (usually youth and early middle age), the positive traits of the first categories in the pairings used by the modernization framework, may subsequently lapse into their opposites; the lapse may be gradual or abrupt.

Within the context of the modernity–tradition polarity this is an important advance. It imparts to the concept of modernization sufficient resilience to accommodate a variety of situations and details produced by the complex simultaneity of change and continuity. And yet it does not go far enough. It remains incapable of understanding terms that are not its own, or a world-view different from its own. While all understanding is eventually in one's own terms, any encounter with the other, i.e. the alien and the unfamiliar, ought to result in a process of questioning, modifying and extension of these terms, and of incorporating new terms from the other. If one merely attempts to comprehend the unfamiliar by translating it in terms of what is familiar, no proper understanding of the unfamiliar can be possible. One needs to be aware that there are no exact equivalents for the other in one's own language. The finer such an awareness, the greater the possibility of the translation being faithful; and the more faithful the translation, the less the degree of violence and mutilation done to the other.

It is this important epistemological effort that eludes the modernization approach. Given its self-besotted belief in the global character of the teleology that it sees itself as embodying, it is immune to the kind of self-doubt required for such an effort.

If understanding is possible only in one's own terms, what are the terms that we — the English-educated Indian scholars who seek to understand the making of a structure of social consciousness that we have inherited — can call our own and employ in order to understand? The question is not posed as a routine exercise. It is a response to the perception of a danger: the danger is that the terms of the modernity–tradition polarity are also our own terms. This is the blunt answer. There is, consequently, the danger that an understanding in terms of the modernity–tradition polarity will help perpetuate the polarity. But human perception is often marked by an effort to break through the perceptual constraints of given cognitive categories, an endeavour that corrodes procrustean constructs. I hope this book makes some headway in that direction.

This hope must be incorporated within my answer to the question of the terms we use, and this may be put like this: the terms of the modernity–tradition polarity are our terms, but the realization that this is so carries the possibility of varying degrees of freedom from these terms. Such freedom is not unlimited, and we shall soon see that it may not include, for the time being, the possibility of formulating an alternative world-view.

Such freedom is not dependent only on the emancipatory potential of human cognition per se. It is also structured in one's distance from the modernity–tradition polarity that has been bequeathed to us as part of our colonially determined social consciousness. In fact, it is largely because of this distance that the continuing hold on us of the modernity–tradition polarity appears, despite its attraction, as a threat.

In foisting upon our nineteenth century forebears the dichotomy of a West, with its civilizing mission, and an East that needed to be 'civilized', colonial mediation helped create in Indian minds the idea of a traditional India. This initiated a momentous epistemological change. At the plane of collective cultural life, time was fractured into past, present and future; and tradition, plucked out of this continuum, was created selectively out of different points in time past. Alienation from tradition — from one's own culture — lay in the consciousness of the need to belong to this newly constructed tradition.

A similar tension marked the relationship with western culture, the nineteenth-century homologue of modernity. Contrary to received wisdom, the Indian response to the West was not along the exclusive lines of either accepting or rejecting the West. Paradigmatically, this is supposedly represented by Raja Rammohan Roy and Raja Radhakanta Deb. But not even the Derozians and the Young Bengal movement, even if they swore by *The Iliad* rather than the Bhagvad Gita, were in fact the deracine souls they are depicted to have been in our textbooks.

The stereotypical image of Radhakanta Deb as the archetypical figure who rejected the West, intriguingly enough, remains unaffected by the knowledge of his celebrated role in the introduction of English education in early-nineteenth-century Bengal, and by his less known initial support to Ishvarchandra Vidyasagar when Vidyasagar wrote in favour of widow marriage.[1]

Similarly, to take an example from the popular notion of the opposite response to the West, Rev. Krishna Mohan Banerji (1813–85) was a rather extreme Derozian who forsook Hinduism and embraced Christianity. Yet all his life he remained an ardent champion of indigenous cultural values. Interpreting Christianity in traditional Hindu terms, he argued in *The Aryan Witness* that the Bible had been anticipated in the Vedas; also that the sacrifice of Jesus was foreshadowed by Prajapati. True to his Brahman-Pandit family tradition, he edited and wrote works on ancient Indian philosophy and culture. Instead of being cut adrift from his community, he became one of its venerable leaders.[2]

In not being dazed by the West and in remaining anchored to his own cultural moorings, Rev. Banerji was a true representative of Young Bengal. Even as a convert to Christianity — converts being another tribe that were supposedly culturally deracinated — his case was not untypical. Illustrative of this fact are the contributions made to the multidimensional national resurgence by patriotic Indian Christians like K. C. Banerji (1847–1907), Rev. Lal Bihari Day (1824–94), G. M. Tagore (1826–90), Pandita Ramabai Sarasvati (1858–1922), and Rev. Narayan Vaman Tilak (1862–1919). The acceptance of Jesus was for such people a rejection of an unsatisfying religion, but not the renunciation of their own culture.[3]

When even 'rebels' and 'apostates' belie the conventional image of having been mesmerized by the West, it would be labouring the obvious to argue that what Rammohan Roy — the archetypical adversary of Radhakanta Deb — embodied was the best of both the West and of his own culture. And similarly, if even Radhakanta Deb did not symbolize a complete rejection of the West, it is reasonable to assume that the dominant Indian responses to the West, as to traditional culture, need to be seen not in terms of exclusive acceptance or rejection, but as different mixes of acceptance and rejection.

As colonialism progressed, a dual tension with regard to the West and to indigenous culture came about. With the intensification of political conflict against alien rulers, the emotional need for cultural belonging deepened. At the same time, and paradoxically, familiarity with indigenous culture diminished progressively. The state of being organically, and unselfconsciously, related to indigenous culture began to be so transformed that it now required consciously designed links for the relationship to exist between individuals and their culture. This was paralleled by a reverse paradoxical development: as the political confrontation against alien rule gained momentum, an intellectual proximity with the West — the centre of modernization — became greater.

The fate of Gandhi's *Hind Swaraj* (1908) is an ironic epitome of this paradox. Within a decade of formulating his radical critique of modern western civilization, Gandhi became supreme leader of the Indian national movement and, barring occasional eclipses and voluntary withdrawals, he held this position for close to three decades. These were the decades when, during the struggle against the Raj, the conception of a free India took shape. This conception replicated the modernization model and bore little resemblance to the civilizational alternative enunciated in the *Hind Swaraj*, a fact that reflects the growing hold of the West upon the indigenous social consciousness that crystallized through the colonial period.

The depth of this paradox is illustrated by the ineffectuality of Gandhi's final bid to have the *Hind Swaraj* blueprint accepted as the pattern for social reconstruction in free India. Realizing that freedom was round the corner, he broached the issue with his 'heir' Jawaharlal Nehru. In a letter dated 5 October 1945 he referred to a 'major difference of opinion between us'. If the difference really existed, he said, he wanted the fact to be known to people, for otherwise the task of *swaraj* would be adversely affected. The difference related to the vision that these two protagonists of Indian nationalism had of India after independence. The vision articulated by Gandhi in this letter was the same as the one he had envisaged in *Hind Swaraj*. In the materialization of this vision, Gandhi told Nehru, lay the true freedom of India, and through India of the world at large. The village was to be the basic unit of the society so reconstructed; the village as a unit within which everyone knew everyone else. Gandhi warned Nehru not to mistake the village he was referring to with actual villages in the country, for then his vision could not be grasped. 'My village today', he clarified, 'exists only in my imagination'; and he added pertinently: 'Eventually every man lives in the world of his own imagination.'[4]

It was an exasperated Nehru who replied to this momentous letter four days later. The exasperation resulted from Nehru's incomprehension of the idiom and categories employed by Gandhi. Even the basic idea that the village invoked by Gandhi existed only in his imagination, waiting to be realized in free India, was misunderstood by Nehru to mean actual villages with their depressing poverty, squalor, disease and superstitions. Was this what the master wanted to build the new India upon, Nehru asked with self-righteous bewilderment.[5]

Barely five weeks after he had first sounded Nehru on this issue, Gandhi reverted to the question of the concrete meaning that was to be given to Indian freedom. He met Nehru on 12 November 1945 and wrote to him the following day to say that their conversation had made him, 'at least', very happy. Nehru's reaction to this meeting is not known. Gandhi's happiness, however, was restrained by his awareness of a gap between himself and Nehru that, he feared, might widen damagingly. For, while granting that the issue could not be resolved in one meeting, Gandhi admitted that, even as they stood on the threshold of freedom after years of intimacy and political association, he and Nehru might have to part company on the issue of what ought to constitute their country's freedom. For the time being, though, Gandhi hoped there were no great differences between Nehru and him. His hope, like his happiness, was tempered with scepticism. Gandhi felt it necessary to summarize, point by point, the previous day's discussions so that Nehru could tell whether his position had been correctly understood by Gandhi.[6]

Little ensued thereafter. The follow-up meetings hoped for by Gandhi as a sequel to their inconclusive discussions on 12 November

1945 never materialized. This was scarcely surprising in view of Nehru's unconcealed chagrin that Gandhi should have chosen to rake up this issue at a time when, with freedom imminent, the Congress leadership was confronted with a whole range of difficult problems. Gandhi gave up quietly. He did not even press his suggestion, made in the letter of 5 October 1945, for a two-or three-day session of the Congress Working Committee to discuss the issue. Neither his political heir nor the national organization that had for so long looked up to him could comprehend his vision of freedom. Nehru's incomprehension was evidently widely shared.

Before coming to what this incomprehension meant, an answer may be suggested for Nehru's objection to the timing of Gandhi's move. The abortive dialogue of 1945 repeated a similar exchange, in 1928, between the two leaders; except that, on the earlier occasion, their roles were reversed. Being impatient with prevailing inequalities and injustices, Nehru wanted the Congress in 1928 to wage a crusade against the dominant interests within Indian society. He told Gandhi that 'we must clearly lay down an economic programme for the masses with socialism as its ideal.'[7] Gandhi's reply was laconic and decisive:' I am quite of your opinion that some day we shall have to start an intensive movement without the rich people and without the vocal educated class. But the time is not yet.'[8]

As colonialism came closer to ending, Gandhi offered an exposition of freedom from the viewpoint of the poor and the oppressed. On the other hand, having fumed in favour of the adoption of socialism as an ideal at a time when the Congress was not required to implement it, Nehru now fretted that Gandhi saw in the prospect of political power an obligation to define freedom from the viewpoint of the masses. This radical difference in the respective priorities that the imminence of freedom impressed upon Gandhi and Nehru, and subsequently its quick resolution, reflect the turn taken by nationalist ideology with regard to the nature of the sovereign Indian state, as well as social relations in independent India.

Though this aspect of the dominant nationalist ideological concern for the poor is important, what is relevant for our purpose is the fact that the timing of Gandhi's move had nothing to do with the Nehruvian rejection of his blueprint for post-independence social reconstruction. Gandhi's view was rejected not because Nehru, representing the dominant world-view, found the move ill-timed — the matter could, in that case, have been deferred to a more propitious time, and not irrevocably settled, as it was. The Gandhian blueprint was rejected because it was seen as completely out of tune with the dominant world-view. It was rejected without being understood. Its supposed 'absurdity' was sufficient argument against the need to understand it.

Gandhi, who had a penchant for manoeuvring his way through seemingly impossible situations, decided to give a walk-over in this case. It was not as though the issue at stake was not important enough. During his leadership of the national movement, even when he believed the time was not ripe for initiating struggles within a colonially beleaguered society, he had been busy elaborating his conception of a free India that would furnish the world with an alternative civilizational model. Yet, as soon as the time was ripe, Gandhi gave up on the issue. He lost out to the imperialist discourse.

The Nehruvian incomprehension of the *Hind Swaraj* alternative defines the extent to which imperialist discourse had succeeded in controlling the minds of the colonized intelligentsia. Despite its debt to western critiques of modern industrial civilization, *Hind Swaraj* represented an aspect of Gandhian thought that — during its refinement from the first enunciation in 1909 to the final formulation in the 1945 letters to Nehru — had become progressively self-assured in its assertion of an indigenous vision. Gandhi's was a language, an ensemble of assumptions and ideals, that lay radically outside the cognitive and normative field of imperialist discourse.

If the fate of the Gandhian alternative is taken as an index, the hold of the colonial modernization world-view upon the minds of the colonized was all but complete on the eve of Indian independence. All but complete because, despite the effectiveness of imperialist discourse, the structure of social consciousness that crystallized in colonial India was one in which notions of both the 'alien' and the 'indigenous' had been inscribed. This meant that even the summary rejection of the Gandhian alternative marked neither the complete triumph of modernization nor the total rout of tradition. It meant that indigenous assumptions and categories gradually receded from the vision of those who continued to feel drawn towards tradition. It is ironic that the advent of freedom was also the high-water mark of the hold of imperialist discourse upon a dominant section of India's intelligentsia.

Colonialism never sought to perpetuate itself via force alone. It created a hegemonic ideology that rested on claims of its own cultural superiority. It was not, thus, entirely open to Indians to challenge or neglect colonialism at the cultural plane. Operating on that plane, India endeavoured in part to appropriate the ruling ideology — especially its double-edged shibboleths of equality, justice, freedom and democracy — in order to buttress the demand for political rights. But this was too derivative to be a satisfying solution; it also implied an admission of the rulers' claim to superiority. So indigenous elements, too, came to be integral to the Indian challenge to the hegemonic culture of imperialism.

In the final analysis, however, this challenge did not question the fundamental assumptions of western culture. It merely attempted to reverse the placement of the West and India on an international roster. The colonizing West was denied any monopoly of characteristics on the strength of which it claimed superiority; and traditions were discovered in order to be invested with the same 'superior' characteristics that were claimed for itself by the West.

This looked like a counter-offensive. It did more than assert equality between India and the West. Advancing the argument that India had anticipated some of the basic features of modern Western civilization, the Indian challenge staked its own claim to superiority. But to the extent that such claims accepted what the West considered signs of superiority, the counter-offensive also marked a surrender to imperialist discourse. Besides the fact that the quest for tradition implied a degree of alienation from tradition, the very circumstances of this quest defeated its emancipatory impulse. This was because circumstances required it to be cast in the mould of the conquering West. Tradition thus refurbished meant tradition lost.

So complete, in fact, was the power of the imperialist discourse to determine the criteria of valorization, that even when a kind of superiority was claimed for tradition by rejecting the West, the terms by which India's superiority was proposed were those that the West valued. This is exemplified by an argument that began during the later nineteenth century and subsequently became fairly common, more so during the decade and a half preceding independence.

At this time, following the rise of the Congress Socialist Party, a socialist veneer was sought to be provided to the dominant nationalist ideology. The argument was that while the West prided itself on its individualism and the spirit of competition that sustained its progress, Indian culture was organized on a principle of co-operation that resulted in harmonious social existence. The argument was further extended towards the conclusion that whereas the West was fumbling its way to socialism, the same ideal had been already woven into the institutional fabric of Indian culture.

Given the reproductive power of imperialist discourse, which could even convert challenges to its authority into instruments of its own perpetuation, it was not easy to recognize or resist the ways in which it corroded the cultural–intellectual sovereignty of the colonized. Gandhi could do this, but only at an individual and therefore localized plane. Among the few like him who understood the cultural–intellectual dimension of subjection was Krishna Chandra Bhattacharya (1875–1949). Addressing his students sometime between 1928 and 1930, when the demand for *purna swaraj* had fired the country politically, this philosopher stressed the need for 'swaraj in ideas' and cautioned against the subterranean working of the cultural subjugation that came in the wake of political subjection. 'Political subjection', he argued, 'primarily means restraint on the outer life of a people and although it tends gradually to sink into the inner life of the soul, the fact that one is conscious of it operates against the tendency.' But the 'subtler domination exercised in the sphere of ideas by one culture on another' was 'all the more serious in the consequence, because it is not ordinarily felt.' 'Slavery', he continued, 'begins when one ceases to feel the evil and it deepens when the evil is accepted as a good. Cultural subjection is ordinarily of an unconscious character and it implies slavery from the very start.'

Bhattacharya did not support an unquestioning rejection of the 'alien' nor a blind acceptance of the 'indigenous'. Cultural autarky was not his ideal. Cultural assimilation, he believed, 'may be positively necessary for healthy progress and in any case it does not mean a lapse of freedom.' Subjugation of one's culture occurred 'only when one's traditional cast of ideas and sentiments is superseded without comparison or competition by a new set representing an alien culture which possesses one like a ghost.'

Such comparison or competition, Bhattacharya continued, was beyond the 'shadow' or 'galvanic' mind 'induced in us through our western education'. Incapable of the kind of 'genuine creativeness' required for cultural assimilation, the 'galvanic' mind could attempt no more than 'mechanical thinking': 'It dares not exert itself in the cultural sphere.' What needed to be done in the circumstances was to recover the 'vernacular mind' which, under the weight of the 'galvanic' mind, had 'lapsed below the conscious level of culture'.

Though he did not put it so sharply, Bhattacharya came very close to suggesting that the secret of the power exercised by imperialist discourse lay in the universality claimed by the West for its ideas and ideals. Aggressive interests were supported by aggressive ideals, and Bhattacharya felt impelled to expose the falsity of such totalitarian universalism. Arguing in general that, despite their assumed universality, western political and social principles were culture-specific, he singled out for refutation, by way of example, one of the cardinal universals put forward by the West — that of rationalism — and showed that the western mode was not the only mode of rationalism.[9]

I

The recovery of the 'vernacular mind', then, was the solution. But that was also the problem. Already, in the 1920s, when Bhattacharya called for 'swaraj in ideas' the 'vernacular mind' had sunk below the conscious level of culture. It had sunk still deeper by the time Gandhi decided to present for practical acceptance his alternative civilizational model. And today, when we English-educated Indians seek to understand our not-so-remote past, we are faced with the task of excavating that buried 'vernacular mind'.

The loss of traditional categories of thought had advanced far enough by 1945 to make the Gandhian alternative generally incomprehensible. Nor, even now, has the hold of the modernization worldview slackened in any significant sense. To cite a sobering example, even Claude Levi-Strauss (whose work has exposed the ethnocentrism of the human sciences in the West and demonstrated the fallacy of treating the 'civilized' mind as superior to the 'primitive' or 'savage' mind) betrays in his conversations with Charbonnier what may be described as a residual faith in the superiority of science.[10] How, then, do we resolve the dilemma?

A propitious starting point is provided by the recent emergence of a concern for alternatives. This has lent respectability to enquiries into 'tradition', as against modernity, that do not *ipso facto* assign an inferior status to tradition. But despite some open-mindedness, the concern for alternatives really springs from the West, the sanctuary of the discourse with global claims. Indeed, the concern for alternatives there is more pronounced than in the Third World, where, in several quarters, it is seen as part of a western design to keep the post-colonial world backward and amenable to manipulation. So, despite the new quest for alternatives, imperialist discourse is far from overthrown and we are still mainly left with a dominant notion of development; development through large-scale industrial modernization. The only admissible debate is whether this ought to be achieved through capitalism or through socialism.

If even the concern for alternatives, on account of its ulterior western inspiration, is suspect and suggests the dominance of, rather than a liberation from, the discourse of modernization, it is no surprise that enquiries directly influenced by the West perpetuate our intellectual submission to the West. For, while displaying some openness of mind, they see tradition predominantly within categories derived from the West. In other words, there has only been a marginal advance on Nehru's classic rejection of the Gandhian alternative. What happens now is that Gandhi's position is considered in terms of western categories and then this position, instead of being rejected out of hand, is found wanting. This is not the only kind of treatment the Gandhian alternative has received in recent times. The centre of a scholarly attention that cuts across ideological divisions, *Hind Swaraj* has also been studied by scholars who, as part of a larger enterprise to recover tradition, have tried to get inside the Gandhian framework. As part of the same enterprise, and also as the inspiration behind it, some of them have been instrumental in rehabilitating Krishna Chandra Bhattacharya. It is significant that these scholars, who believe that their tradition presents a viable alternative in the world today, are often clustered together as 'non-progressive'. Assuming that there are plausible ideological considerations for such a classification, it cannot be a mere coincidence that 'progressive' scholars have not even attempted anything more than an understanding of their own tradition in western terms.[11]

Important though it may be as a starting point, something more than the will to understand tradition is required. A project involving the recovery of a world that remains ours, despite having been nearly lost to us intellectually, is needed. This should attempt an understanding of the world of tradition in its own terms, although it may thereafter reject that world as anachronistic. Given that the terms we use cannot be too different from those within the modernity–tradition frame, any project to understand tradition in its own terms can hope at best for partial success.

Fortunately, our nineteenth-century forebears retained organic links with their own culture, even as they began to drift gradually away from it. The generations of Indians from Rammohan Roy and Radhakanta Deb to Mahadev Govind Ranade and Bharatendu Harishchandra were more or less steeped in their culture. They were conversant with its classical as well as popular aspects. Though they recognized this distinction, it mattered little to them in actual life because, in the culture to which they belonged, classical and popular elements were inseparably fused.

For example, Bharatendu Harishchandra, who will loom large in this book, had imbibed, through conscious learning and cultural osmosis, the wisdom of scriptural, philosophical and classical literary texts. He was, besides, at home with popular cults, mythology, legends, tales and fables. His vast corpus, comprising a variety of literary forms in both prose and poetry, exhibits a familiarity with the Mahabharata, the Ramayana and an impressive repertory of literary masterpieces from Kalidas, Bhavabhuti, Shri Harsha, Chandrashekhar, Vishakhadatta, Shudrak, Krishna Mishra and others; Bharatendu was equally conversant with contemporary folk forms like the *baraha masa*, *khyal*, *lavani* and *hori*.

The world of later-nineteenth-century Hindi literature, with Bharatendu Harishchandra as its presiding genius, reflected, *mutatis mutandis*, the reality in the rest of the country. Thus, in a survey of modern Marathi literature undertaken at the turn of the century, Ranade hoped that soon 'the national mind' would 'digest the best thoughts of Western Europe with the same intimate appreciation that it has shown in the assimilation of the old Sanskrit learning.'[12]

Ranade's hope was more than fulfilled. Soon, educated Indians were showing signs of an acquaintance with western literature and a learning that was better than their understanding of their own literary and intellectual stock. This happened because of the growing distance from traditional culture, a process which started in Bengal well before Ranade envisaged for the national mind the ideal of a cross-cultural equilibrium.

An upshot of this process is that creative Indian writers today have to make special efforts to employ traditional themes and popu-lar forms — and in the bargain end up, paradoxically, with an avant-garde and elitist literature — while Harishchandra and his generation handled traditional themes effortlessly because they were born in a world of which these themes and forms were organic constituents.

The triumphal course of the imperialist modernization discourse is one of the subjects of this book. A generation, which is the product virtually of this discourse, is seeking to understand the discourse of its ancestors, in their terms, and looking at people who were among the first to be exposed to this discourse. Still one with their own culture, these people faced an alien culture and were forced to adjust. Much happened in their own day that was beyond their ken, but there also happened things that they either consciously chose or were keenly aware of. Irrespective of the extent to which they were conscious of the political and cultural world around them, or of the nature and implications of their own positions, their idiom was predominantly indigenous.

Their idiom produces in our minds resonances that are tantalizingly familiar. The familiar tone, we realize, is not related to the space that colonialism had begun carving out within this idiom. It is related, rather, to the parts of our being that still reverberate to indigenous idioms at a subconscious plane. Some of these we recognize fleetingly — at least some of us do — in those rare moments when we seem to apprehend the point of view of our grandmothers, though not without being struck by the difficulty of making out where they figure in our own selves. Even this is changing fast. Not many grandmothers in the coming generations will have escaped being overwhelmed by the modernization discourse. Be that as it may, the tantalizing resonances do not amount to intelligible patterns that we may call meanings. But nor are they devoid of suggestive traces that can be made intelligible by careful analysis.

Vague and tenuous though they may be, our links with the fast disappearing world of our nineteenth-century forebears offer us clues to work our way back into their idiom. As a possible beginning towards the retrieval of that repressed and powerful stratum of our being, we need to watch out for those moments when familiar resonances tend to leave us as we fail to follow their trail, and to see that we do not treat what we do not comprehend as irrational or obscurantist. We could learn also to be wary of yet another sequel to this failure of understanding: the tendency to ascribe our own meanings to terms that we do not quite understand.

The material world is changing fast from the times of our nineteenth-century ancestors, but the structure of social consciousness that began taking shape with them has not undergone anything like the same rapid transformation. Our attitudes, in certain basic respects, have shown an amazing persistence. This similarity over generations often escapes attention because of our only too obvious submission to modernization. The fact of this similarity, nevertheless, constitutes a primary premise of this book.

My formulation of the persistence of a dominant structure of social consciousness may seem objectionable on the grounds of there being an ideological–theoretical correlation, which is believed to exist axiomatically, between a given socio-economic reality and its universe of values, beliefs and attitudes. But I argue that this, by itself, cannot be a reason for revising the argument about the persistence of a dominant social consciousness. Nor is this an argument for the total autonomy of the world of ideas, attitudes and beliefs. What my formulation does is attempt to support the shift towards arguing for a more dialectical relationship between the material and cultural–ideological realms of Indian society.

♣

I
Crushed by English Poetry

♠

No generation lives and dreams for itself alone. It engages also in ventures that it knows will benefit and be carried on by its descendants. But history also shows generations that seem doomed to work consciously and almost exclusively for hopes and objectives which can only be realized by successors still unborn. Those who came of age in later-nineteenth-century India and felt concerned about the state of their country and society were all too conscious that this sort of tragic destiny was theirs. Whichever way they looked, the present seemed oppressive to them. The problems facing their society seemed so insuperable that the present could acquire a meaning only with reference to the past and the future. The past alone held out, in terms of its glory, a promise on behalf of the present; and its fulfilment lay a few generations away in the future. This was so, in the final analysis, even for those who viewed in the contact with the West signs of a new national awakening. What caused this oppressiveness was the awareness of subjection and the realization that freedom was not possible in the foreseeable future.

The conviction that their actions would bear fruit only posthumously did not, however, result in any deferment of action. Socially aware Indians of the period grappled with the oppressive present in the belief that their efforts would facilitate the work of later generations. In the process they betrayed moods, attitudes and tones within which were fused escapism and romanticism, idealism and realism, passive deliberation and a determined exploitation of the little space available for action. Their responses to their situation revealed a stern matter-of-factness and opportune myth-making, as also a certain kind of ambiguity as well as paradoxicality that characterized the structure of social consciousness in their times.

I

We may begin with a striking observation made by Vishnu Krishna Chiplunkar (1850–82). A distinguished man of letters who inspired such illustrious patriots as Tilak and Agarkar, Chiplunkar was driven by his desire for independent public work to give up his job as a teacher in a government high school. In 1874, while still in government service, he started a monthly which soon became a force in the political and literary life of Maharashtra. Called *Nibandhamala*, the journal was designed to devote a whole issue or series of issues to the discussion of a single important problem of the day. After bringing out seventy-six issues, Chiplunkar decided to take up, in May 1881, one last theme before winding up *Nibandhamala*. The theme he chose as his journal's swan song was, significantly enough, 'Amachya Deshachi Sthiti' (The State of Our Country) and it took him no less than eight issues to complete the discussion on it. It is as part of a sentence in 'Amachya Deshachi Sthiti' that the following observation occurs: 'Crushed by English poetry, our freedom has been destroyed . . . '. The rest of the sentence reads: 'under their laws we have become bankrupt'.[1]

'Crushed by English poetry' is a formulation that can be explicated at length in modernist discourses on the hegemonic hold exercised by British colonialism. It is, in that sense, not surprising that the observation runs counter to most of what was explicitly written by later-nineteenth-century Indian beneficiaries of English education, including Chiplunkar himself, on the impact of western knowledge upon their minds: mostly, what they did explicitly was celebrate the liberating and egalitarian ideas brought to them by the new knowledge. At the same time, however, Chiplunkar's observation captures with uncommon fidelity an underlying assumption of the contemporary Indian attitude — complex as it was — towards the colonial connection.

Using the term 'English poetry' as a shorthand or synecdoche to denote the entire range of western intellectual influences, Chiplunkar's formulation is far more penetrating than a plain statement such as 'our freedom has been destroyed'. Occurring with the suddenness and brevity of a revelation, it shows how profoundly the British had succeeded in holding not only the physical territory of

India but also the minds of those whom they ruled. However, this aspect of British colonial control over the thinking processes of Indians was understood only intermittently and vaguely; Indian intellectuals were aware of it, but only rarely did they comprehend and articulate it clearly. Chiplunkar's comment, which made India's fascination with English poetry a metaphor for British rule, was one such moment of clarity. It was a brilliant and audacious comment, for it inverted the whole significance of 'English poetry' — which was usually viewed as the source of freedom and democracy — and presented it as the hidden instrument of an alien dispensation. In this moment of insight both English poetry and the rule for which it was used as a metaphor were divested of their attractiveness.

Still, this moment of insight did not neutralize different impressions of the colonial connection, namely those that celebrated the advent of liberating and egalitarian ideas as the concomitant of British rule. Thus, Chiplunkar himself, in the same text, 'Amachya Deshachi Sthiti', considered it a 'matter of great good fortune' that 'without our doing anything we have been destined to come into contact with a country possessing such incredible efficacy.' Among the advantages he listed, were the acquisition of a vast capital of knowledge; practical gains like the railways, the post and telegraph; and the coming in of law and order following the anarchic years of Mughalai and Peshawai.[2]

'How lucky we are', Chiplunkar declared, 'that this vast body of knowledge from the West has just walked over into our land on its own.' Explicating the 'mental progress' that began with the fortuitous coming in of this knowledge, he selected for special mention the infusion among Indians of commendable new traits such as a desire for independence, national pride, pride in one's self, a revulsion against improper conduct, and the abandonment of obsequiousness. 'This', he wrote, 'is essential for the country's advancement.' He also added the warning that 'without it [the new knowledge] the country would remain backward.' 'As English education advances in our country', he confidently predicted, 'progress, independence and happiness will definitely spread!'[3]

The syntax suggests the hope of gradual, though certain, realization of the potential benefits of British rule and English education. The hope also has a base in the present. Chiplunkar talks also of the intellectual freedom that the British had already brought along with them. 'Even under the best swadeshi rajas', he assured his readers, 'such freedom was not available.'[4]

Chiplunkar's view of the likely benefits of British rule may be seen as a negation of his insight on the enslavement effected by 'English poetry'. But viewed differently, this apparent contradiction appears the manifestation of a pragmatic general belief that British rule was, in actual fact, producing contradictory effects. This was the sort of belief that created the sanguine feeling that India's subjection to the British would lead also to the country's eventual liberation. In 'Amachya Deshachi Sthiti' Chiplunkar articulated this belief along the following lines: 'Once we possess the weapon of English education, we shall pay no heed to Lyttonshahi, Templeshahi ... and a hundred such other shahis.'[5]

This seems a plausible reconciliation of two seemingly opposite positions *vis-à-vis* British rule. But it is rendered problematic by something else in 'Amachya Deshachi Sthiti' that cuts at its very basis. The reconciliation rests on an admission by contemporary Indians of their being unfit for independence — no matter who destroyed their freedom — and on their belief that this want would be made good by a continued exposure to English education. Having written in a way that suggests and supports such a reconciliation, Chiplunkar takes away its viability when he writes, at another point in the same essay: 'That we are unfit, at the moment, for freedom and our subjection is good for us is an erroneous opinion.' He even holds forth on the falsity of the freedom that is supposed to have come in the wake of British rule: 'In Britain it is people who possess real power. But here people are mere cattle and the government is the Supreme Power. We have the facade of freedom — councils, municipal boards, juries, native officials ... free press. ... But whereas the freedom enjoyed by the British is like free flowing water, ours is mere mirage.'[6]

A constant tension thus underlies Chiplunkar's essay. In it are to be found an acute sense of subjection and a consequent urge for freedom, along with a feeling of grateful loyalty to British rule. There are other examples of this within the essay, for, besides welcoming the coming in of law and order in the country as a relief from the ravages of internecine wars, Chiplunkar condemns the same law and order as the instruments of alien rulers to make Indians effeminate: 'The English historians may extol the peace they have brought to Hindustan. This may have benefited them. But there is no doubt that it has been extremely baneful to us.'[7]

The insight of 'crushed by English poetry, our freedom has been destroyed' lies in encapsulating the operation of hegemony, the mental enslavement that denies the enslaved any realization of their own enslavement. There have been, observes Chiplunkar, other examples of foreign rule in the world, but such total domination has been unprecedented.[8] To the extent that British colonialism succeeded in its objective of conditioning the minds of its victims, it rendered them incapable of perceiving the reality of their condition. Even when they got a glimpse, as Chiplunkar did, of the scale of their subjection, their perception was blurred by something resembling its opposite. Hence the paradox of celebrating the 'freedom' brought in by the British, along with the perception of this for what it was — a curse and a mirage.

This is the paradox that defines the Indian attitude towards British rule. At one level this paradox led to constant shifts between what existed and what might exist, between the enslavement that was and the freedom that would be. At another level, freedom and slavery seemed to coexist within the present.

I may have over-read Chiplunkar's epigrammatic formulation. But in retrospect, the reading does not seem entirely invalid. Chiplunkar himself begins 'Amachya Deshachi Sthiti' by admitting that his readers had found him guilty of many contradictions in the preceding seventy-six issues of *Nibandhamala*. He admits that at times he had praised the English and at times written critically about them. Similarly, there were occasions when he had supported proponents of new ideas at the expense of those who stood for the old order, while on other occasions he had said the opposite. Given this inconsistency of views, he appreciated his readers' demand that he unequivocally state his own considered position. For, he further conceded, it would not do to be constantly finding fault with everything and everyone. Instead of mere refutations, which were in their very nature negative, he had to come up with positive assertions as well. Chiplunkar does not, in essence, accept the charge of inconsistency. By way of defence he makes a remarkable observation. The contradictions noticed by his readers, he argues, reflect not the fickleness of his mind but the inconstancy of truth. And truth, in this context, means the objective reality of his society. It is this that he seeks to comprehend; and it is this that he finds in a state of flux. He says something about this objective reality, but soon discovers yet other facets of it that oblige him to say something else that seemingly contradicts the earlier statement. Only through a series of mutually irreconcilable propositions can he comprehend this reality. This mode of rationalization, which permitted Chiplunkar to argue away contradiction per se, must have been very comforting to a generation that, inferring from Chiplunkar's own testimony, saw no clear way out of its complex and contradictory reality.

It is possible that, in comparison to most of his contemporaries, Chiplunkar was more conscious and less unaware of the underlying tension in his response to British colonialism. Nonetheless his response was typical of that of English-educated Indians. Regional variations relating to such matters as the exposure to English education and to new political ideas and institutions do not appear to have impeded the growth of a similar colonial consciousness in the country as a whole. This similarity also cut across the apparent politico-ideological divisions between 'moderates' and 'extremists'. At the level of political organization and action, these divisions might have manifested real differences of perception with regard to the most effective and feasible means of struggle. In terms of implicit assumptions, however, both 'moderates' and 'extremists' shared an uneasy tension vis-a-vis the colonial connection. A rejection of the connection progressively got the better of its acceptance. But, at the level of consciousness — as distinct from tactically inspired political goals — this rejection was never total.

Let us turn, within the Bombay Presidency itself, from Chiplunkar to Govardhanram Madhavram Tripathi (1855–1907). A Nagar Brahman who rose to be one of the leading advocates of the Bombay High Court, Govardhanram was a formidable thinker and one of the makers of modern Gujarati fiction. A fiercely earnest man, and devoted to the life of the mind, he was essentially a patriot. But he was a patriot with a difference. His singular aspiration was to be able to mediate effectively in shaping the destiny of his nation. He saw his goal in moulding the pattern of change by training people. In defining to himself his 'duties in regard to the country', he wrote:

> To produce a particular event — be it a rebellion, or be it a political constitutional agitation or a social reform effervescence — this is too little for my mind and aspirations. . . . I wish to produce, or see produced, not this or that event, but a people who shall be higher and stronger than they are, who shall be better able to look and manage for themselves than does the present helpless generation of my educated and uneducated countrymen. What kind of nation that should be and how the spark should be kindled for that organic flame: these were, and are, the problems before my mind. I lay down this as, for the present, the only fixed objective before me, and my studies will be my 'skirmishers' and 'support'. . . .[9]

Convinced that 'seeing must precede acting', and worried about 'the evil consequences which we may inflict on our country by our well-meaning follies', Govardhanram would 'attempt or wish to assist nothing' before proper study. He looked upon himself as a *sakshi* — witness — who, unaffected by the 'nameless storms' of life, must be able to understand the reality around him with perfect equanimity. He wanted his 'thoughts and opinions' to be given 'public or permanent currency' only after adequate 'external research and internal deliberation'. In order to acquire such clarity he needed to closely follow, in the raw, the incessant working of his mind. Periodical 'notes' had to be made of his 'concerns so as to preserve their history' in order that, whenever necessary, he could trace the working of his own mind 'with greater continuity'. To be useful, these notes had to be marked by a ruthless objectivity that could entitle Govardhanram to talk of 'my judgment against myself'.[10]

During the last twenty odd years of his life Govardhanram was driven, by this manic quest for clarity, to maintain a private journal which he called his *Scrap Book*. Since it was not meant for publication — except for a vague and unrealized suggestion to this effect towards the end — he could strain in this *Scrap Book* the very limits of his thought and express himself with a nakedness almost uninhibited by the fear of being seen.

Because his 'ultimate' objective — 'one which never ought to be lost sight of — was to 'mould the people of my country . . . into a great people who would be able to take care of themselves',

Govardhanram grappled with the meaning of British rule. In an entry dated 13 April 1891 he wrote:

> India is invaded and subdued already. There is no question of Offensive or Defensive here, and Elasticity would be a nice helpmate in Constitutional warfare. The rulers are a clever set of people — an admixture of selfish aggressors and disinterested, benevolent helpmates. India is worked by 'push and pull' among these, and naturally the Home Interests generally carry the day. Yet even here we win morsel by morsel, though often it is snatched away — sometimes even from near the lips. I think people are on their way lo elasticity. The Congress History is just that.[11]

This is by no means an unequivocal passage, even though Govardhanram is not equivocating. It is, rather, another example of the ambiguity inherent in understanding the nature of British rule.

There is in this passage only one unqualified statement, and this relates to the most basic fact about the country's political situation: its subjection. 'India', Govardhanram says, 'is invaded and subdued already.' What draws attention within this otherwise plain formulation is the word 'already'. For someone seeking, in 1891, to comprehend the contemporary political situation, already indicates the necessity of accepting subjection as a hard reality about which little can be done. So, after noting that the country has been invaded and subdued, the course of action Govardhanram prescribes his countrymen is the cultivation of elasticity. Coming after offence and defence have been ruled out, 'elasticity' becomes the very epitome of ambiguity. The term seems to suggest here a pragmatism, an avoidance of confrontation, the settling into a long-drawn-out trial of strength which will involve a good deal of compromise and adjustment with the other party. That this is the sense in which Govardhanram has employed the term is clear from the context: it is in the conduct of 'constitutional warfare' that elasticity will prove to be useful.

Warfare, as defined by Govardhanram, may seem the ultimate logic of the relationship between India and Britain. It evokes the image of a confrontation with the lines between the combating parties clearly drawn. However, warfare is not for him the most dominating or final metaphor for the British presence in India. The notion of warfare is modified when Govardhanram uses the words 'constitutional' and 'elasticity'. The notion of a 'constitution' is what the British have made available to the ruled; and elasticity is what responsible Indians ought to cultivate. There is, consequently, ground for the hope that both parties will work for the gradual and smooth resolution of the underlying logic of 'warfare'.

Govardhanram then discusses the rulers. He sees in them a mixture of contrary qualities. A clever set of people, they are selfish aggressors as well as disinterested and benevolent helpmates. India is torn between the contrary pulls exercised by their qualities. Unfortunately for the country, the balance is tilted against India by the intrusion of 'home interests' which, 'naturally', carry the day. The despair caused by the decisive hold of 'home interests' is marginally allayed as Govardhanram notes that 'even here we win morsel by morsel'. Small as the relief is, it is neutralized by the admission that even these morsels are snatched away.

A pattern can be discerned in this excerpt from the *Scrap Book*. It contains three statements in which an assertion is made on British rule, which assertion is then seriously modified. In all these cases the passage is from faith in the British, towards its negation. In the first statement, 'elasticity' and 'constitutional' lead to 'warfare'. In the second, the mixture of oppositive tendencies among the rulers, offering some hope to Indians, ends with 'home interests' generally carrying the day. In the last statement, even the morsels won by the Indians are snatched away from their lips.

It is improbable that Govardhanram is conscious of this pattern in his attitude towards British rule, else he would not have said, without a note of anxiety, that 'people are on their way to elasticity' and that the Congress, too, is moving along the same path. Clearly, there are contradictions that Govardhanram is not quite able to grasp.

Govardhanram sees subjection as the most critical factor in the political situation of the country. However, while the fact of subjection is the constant factor against which all other calculations are made, these calculations are at variance with his perception of the underlying logic of the British presence. Thus, in the *Scrap Book* passage quoted above, the pragmatism that dictates constitutional struggle is articulated in response to the awareness of subjection; but the fact that British presence really means war between India and Britain is stated in a manner which suggests that the fundamental truth about British rule has slipped into the recesses of consciousness.

Moving on from Chiplunkar and Govardhanram to Bharatendu Harishchandra (1850-85) and his contemporaries in the North West Provinces, we discern a similar response to colonialism even in a region that was just beginning to respond to the new associational and agitational nationalist politics that had already made some headway in the three presidencies, especially in Bengal and Bombay. Born in a rich and ancient Bania family of Banaras, Harishchandra was a man of varied interests and restless energy. Though he died very young and was often plagued by ill-health — not an unusual phenomenon for his times in India — he wrote enough and in a wide variety of genres to have his works published, long after his death, in three separate volumes of prose, poetry and drama. These together comprise more than two thousand pages. Without altogether breaking away from received literary conventions with regard to themes, forms, diction, syntax and orthography, he self-consciously created new forms in Hindi literature. He also inspired a nucleus of writers, known as the Bharatendu *mandal*, who carried on the development of the Hindi language, as well as of literature and journalism, along lines indicated by him.

As a devout Vaishnava and a rich aesthete, Harishchandra wrote some devotional, erotic and epideictic poetry which was conventional in form and design. But most of his work, like that of his contemporaries, was imbued with a social-patriotic concern. In fact, even his devotional poetry at times carried a political message. He entreated and admonished God on the state of the country. He set an example for his followers to utilize the conventional form of devotional song for non-metaphysical and patriotic ends. Not content with appealing only to the educated sections of society, he stressed the need for, and demonstrated the possibility of, employing popular literary forms like *hori* and *lavani* in order to reach out to the common people.

Further evidence of the social commitment of Harishchandra and his contemporaries is provided by the fact that nearly all of them were practicing journalists. Some of them courted risk and losses by carrying on their own journals at a time when serious journalism — serious vernacular journalism at any rate — was a mission rather than a profitable business. In fact the distinction between journalism and literature had not yet crystallized and a convergence of the two was particularly well-suited to a situation in which the free expression of social concern was inhibited by the constraints imposed upon a subject people.

Harishchandra's *Kavivachansudha, Harishchandra's Magazine*, and its sequel, *Harishchandra Chandrika*, set new standards for Hindi journalism. In the process he not only lost a great deal of money, which added to his mounting debts, he also earned a degree of official displeasure, which testifies to his success as a journalist in a region that had barely begun to feel the tremors of nationalist politics.

At the level of agitational politics, too, Harishchandra involved himself with whatever public movements managed to reach the North West Provinces. He was actively associated with the public meeting which was organized when Surendranath Banerji reached Banaras in the course of his tour from Calcutta to Lahore; this he had undertaken, under the auspices of the Indian Association, as part of the famous civil service agitation. Harishchandra also addressed public meetings outside Banaras and spoke about the problems of the country.

All social concern eventually got interlinked with the question of subjection and freedom. Not surprisingly, therefore, Harishchandra turned again and again in his writings and speeches to the current discussion on the problems of taxation, tariffs, famine, 'drain', swadeshi, representation, employment in the upper echelons of the administration, racialism, and the like. All these stemmed from an awareness of subjection and, inexorably, deepened a realization of the need for a national organization that could advance the country's cause. He died early in 1885, towards the end of which the Indian National Congress was formed.

How did this politically conscious pioneer of modern Hindi literature respond to British rule and to the question of subjection and freedom? Harishchandra was less than twelve years old when he wrote one of his earliest poems. Despite its literary shortcomings, the combination of its mode and occasion makes the poem historically significant. Cast in a conventional mould, it was composed on the death of Prince Albert (14 December 1861), the husband of Queen Victoria.[12] At nineteen, Harishchandra wrote another loyal poem, again in the conventional hyperbolic style. This was prompted by the Duke of Edinburgh's visit to India. Harishchandra even convened a meeting of the notables and poets of Banaras on the eve of the Duke's visit to the holy city. The following excerpt from his preface to *Sumanonjali*, the collection of poems presented on this occasion, conveys something of his attitude towards the British connection:

> With the co-operation of some of my esteemed friends, I convened a meeting at my house on the 20th January and invited many respectable and learned Pundits and Gentlemen lo attend it. The meeting was formally opened by me by reading the biography of the Royal Prince in Hindi, and in conclusion requesting the gentlemen present on the occasion to adopt suitable measures for the address. The Pundits of the city expressed their great satisfaction, and read individually some Shlokas Sanskrit [*sic*] expressing their heartfelt joy on the advent of the Royal Prince to this city. The verses are entered systematically into this book. The meeting then broke up. The gentlemen present on the occasion evinced great joy and loyalty to the Royal Prince for which this small book containing the expression of their sincere loyalty, is most respectfully dedicated to his Gracious feet.[13]

The preface, it may be remarked, was originally written not in Hindi — which would have lent a degree of naturalness to the exaggerated obsequiousness of its idiom — but in English which was ill suited to expressions like 'most respectfully dedicated to his Gracious feet'.

In 1871, when the Prince of Wales was taken seriously ill, Harishchandra wrote a poem to pray for his speedy recovery.[14] Three years later he wrote a poem of twenty couplets on the occasion of the marriage of the Duke of Edinburgh with Princess Mary of Russia. This poem marks a very slight departure from the earlier loyalist panegyrics. It suggests feebly that Indians might be rewarded by the Queen if they manage to salute her unitedly. Coming at the end of a stylized felicitation, in the last but one couplet of the poem, the suggestion is at best an indirect exhortation to the people to be united.[15] There is no hint of any criticism of British rule. But, howsoever slight, this variation presaged a new pattern.

Harishchandra was twenty-four when his poetry celebrated the royal wedding. In the remaining eleven years of his life, too, loyal poems flowed from his pen. But these were no longer unadulterated panegyrics. They were, rather, used as occasions to voice Indian grievances. The first in this series was a poem written to welcome the Prince of Wales to India (1875). Conventional in form, like the earlier loyal poems, it was more directly indicative of India's plight. The country was described as a wreck, and its progeny as emaciated and destitute. After profusely welcoming the prince, the poet tells him:

> Although the people of Bharat no longer possess the qualities of old ... and its cities lie ravaged and cheerless; although the country is in ruins and miserable ... yet, seeing you, the people have suddenly become happy and the land of Bharat once again looks lively.[16]

In yet another, and much longer, poem written on the same occasion, Harishchandra provides a more forthright, though guarded, description of India. Interspersed with loyal panegyrics, this poem was inspired by and modelled after one by Hemchandra Banerji (1838–1904), a leading poet of Bengal. Harishchandra here asks the princes and people of the country to welcome the Prince of Wales, and invokes *Bharat-Janani* — 'Mother India' — to arise and rejoice as the sun has at long last shone on her land, and hold the prince in her lap, bless him, and recount to him her tale of woe. Poor *Bharat-Janani* is baffled. She cannot comprehend why the prince has come to India, a land plunged in darkness. Alluding in detail to her former glories, she points dejectedly to the revival of her old friends, Greece and Rome. She contrasts their revival with her own condition and laments that she continues to be the mother of slaves, forever nursing the agony of subjugation. The British, she suggests, should forget their mighty position and feel affection for the people of India. She asks the prince to assure his mother, the Queen, of the steadfast loyalty of Indians whose sufferings she should remove. With this plea, and with tears in her eyes, *Bharat-Janani* blesses the prince and disappears.[17]

Though two years later, in the preface to a long loyal poem, Harishchandra observed that Indians were intrinsically loyal, the critical tone of his loyal poems continued to sharpen. On the outbreak of the Anglo–Afghan War (1878), he exhorted Indians to side loyally and bravely with their rulers. He defied those 'fools' who had called the Hindus 'disloyal' — the English word is used in the Hindi poem and the Hindus here denote the Indian people — to now bear witness to their loyalty. But the exhortation soon became a dirge on the decline of a people who had once been famous for their valour.'[18]

By the time the Afghan war ended (1880) and Harishchandra wrote to welcome its termination, the dirge had become a direct indictment of British rule. Beginning with an expression of astonishment that there should be such jubilation throughout the country, this poem asks a series of damning questions — What is this rejoicing through the length and breadth of Bharat? Why are people's hearts overflowing with joy? Have the taxes been repealed and the land revenue abolished? Has the entry of Indians been facilitated into the civil service? Have the curbs on newspapers and dramatic performances been lifted? Telling as they are, these questions culminate in a forthright assertion — the war has brought glory to the English and given a new fillip to their trade; for Indians it has been productive of nothing but sorrow. The indictment, however, tapers off into a listless optimism that, while solving the mystery of country-wide jubilation, reiterates Indian loyalty: now that the generous and peace-loving Liberals have come to power in Britain, they will rectify past errors and work for India's welfare; no more loans will be raised and no more taxes imposed. This, and not the termination of the war, is the cause of people's rejoicing.[19] Obviously, they have reasons to be loyal.

The increasingly critical tone of Harishchandra's later loyal poems was for once blunted in the poem he wrote to hail the British conquest of Egypt (1882). Recited at a largely attended public meeting where local notables and the district collector were present, it drew a vivid contrast between the past and present conditions of India. The contrast, however, was drawn not so much to bemoan present plight as to express joy at the revenge of the past: it was for Harishchandra a belated nemesis that Indian soldiers should contribute to the British success over Muslim Egypt. India had for centuries been trampled upon by the *yavanas* — meaning, in this context, the Muslims — but now Indian soldiers had 'once again brightened the face of Bharat-Janani'. 'With iron pens they had engraved the Aryan might on the *yavana* heart.'[20] The apparent break that this poem presents in the pattern of sentiments expressed in Harishchandra's later loyal poems can be attributed to its peculiar structure, whereby Muslims became the arch villains and the centre of attention is shifted to them. To this process we shall return in chapter three.

Harishchandra's loyalty was not limited to poems prompted by specific events. His works in general, like his later loyal poems, combined expressions of loyalty with an increasing discontent and his awareness of subjection. For example, two of his patriotically political plays, *Bharat-Janani* (1877) and *Bharat Durdasha* (1880), dwell on both the destructive consequences and the regenerative possibilities of British rule in India. Despite their elegiac tone and pessimistic thrust, they reiterate and lend credence to the contemporary belief that, but for British mediation, the ruination of India would have gone on uninterrupted. For example, in the play named after her, Bharat-Janani — Mother India — says: 'But for English rule I would have been dead by now.' She asks her children, the people of India, to awake from their long slumber and, with Victoria there to protect them, shed their fear. She tells them: 'Listen to me, my sons, and call aloud once to the merciful Empress. She can, if she so pleases, hear everything, and there is no doubt that she will listen to you patiently and remove your sorrows in no time.' At the same time, however, in a verbal see-saw as it were, Bharat-Janani bemoans that her poor miserable children cannot even cry or complain. And still, as the see-saw continues, Victoria is said to be even more solicitous about people's welfare than was the fabled Lord Ram.[21] *Bharat Durdasha*, too, is characterized by a similar ambivalence.[22]

But it is a small six-line song that encapsulates the underlying tension of Harishchandra's attitude towards British rule. Coming at the end of *Vishasya Vishamaushadham* (1876), a play relating to the deposition of Malharrao Gaekwad, the ruler of Baroda, the song is in the form of a conventional prayer. It begins with the wish that kings — implying Indian ruling chiefs — may not covet others' wealth and wives. It goes on, in the fourth line, to ask God 'to render eternal the Englishmen's rule in this land'. This plea for eternal British presence is followed, in the last line, with the prayer: 'May Bharat be ever victorious.'[23] The tension epitomized by the song runs through the whole play. Loyalty operated strongly also in his Hindi adaptation (1878) of Vishakh Dutt's *Mudra-rakshas* — the Sanskrit play on Chandragupta's accession to power during the fourth century BC — where Harishchandra had little hesitation in inserting between two acts a song wishing Queen Victoria eternal life.[24] Anachronism notwithstanding, any occasion, it seems, was good enough for expressing loyalty.

It is a coincidence full of historical significance that, like one of his early poetic efforts, two of his last literary ventures were preeminently loyal compositions. When the British national anthem — Harishchandra typically looked upon it as the national anthem — was sought by the rulers to be rendered into Indian languages in a way that would make it meaningful to native audiences, he volunteered a Hindi adaptation of it in 1884. In this year he wrote another loyal poem, 'Riponashtaka', which, as its title indicates, was addressed to Ripon and contained eight purely eulogistic stanzas.[25] This was the last working year of Harishchandra's life. He died on 6 January 1885.

Alongside this consistently expressed loyalty was a critique of British rule. Initially, as is clear from the *Kavivachansudha*, which Harishchandra started in 1868, and *Harishchandra's Magazine* (1873–4), British rule was criticized with respect to isolated grievances. But a public lecture that he delivered in verse on the promotion of Hindi in 1877 shows how a growing apprehension in relation to the alien presence was transforming isolated criticisms into a critique with a central thrust. In a poignant question he asked the people: 'How come, as human beings we became slaves and they kings?'; and exhorted them with a rhetorical question: 'How long will you suffer these sorrows as slaves?' He warned against India's debilitating tendency to rely on foreigners for salvation, and spurred the people on to cast aside fear and dissensions, as well as to uphold the dignity of their language, religion and culture. (Here are intimations of Gandhi's observation that fear formed the basis of British power in India.) And, in two sharp couplets, Harishchandra singled out 'drain' as the raison d'etre and the chief evil of foreign rule: 'People here have been beguiled by the power and trickeries of the machine. They are daily losing their wealth and gaining in distress. Unable to do without foreign cloth, they have become the slaves of foreign weavers.'[26]

'Foreign weavers' denotes here the powerful industrial magnates of Manchester and their connection with Indian enslavement. Clearly, Harishchandra is able to relate the larger verities of imperialism with the life of common men and women. He can translate into everyday language and, through it, slowly into everyday consciousness, the twin symbols — Manchester and 'drain' — of an exploitative relationship which were becoming embedded within the incipient nationalist discourse. Harishchandra's presentation could command the simplicity and force of traditional narrative.

The idea that Britain was draining away Indian resources appeared almost obsessively in Harishchandra's work. Three years after the lecture in verse, in an extraordinarily pithy line in the *Bharat Durdasha*, he described 'the flow of wealth to a foreign land' as the worst sorrow caused by the 'Angrej Raj'. Rising prices, recurring famine and disease, and ever growing taxation, too, harassed the people. But these were mere corollaries of the ceaseless outflow of wealth. Even in a play like *Nil Devi* (1881), located in medieval times and concerned primarily with the Hindu–Muslim question, he felt impelled to speak about the foreign extraction of wealth. Employing the stratagem of a prophecy in order to comment on contemporary India, he listed increasing irreligion, ignorance, lethargy, superstitiousness, cowardice, and proneness to slavery as the evils that would plague the country. But he chose for special stress the harm caused by the craze for foreign goods and by the emulation of foreign ways.[27]

He saw a link between the British presence in India and the mental habits of the ruled. The 'drain' was, indeed, an essential requirement of this presence. But what sustained this unceasing loss, and with it British rule, was the eagerness of Indians to buy imported goods. It seemed logical, therefore, to hope that a curbing of habits which made it profitable for the British to stay in India would sap the imperial connection. This, in turn, gave a stimulus to the urge for swadeshi. Harishchandra wrote fervently to promote this cause. He even formed a society, called Twadiya Samaj, the members of which were bound by a vow to use and propagate the use of things indigenously manufactured.

Though the link with the mental habits of the ruled seemed real, it is intriguing that Harishchandra missed another powerful connection between the material interests of certain sections of India, and imperial rule. More than most politically conscious Indians of the period, he might have been the one to grasp this clearly. It is ironic that he could, without qualms, insert in *Harishchandra's Magazine* (in which he was writing to promote the idea of swadeshi), an advertisement saying that his own firm, M/s Harishchandra and Brother, had 'received various fresh goods direct from England per steamer Cathay, consisting of new and choicest novelties of the season that are not to be had in the Indian markets.'[28] Having dealt earlier on the divergence between belief and practice in the making of an Indian nationalist consciousness, I shall here concentrate on the tension within the structure of consciousness itself, of which the divergence between belief and action was often only a manifestation.[29]

Personal factors and limitations apart, Harishchandra's critique of British rule continued to develop around its exploitative economic aspect. In 1881 he wrote *Andher Nagari Chaupatta Raja*, a political farce based on a popular tale. A thinly veiled indictment of British rule in India, it exposed the reality of corruption, exploitation and capricious lawlessness that lay behind the facade of Pax Britannica. Written in the language of the street and making generous use of humour, it preached even as it amused. It also employed conventional song forms, along with popular musical tunes, which were likely to linger or be hummed long after the reading or the performance was over. A written text that could be read at will, it also possessed in its songs something of the quality of the 'remembered' texts of popular theatre. It was one such song in *Andher Nagari* that described, among other things, how the English 'saheb' could 'digest the whole of Hind' in order to fill the coffers of Britain.[30]

In a small poem written in 1884 — the year in which he translated the 'national anthem' and wrote in praise of Ripon — Harishchandra contrasted the seductive facade of British rule with its exploitative reality. For this *exposé* he chose a conventional verse form, called *mukari*, in which the first three lines are predicative and the last reveals the subject of the poem in a way calculated to shock or startle. Called, appropriately, 'mukari for modern times', the deadly simplicity of this poem is difficult to convey even in a free translation:

Sucking stealthily the entire juice from within;
Smilingly grasping the body, heart and wealth;
So adept in making glib profession,
Is it your husband? No, the Englishman.[31]

This seems to herald a final loss of faith in the British; even the persistent expression of loyalty seems, in the light of this, to have been tactically motivated. I shall discuss later the pragmatic aspect of loyalism. At the moment we need to ask if this exposure of British rule, and especially the loss of faith in its value or goodness, was as total as we are, prima facie, led to believe. It is possible that what the *mukari* reflects is the very ambivalence that we are tempted to see as resolving in favour of the certitudes of nationalism.

The *mukari* poses and answers a riddle. An ersatz subject is described in order to tease the reader. The way to reach the real subject is through the description of the ersatz. They form two separate associational patterns so that the qualities it assigns to a 'husband' are also those of an Englishman. The qualities of a husband, as described in this poem may induce the present-day reader to imagine a completely exploitative relationship which is acquiesced to by a vulnerable wife out of sheer helplessness. But there is reason to think that this is not what is implied by the poem. It is, we need to remember, cast in a conventional mould. And in conventional poetry, certainly in Hindi and perhaps in all Indian languages, there existed a stereotypical opposition of husband and lover. The woman, in this stereotype, loved the husband, waited for him while knowing about his infidelity, always succumbing to his myriad charms. Their love remained unscathed.

It is difficult to say whether Harishchandra chose the simile of the husband deliberately in order that something of this stereotype image of the husband might pass, through a transference of the specified attributes, from the ersatz on to the real subject, i.e. to the English rulers. Steeped as he was in the sensibility which informed conventional forms, and writing as he did when most of his contemporary readers shared that sensibility, the transference from the husband to the English must have carried traces of the conventional connotations of this particular simile. But even if he employed the simile without being overly conscious of these connotations, the transference could not have been devoid of their traces. In this transference, the analogue of the wife's persistent love for the unfaithful husband was analogous with the Indians' continuing faith in the British despite exposures of their exploitative character. Irrespective of what Harishchandra consciously meant, the simile carried resonances of a continuing fascination with English rule. This fascination had become a part of the consciousness of the ruled and could, hence, remain thus, despite criticisms of British colonialism. The disillusionment with British rule was never total, being so frequently accompanied by an appreciation of its beneficent aspects.

Yet, despite their ambivalence, the dominant note of Harishchandra's patriotic writings was pessimistic. Gloom runs through *Bharat Durdasha*, perhaps his most overtly political play. Similarly, in *Bharat-Janani*, adapted from a Bengali play and concerned with the political state of the country, he omitted from his version two characters present in the original: Unity and Enthusiasm. He argued that, even if valid for Bengal, in the North West Provinces neither unity nor enthusiasm could realistically be assigned any role.[32]

Harishchandra's response to British rule, both in its tone and substance, presaged and set the pattern for the attitudes of his fellow Hindi litterateurs. This was perhaps as due to the force of his personality and work as to the prevalent conditions which evoked similar responses elsewhere in India. In varying degrees, these responses betray the same ambivalence.

The man who came closest to Harishchandra, in form if not in the spirit of his response, was Chaudhari Pandit Badari Narayan Upadhyaya 'Premghan' (1855–1921). Belonging to a rich Brahman family of Mirzapur that owned zamindaris — besides other lucrative commercial interests — Premghan came to literature through his fondness for a life of luxury and culture. What began, in conformity with the traditional image of a cultivated *rais*, as dilettante dabbling in erotic poetry, turned into a socially committed and politically alive sensibility soon after its contact with Harishchandra. Though not possessing the latter's intensity and missionary zeal, Premghan wrote with feeling and discernment about his society. The thrust of *Ananda Kadambini*, a journal he brought out in 1881, was a shade less sharp than that of *Hindi Pradip* or *Brahman*, to which we shall turn later. But the adoption of a relatively restrained tone did not preclude frank discussions of sensitive political issues.

For a rich and comfortable zamindar to have been so concerned is not without significance. But perhaps more relevant is the fact that Premghan's reactions were similar to those of his contemporaries who belonged to different and less privileged social strata. It is possible that this similarity of attitudes was, in some ways, facilitated by the crystallization of a nationalist critique of British rule following the birth of the Indian National Congress.

Premghan's *Bharat Saubhagya* illustrates the fusion of faith in, and condemnation of, British rule better than any other work of the period. Dedicated to the president of the fourth session of the Indian National Congress at Allahabad (1889), *Bharat Saubhagya* was specifically written to be staged for the Congress delegates. It could not eventually be performed, though not because the local organizers of the Congress found anything objectionable in it. In fact, Raja Rampal Singh, the leading organizer of the session, was perfectly satisfied with the script. He was particularly happy with a song, addressed to Queen Victoria, which included: 'May you, O Queen, live for a hundred thousand years.'[33]

Bharat Saubhagya shows 'British Nation', one of the main characters of the play, busy restoring order and peace in the country. He is assisted by three chief agents: 'British Policy', 'Education' and 'Freedom'. The restoration of order, which shows the provision of relief after centuries of turmoil and oppression, is unfortunately disturbed for a while by the outbreak of 1857. The leaders of the outbreak, Bahadur Shah and Nana Saheb, are chastised for causing the disturbance. Nana Saheb, a Hindu, is described as 'Aryakula kalanka', a blot on the fair name of the noble Aryan family. Implicit in this is an assumption of the incapability of Indians for self-rule. At the same time, paradoxically, there is a sympathetic description of the 1857 outbreak in *Bharat Saubhagya*.[34]

It seems ironic, in retrospect, that a play intended for the recreation of the Congress delegates should have suggested India's incapacity for self-rule. It is even more ironic that Premghan should have made the character 'Freedom' say: 'What vain thinking it is that those who can't hold together their loose dhoti will govern the country.'[35] Even though Anglicized delegates to the Congress during its early phase were unlikely to have appeared in dhotis, the sarcasm on Indian limitations is clear enough. But because it comes from 'Freedom', the gibe is not without the assurance of better things to follow. It epitomizes a several belief in the eventual bestowal of freedom, as well as recognition of the need for its temporary and partial negation.

The description of British rule in *Bharat Saubhagya* tallies with the popular image of Ramarajya. (Nine years later Premghan would, in a poem, explicitly compare pax Britannica to Ramarajya.) The play provides an inventory of the boons granted by the British to India. It singles out Ripon for special praise and, in a song set in a conventional mould, commemorates the generosity of the Liberals. While mentioning the House of Commons it also shows that the other British political parties feel like the Liberals on the question of justice for India. So moved is Bharat, the leading character of the play, with this unanimous display of kindness that with folded hands he tells the Rajapratinidhi (Viceroy): 'By giving us surfeit of joy, you have given us dyspepsia.'[36]

However, *Bharat Saubhagya* also provides a commentary on the disastrous consequences of British rule. Saraswati and Rajashri — symbolizing learning and political power — are shown as departed from India long ago. But following the restoration of peace and order by the British, even Lakshmi — the goddess of wealth — is now resigned to being taken away to the West because technology, railways and ships leave her no other option.[37]

This was Premghan's way of broadcasting the idea of 'drain' by phrasing it in picturesque mythological terms. But there were occasions when he was more forthright, even uncharacteristically blunt, about it. In a poem composed in a popular literary form and meant to be sung in public, he described Britain's economic transactions with India as 'loot'. If Britain flourished, it was at India's expense. Again, in 1889, in the same poem where he compares pax Britannica with Ramarajya, he says plainly: 'Very cruel, indeed, are those who carry off wealth and grain from here.'[38]

Even the moderately toned *Bharat Saubhagya* has a convincing description of how, as an inevitable consequence of the 'drain', commerce and agriculture have fallen on evil days and people are reduced to starvation on account of rising prices, famines and taxation. Neither God nor the Queen Empress seems to care for the Indian people. Agriculturists are obliged to take loans to pay dues to the government. The salaried classes have fixed incomes which are devalued by an unchecked rise in prices. There is commotion all around. Even charity and religion, the traditional anchors of culture in society, are enfeebled by material debasement.[39]

The simultaneous appreciation and condemnation of alien rule does not make the feeling of subjection less acute. In a poem addressed to his progenitors, and written the year the Congress came into being, Premghan implores them not to return to their once glorious land for the annual *shraddha*: they will, he says, not be able to bear the sight of their descendants carrying with bowed heads the burden of slavery. Impotent, ignorant, poor and slothful, these descendants do not recognize their own interests. Averse to new technology and reluctant to conduct independent trade, they are incapable of making any effort or sacrifice for their own regeneration. Leading an animal-like existence, they have been culturally uprooted. God alone can save them.[40]

Like Premghan, Radhacharan Goswami (1859–1923) was inspired by Bharatendu Harishchandra. Coming from a sacerdotal family of Vrindaban which owned a chain of temples in a number of north Indian cities, Radhacharan was an orthodox Vaishnava with pronounced reformist leanings. At times openly, and at other times surreptitiously, disregarding the injunctions of his family and vocation — his father considered it sacrilegious to utter even a word of English or Persian — he managed to acquire a rudimentary knowledge of English and educated himself about the state and affairs of his country. He was actively associated with the Indian National Congress during its initial phase and attended its annual sessions in Calcutta (1886), Allahabad (1888) and Lahore (1893). When the Indian National Social Conference was founded in 1887, Radhacharan became enthusiastically involved with its activities and wrote two pamphlets in support of sea voyages and widow marriages. He acted for some years as secretary of the Mathura circle of both the Congress and the National Conference. He was also connected with the Hindi editors' association, which was formed at Allahabad in 1884, and was for a year its secretary. He took a keen interest in local affairs and successfully fought the municipal elections in 1885 and 1894. As a token of the debt he owed his literary mentor, Radhacharan named his monthly journal *Bharatendu*. During the three and a half years of its existence (1883–86), the journal was candid and fearless — though not always intelligent — on a variety of public issues. Radhacharan, in fact, believed that it was against his nature to forsake, for any consideration, the 'independence of his heart and views'. He considered 'national progress, the Indian National Congress, social reform and women's freedom as dear to me as life'. In matters relating to the welfare of the country, his self-image was that of a 'liberal'. This for him was a matter of some pride because he had become a liberal in spite of having been born in an 'orthodox' family ('orthodox' is the word used by Radhacharan in his Hindi text).[41]

In 1880, Radhacharan wrote a fantasy called *Yamalok ki Yatra*. Serialized in the *Sarasudhanidhi*, a prominent Hindi periodical of the time, it described the visit of an 'enlightened' young man to the kingdom of Yama, the god of death. Interestingly, of the many hells described in this fantasy, one was reserved for those who had risen against 'our mighty government', although there was nothing in the theme of *Yamahk ki Yatra* to warrant a hell for the enemies of the British. The fantasy was intended to tackle a critical issue that was virtually tearing Radhacharan's insides, just as it was tearing contemporary Indian society, into hostile camps: the conflict between the old and the new. A special hell, moreover, was imagined for those who had fought against the British in 1857.[42]

Though he consigned their enemies to perdition, Radhacharan considered it justifiable to criticize the British in the strongest terms, for they had occupied India through deception. There was not a single issue of *Bharatendu* in which some aspect of British policy and administration in India was not assailed. It is a measure of the bitterness of Radhacharan's criticism that he could say that the oppression of the Muslim rulers — from which the British were supposed to have provided relief as part of a divine design — paled beside the enormities of the British. Besides, in keeping with the contemporary vogue of employing mythological imagery, he wrote a short play in which the rulers were shown as demons — *rakshasas* — mercilessly exploiting their subjects.[43]

Radhacharan was not always so unbridled in his choice of expression. He could also convey a great deal through mere suggestion. For example, in one issue of *Bharatendu*, he posed 'three new questions' and asked his readers to furnish a common answer to all of them. One of these questions was: 'Why is there not a single independent representative of the twenty-five hundred million Indian subjects in the Parliament?'[44] (Like Harishchandra's use of the national anthem for the British national anthem, Radhacharan talks of the Parliament rather than the British Parliament.) Whatever the answer to these questions, the thrust was unmistakable. It stressed the subject status of Indians.

The awareness of subjection found particularly impassioned expression when Radhacharan joined issue with Raja Shiv Prasad (1823–95) for giving currency to the view that 'patriotism' — the word used in the course of the controversy — was a notion unknown to Indians until they came into contact with the British. With the blindness to logical consistency that intrudes when passions run high, Radhacharan put forward a whole series of arguments to expose the absurdity of Shiv Prasad's contention that 'patriotism' was a word without any synonym in Indian languages. He reacted with a fierceness that stemmed from helpless anguish at subjection, and sought relief in an imagined past. The following excerpt is revealing:

> If one were to say that political progress is real national progress, then the king was always under the control of the public. Whoever the public preferred became the king; kings who opposed the public were dethroned. . . . It is well known that people's representatives would go to the royal assembly and present their views on matters of importance. If the king could not go by their advice, he arranged to have the matter sorted out by arbitration. There were even occasions when kings left the country. All this was political activity. [The English word 'political' is used in the Hindi original.] Now the question is whether there existed at that time the kind of modern political activity in pursuit of which people now move from one city to another and deliver lectures on matters of national welfare. The gist of these lectures is: Free the country! Prevent the flow of wealth (Lakshmi) to Britain! Purify your social conduct! But these things were irrelevant then. The country was independent; there was ample learning; wealth used to flow in from other countries; social conduct was pure. It was superfluous then to endeavour to improve our lot here and now; all energies could be diverted to the betterment of the hereafter. . . . As for patriotism and devotion to the country, the sacred sentence that your mother and motherland are higher than paradise coursed its way through every vein among Indians. Attachment to the motherland was so intense that our people would rather die of hunger than leave the country. To say, then, that passion for national welfare and progress came in the wake of English education is thoroughly fallacious. That India gave birth

to the idea of social and national welfare would, instead, be freely admitted by all.[45]

But the same Radhacharan, writing in the same issue of *Bharatendu* — though in the changed context of a possible Anglo-Russian war over Central Asia — had no hesitation in saying: 'Such is the cleverness, intelligence and learning of the English that all India is willing to remain their slave.'[46] It was this ambivalence towards the British connection that made it possible for Radhacharan, as for his contemporaries, to welcome the Duke of Connaught to India (1883) in the most loyal terms, and to simultaneously provide a critique of British rule.[47]

If Harishchandra is taken as the norm for the expression of appreciation and criticism of foreign rule, Premghan and Radhacharan would appear to have been rather generous in their appreciation, without ceasing to be severely critical. In Pratapnarayan Misra (1856–94) and Balkrishna Bhatt (1844–1914) the tendency was reversed; their nationalist fervour all but eclipsed their sense of loyalty.

Born in a Kanyakubja Brahman family of modest means, Pratapnarayan combined in his life and literature an air of devil-may-care alongside a refined sensibility and solicitude for the oppressed. In his *Brahman*, a monthly that exemplified fearless and informed journalism, he assiduously nursed an instrument of public service that was to him a perennial source of material, physical and mental strain — more so as he disdained improving his indifferent health and slender finances, and hated curbing the natural ebullience of his pen. While Harishchandra, his literary guru, died a despairing patriot at the beginning of the year that witnessed the birth of the Congress, Pratapnarayan had the advantage of being wholeheartedly associated with the national organization during its early years, and this gave him a degree of confidence in the face of heavy odds. However, his passionate concern for his country and his assessment of the British were, by and large, the same as his guru's.

It was rather early — in 1883 when he was twenty-seven — that Pratapnarayan saw through what he called 'English policy', and anticipated by a year Harishchandra's *exposé* of British rule in his 'mukari for modern times'. The essence of this policy, Misra says in a couplet, is that Indians should suffer the white man's 'kicks' and lose their wealth.[48] This pithy summing up points to racialism as being integral to British rule, and was possibly inspired by the Ilbert Bill controversy. Whatever the circumstances, his convictions against alien rule became stronger over time. By 1884 he expressed his anger in the form of a proposition: 'Has ever a conquering nation anywhere done good to the vanquished? And how can it?' Referring specifically to the British, he added: 'We should not cry on account of the oppressions of Englishmen, and should give up the hope that they have come here to do good to us.' Stressing that 'everyone helps the strong, no one supports the weak', he warned: 'So long as we remain what we are now, our cries and protestations will have no effect on anybody.'[49]

Like Harishchandra, Pratapnarayan saw that the British were keen to maintain an attractive facade behind which to carry on the seamy business of empire. In a poem written towards the end of 1884, he says that 'all that the English pray for' is that the flow of Indian wealth to their country should go on uninterrupted, and that their 'criminal' machinations remain unexposed. Utterly selfish as they are, he wrote in an article the same year, 'how can they see us progress as against their own countrymen?'[50] He defied his readers, appropriately in an essay on 'Selfishness' (1889), to cite any examples of measures taken by the government purely for the people's welfare; or to demonstrate any instance of even trivial gains to the English being foregone in order to avert substantial damage to Indians.[51] It was senseless to expect, he wrote two years later, that a government which thought nothing of making its rupee while people perished in famines would accede to Indian prayers for just rights. India was held and defended 'only in order that it may be exploited for the sake of the British'. 'What good will they do', he asked, 'who have grabbed your land and wealth?'[52]

Pratapnarayan was particularly troubled by the 'drain', poverty and the general socio-cultural disorder that arose from alien rule. In a long poem, addressed to the gods and to dead ancestors, which explains how propitiatory offerings made since time immemorial were no longer within the means of the poor Indians, he depicts the fallen state of the country. Addressing the sea-god, for example, he bemoans: 'Lakshmi has gone across your vast expanse [to England]. How can we, then, make arrangements for your worship? Drown this country into your depths — this is what we pray to you with folded hands.'⁵³

Besides devotional songs, Pratapnarayan employed other popular poetic forms to spread the idea of increasing impoverishment. In one such poem he wrote in 1890: 'Destitution shrouds the country as its wealth is carted away to England.' 'All the collections made from us by way of taxes, octroi and donations have gone across the seas. The remainder also is going away.' Emphasizing the irretrievability of the 'drain', he added: 'Having once gone away, it never comes back. That, simply, is why poverty, sorrow and evil conditions plague us.'⁵⁴

In an essay on 'Truth', he says: 'Whatever the starving crores of this country earn from agriculture, trade, crafts, and services is sent to England through the instruments of taxation, donation and trade.' Manchester, in his poetry, symbolized this exploitative relationship.⁵⁵

Poverty is another theme that recurs in Pratapnarayan's writings. He pointed to the scale of starvation, to the fact that a quarter of the population was forced to survive on tree bark and fruit stones, adding this staple to whatever coarse grains or wheat flour it was able to scrape together.⁵⁶

A situation of pervasive scarcity, Pratapnarayan argues, has made Indians 'the slaves of their bellies'. This phrase occurs repeatedly in his work.⁵⁷ Through it he wished to show that this single circumstance of scarcity rendered people incapable of co-operation, unity and any exertion for the common weal. The peasant was without land, the trader without business, the professional without jobs, and the beggar without alms. The consequent struggle for bare survival made for mutual suspicion,⁵⁸ and corroded the sense of community that had held the people together even during the centuries of 'Muslim oppression'.⁵⁹

Like Harishchandra, again, Pratapnarayan regretted the loss of what he called 'selfhood', and the suicidal craze for imitating the rulers' culture and way of living. Both writers used the same words in the context of the cultural erosion that set in as a result of foreign domination. Harishchandra described this 'selfhood' as *apunapau*, while Pratapnarayan used its modern variant *apanapan*. The latter also employed, in the same context, other terms like *nijata*, *nijatva*, *jatiyata*. If Harishchandra lamented that Indians had shamelessly forsaken their own identity, Pratapnarayan felt anguished that, wasting away in the struggle for mere survival, they had forgotten their true self and wallowed in slavery. In *Suchal-Shiksha* (1891), a small book for the moral instruction of the Indian youth, he made a moving and reasoned plea for recovering pride in being Indian. This, he felt, was a prerequisite for national regeneration.[60]

Subjection was for Pratapnarayan a tormenting refrain from which there was no escape. Whether he wrote conventional prayers or folk ditties, nationalist poems or verses addressed to visiting British dignitaries, plays or essays that touched upon a large range of subjects and evoked moods from the humorous to the sombre, the pain of subjection always emerges in his writings. Very often the pain is tinged with nostalgic pride in India's old past and expectations for its future. Unable to bear the spectacle of Indians 'grovelling at the feet of the foreigner',[61] Pratapnarayan tries to arouse whatever vestiges of self-respect they still possess by provoking or shaming them. This country, he says, has no man. Populated only by 'women' — the common epithet for cowards — it has become the laughing stock of the entire world.[62] If Indians wanted to become 'men', they must cultivate patriotism, else they may be written off as 'feeble animals'.[63]

Pratapnarayan adopted a variety of tones, ranging from entreaty and exhortation to taunts and provocation. Hope rarely deserted him. An uncharacteristic despair, however, crept into his writing when he sought to pinpoint the cause of the country's decline. The decline, he observed, was due to 'our folly', and, failing to find cogent explanations, he ended by saying to the reader: it is due to 'whatever you may say'.[64] Frustrated in the search for perceptual clarity, he could do little more than place his final trust in God, as did most of his contemporaries.[65]

Notwithstanding his understanding of exploitation, Pratapnarayan was also loyally disposed towards the British. It is true that he wrote no wholly loyal encomiums. His manifestation of loyalty invariably combined with a criticism of British rule. Yet he reacted sharply to official suspicion of loyalty in Indians. These suspicions, he argued, were ill-founded because Indians treated their rulers at par with God, inasmuch as the rulers were seen to constitute a link between individuals and God. As evidence of Indian loyalty, he recalled the days of the 1857 rebellion, when Indians risked property and life for the sake of their rulers. He compared Ripon not only to Akbar but even to Ram, and hoped the British would strengthen the natural loyalty of Indians by giving them their due.[66]

The complex character of Pratapnarayan's response to the British in India is brought out by six lines in a very long poem which was serialized in the *Brahman* between August 1884 and December 1885. After recounting the horrible atrocities perpetrated by the Muslim rulers, he says it was because of such sins that Muslim rule in India was destroyed. As the agent of this destruction, the 'English government' had saved the Hindu religion and made Hindus feel as though they were living in Ramarajya. But the appreciation is qualified by the view that, under the English government, people 'are experiencing joys and sorrows in accordance with their karmas'.[67]

Why, in this instance, did Pratapnarayan not write with his usual candour? Why did he make the obviously exaggerated comparison with Ramarajya, specially as the comparison is all but negated in the preceding line with the thought that, except in the loss of wealth and the plague of taxation, the British Raj resembles Ramarajya. Resonating Harishchandra's famous couplet in *Bharat Durdasha* ('barring the flow of wealth to foreign land, the Angrej raj is teeming with great happiness'), Pratapnarayan's enigmatic line embodies the Indian dilemma over their connection with British rule. It is tempting to argue away the enigma by construing the six-line fragment as an elliptical attack on British rule. More so as Pratapnarayan did have a penchant for irony. But the context in which the comparison with Ramarajya is made invests these lines with an ambiguity that rules out such a reading. Inasmuch as the lines include the notion of a relief from Muslim tyranny, the context is imbued with feelings which, as we shall see later, were for Pratapnarayan and his contemporaries too strong and discrete to permit any simple irony.

As intrepidly critical of British rule as Pratapnarayan, though not equally penetrating in his perceptions or pointed in his expression, Balkrishna Bhatt was a writer who devoted himself to the service of his country. Making his living as a teacher, and supplementing his meagre salary through petty trading in stationery and the occasional practice of astrology and indigenous medicine, this proud Brahman from Allahabad never rose above want. Steeped in Sanskrit learning and tutored in English, he was willing to promote social change even as he was determined to preserve the rich cultural heritage and fabric of his society. While most of his contemporaries who have been discussed above took to writing and public affairs rather precociously, Bhatt did so relatively late. He launched *Hindi Pradip* when he was thirty-three. Perhaps the uncertainties of a chequered early career and the vexations of a turbulent joint family — with which he was later obliged to sever his connections — held him back for a while. But once he had decided to embark upon the venture (1877),[68] nothing deterred him. The difficulties that came his way in the course of a long life of struggle were not of the ordinary kind. His outspoken writing in *Hindi Pradip* antagonized both the authorities and his contemporaries. When, once, he was waylaid and beaten up, the authorities revelled in his discomfiture and refused to take any action against the culprits.[69] Bhatt was forty at the time of this assault. Age did not mellow him. At sixty-four he made a stridently critical speech to condemn Tilak's deportation, and, rather than apologize or submit to a token disciplinary action by his college authorities, he chose unemployment.[70]

Bhatt knew that the life he was choosing for himself would bring him nothing but trouble. The appeal he made to his readers in the inaugural number of *Pradip* leaves no doubt as to the missionary fervour that inspired him. Warning them that the mood of the monthly was not calculated to please the government, he said he had been driven by faith in the goodwill of his countrymen, and in his own capacity for hard and sustained effort.[71] Judging by the small circulation of *Pradip*, his faith in public goodwill does not appear to have been vindicated.

Besides the trenchant tone, Bhatt was ever willing to displease those in power. He distrusted all Englishmen — even those who were hailed as India's friends. For example, when John Bright said that the British administration had reduced Indians in their own country into mute creatures, Bhatt wrote bitterly in 1878: 'If the selfsame Mr Bright were to come here as governor-general, he would lose this kind of understanding and no more be able to see such things.' This distrust arose from his conviction that, however well-intentioned they might be, individual Englishmen could not be more powerful than the exploitative system of which they were a part. 'What, apart from loss of honour', he asked, 'has India gained by surrendering everything it possesses and lying at the mercy of England?' It was at India's expense, he firmly believed, that 'England has become a red rose'. In return, deprived of all dignity, courage and self-reliance, the people of India had been transformed 'from sword-wielders to pen-pushers'. 'To be the patient butt of white men's shoes', he continued, 'has become their habit ... contempt and dishonour have become their badges.'[72] From economic exploitation to racial hauteur, the picture of alien presence was clear in Bhatt's mind. Trust in this kind of a relationship seemed to him misplaced.

In a short play (1878) consisting of a series of dialogues between Englandeshwari (Queen of England) and Bharat-Janani, Bhatt painted the reality of colonial India with a sombre vividness that neither Bharatendu Harishchandra nor Pratapnarayan Misra ever achieved. The dialogue begins with Englandeshwari telling Bharat-Janani about a sum of five million rupees that her (Englandesh-wari's) sons 'had to send' for famine relief in India, and asking her if she felt grateful to them for this generous contribution. Though she expresses her gratitude, Bharat-Janani says that this was a mere discharge of duty. Englandeshwari thereupon points out that famines being an annual occurrence, she could neither prevent them nor contribute money for relief each time. To which, in an aside, Bharat-Janani reacts: 'How can you give? You only know how to take.' Ostensibly, she only asks Englandeshwari: 'What can be done then?', and the latter suggests the creation of a famine insurance fund which could be used to construct public works designed to meet the menace. Worried that, in addition to the famines, there will now be this new financial burden, Bharat-Janani asks from where the money for the proposed fund will come. Englandeshwari replies: 'Why, my sons will advance you a loan. It does not matter if you have become old. Your pores are still filled with juice, and your flesh has such an aroma that everybody likes you. Let your sons be ready to take the loan.' Again in an aside, Bharat-Janani reacts: 'Your sons have taken away every bit. Now only the flesh remains. Let them slice and eat it if they find its aroma so irresistible.' This time in her address to Englandeshwari, however, she manages to be more forthright: 'My sons, poor souls ... you can squash them as much as you like. ...'

Englandeshwari then complains that the educated sons of Bharat-Janani are forever finding fault with her sons, and trying to be their equal. As a simple prescription for amity, Englandeshwari suggests that 'native' sons accede to the orders of her sons. The dialogue ends with Bharat-Janani saying: 'What else can my sons do? Speaking out does not help. . . . Let us see how long this tyranny lasts.'[73]

Recalling a maxim of Manu, the law-giver, to the effect that there is no pain like the pain of slavery, Bhatt asks if death did not hold in store greater relief than a life made up of taxation and suffering police atrocities. He even questions the wisdom of relying on God, which, for a believer like him, was the limit of despair. For all their circumspection and reliance on God, he says, Indians have for centuries rotted in slavery.[74]

But for Bhatt despair was never more than a passing phase. He knew that the struggle would be long drawn, and that repeated failures were inevitable in this struggle. But every failure had to be viewed as an essential step towards ultimate success. 'Whenever a weak nation has fought against a powerful nation to achieve any kind of independence', he says, (the formation of the Indian National Congress was still seven years away), 'it has very often met with defeat. But the defeat has without doubt proved a means of great benefit later on.'[75] There could not have been a more satisfying justification for a generation that seemed aware of being born to make collective efforts that could only bear fruit for succeeding generations.

Bhatt's conviction that British rule could not benefit India co-existed with the belief that it was divinely willed.[76] In a novel entitled *Nutan Brahmachari* (1886), he described the state of anarchy that had prevailed in the country until the British restored law and order. The Pindari rampages and the turbulence caused by the Marathas and the Muslims had exposed the countryside and the towns equally to the law of the jungle. A proverb had gained common currency during this lawlessness: One who does not guard his belongings is a fool; but a greater fool is one who does not grab the unguarded belongings of other people.[77] That such sentiments were expressed in what was intended to be a didactic novel for young boys and girls would suggest that Bhatt not only believed, but was also willing to transmit the belief, that following God's grace the British had 'saved' India from anarchy.

Even the article on Bright — in which his governor-generalship is hypothesized in order to bring home the eventual meaninglessness of any solicitude for India that came from public men in Britain — contained a loyal assertion that did not square with its explicit argument and implicit assumptions. Referring to Bright's proposed division of India into a number of presidencies which were to be governed so as to enable self-rule in the event of British departure, Bhatt commented: 'This, our prayer to God is, may never happen. It is impossible not to be the subjects of a kind and just government like the present one.'[78]

Despite his understanding of the imperial system, Bhatt exhorted his countrymen to press for the redressal of numerous grievances because there were sincere well-wishers in England who would ensure that Indians were not denied justice indefinitely. He also proudly reminded the British of the steadfast loyalty that many Indians had shown during 1857.[79] And, like most of his contemporaries, he did this without being struck by the underlying incongruity and ambivalence of his attitude.

II

Faith in colonialism despite an understanding of its exploitativeness — this was the paradox of educated consciousness in colonial India. This was a result of the depressing realization — from which there was no escape for the generation that came of age after 1857 — that the struggle against British rule would go on beyond the foreseeable future. To the extent that this paradox was perceived by the colonized, it only presented to them a dilemma regarding the specific strategies and programmes that might be the starting point of this struggle.

But the paradox was never fully perceived. The reality of exploitation was seen, and so was the futility of relying on colonial masters; yet the British were appealed to for relief and reform. Faith in the rulers had been internalized, and this influenced not only tactical calculations but also the very perception of colonial rule. This really means that the understanding of its reality was, at one level, nullified. It was this that impaired the capacity of the colonized to be free, and facilitated the operation of 'English poetry'.

Much of the manifestation of loyalty was no more than an empty ritual. A matter of form — a necessary preface for addressing rulers even when the aim was to present a grievance — the ritualized expression of loyalty seems to have become a habit with people. A typical illustration is a review in *Harishchandra's Magazine* (1874) which assailed Raja Shiv Prasad's *Itihasatimirnashak* for favourably comparing conditions in British India with the dark days of Muslim rule. Before exposing the Raja's pro-British bias, the reviewer says: 'We will be guilty of the blackest ingratitude if we do not acknowledge the blessings we enjoy under the British Government.' The formality of a loyal preface completed, he comes to the point: 'but it has excelled all the former governments of the country in the variety and number of its taxes on the people.' Though maintaining a civilized exterior it has, he says, surpassed the worst elements of Muslim misrule. He adds that 'the system of local taxation in India seemed to have been devised to produce among the people the maximum torment and terror.' The reviewer concludes: 'Still Babu Shiv Prasad thinks it fit to sound the praises of the British Government in this respect.'[80]

The equation of British rule with Ramarajya was not confined to the small community of Hindi writers who knew one another's writings intimately. It was also evident in writers from different and far-flung parts of the country who had little chance of interaction or of directly influencing each other. While this undoubtedly reflected a broad similarity in Indian response to British rule, the similarity was by no means exhausted by ritualized expressions of loyalty.

Dalpatram Dahyabhai (1820–98) and Narmadashankar Lalshankar Dave (1833–86) provide examples. Rival figures in their own day, these two architects of modern Gujarati literature continue to be seen as symbols of opposed trends in the literary as well as general sociopolitical development of Gujarat. Dalpat is seen as the circumspect conservative who stood for gradual change in society and politics. Narmad is remembered as the very picture of defiance. Dalpat, naturally, figures as a loyalist, and Narmad as a fiery patriot. However, their works reveal, with different stresses, the same general attitude defined as loyalty and an awareness of subjection. If Dalpat welcomed British rule in India with the image of sunrise, he also provided in his long poem, entitled 'Hunnar Khan ni Chadhai' (1851), one of the first graphic accounts in modern Indian literature of the devastation caused by the British.[81] Similarly, while Narmad formulated the idea of swaraj, he also prayed for eternal British presence in India.[82]

Dalpat used the fabled attributes of Ramarajya to describe British rule; besides, he also linked British rule to *satyuga*. Convinced that 'by God's grace true satyuga has come about', he wrote: 'It was in Ramarajya that lions, goats and sheep played together. But such is the prevailing justice that rabbits drive lions while frogs hop along, and goats leash elephants.'[83] Narmad, too, referred to Ramarajya, and only with a slight variation in detail. Instead of goats and lions, he showed goats and wolves together peacefully under the protection of British justice.[84]

The widespread equating of British rule with Ramarajya, even down to a similarity in the details with which this was done, confirms this as one of the ritualized expressions of loyalty. Coming back to Hindi, in *Bharat Saubhagya* Premghan wrote thus in praise of Pax Britannica: 'Both the lion and the goat now amiably drink water at the same bank.'[85] Radhakrishna Das (1865–1907), first cousin of Harishchandra and a man of letters in his own right, further embellished the standard portrayal in his elegy on Queen Victoria: 'The lion and the goat drink water together'; and added: 'With folded hands the lightning waits in attendance.'[86] A correspondent writing in the *Hindi Pradip* echoed these words.[87] Even Balmukund Gupta (1865–1907), a relatively militant writer who had served his literary and political apprenticeship under Pratapnarayan Misra and made *Bharatmitra* a fairly trenchant paper during his editorship, employed this imagery in his politically trenchant *Chitthe aur Khat* (1901–7).[88]

The imagery obviously rested on exaggeration. Not meant to be taken literally, it was part of the popular Indian mode of perception and articulation. Exaggeration and fantasy constituted two essential ingredients of this particular mode. Exaggeration, as Radhakrishna Das noted, came naturally to the traditional popular sensibility.[89] Analogies from mythology were a recognized way of understanding and explaining social phenomena. Consequently, depending upon the context, certain aspects of a given situation or human qualities were dramatized, to the virtual exclusion of other qualities, and apparently with little regard for any balanced statement. For instance, antinomies such as *sura* (god) and *asura* (demon) were employed to describe several situations and people. But the lasting impression was not meant to be the irreconcilable distance between rival positions or points of view: the dichotomization dissolved in experience. After all, Ram had his flaws while Ravana, his prime antagonist, had a generous share of virtues. The articulation of this sensibility thus comprises, in part, sharply opposed pictures which do not extend with any finality into suggesting any irreconcilable opposition. The use of exaggeration in both praising and condemning foreign rule allowed a measure of freedom to reject or accept parts of the broad characterizations that were made, depending upon the situation. It permitted the construction of a stereotype of British rule that could credit the British with intrinsic goodness, even while imputing to them the vilest intentions. Both these aspects were very frequently dramatized, without either one being shown as more true or valid than the other.

In this stereotype, the Angrej Raj was *suraj*. This suraj (good rule) was distinguished by peace, freedom and rule of law. 'Even in Angrej Raj' was a familiar prefatory strain in many writings of this period. In the opening scene of *Bharat Durdasha*, the inventory of the country's ills is preceded by the remark: 'Angrej Raj teems with happiness.'[90] In *Bharat-Janani*, similarly, Mother India cajoles her sons: 'This is Queen Victoria's reign. Wake up, my children, and be rid of your fear.'[91] In a long poem detailing the wretched condition of Indians, Pratapnarayan Misra made them say: 'Even in this suraj we are living out our days with the name of God on our lips.'[92] Pratapnarayan may have dismissed the idea of freedom under the British as 'the horns of an ass',[93] yet he did not quite believe his own simile when he moaned on behalf of the victims of *begar* (forced labour): 'Everybody has freedom in the English Raj; but lightning has struck our destiny and slavery is our lot.'[94] Premghan, too, regretted that the poor of the country had known nothing of the happiness of 'this good rule'.[95]

The frequent expression of loyalty can be ascribed partly to anxiety at possible official displeasure. Most of the creative writers of the period were not only politically inclined but were also practising journalists. In both capacities they wrote things that the authorities might find less than palatable. The situation called for a discursive strategy by which dissenting ideas were couched within a bed of loyalist phrases which minimized the risk of an outright clampdown on disguised dissent. Hemchandra Banerji, whose poetry offers no exception to the usual combination of loyalism and patriotism, wrote in his *Birbahu Kabya* (1861–6): 'With fear I write, and so I can write little. But if there were no fear, you could have listened to the angry strains of my lyre sending thrilling sensations to the lacerated heart of India.'[96]

Though he occasionally borrowed from Hemchandra Banerji, Bharatendu Harishchandra probably realized on his own the constraints upon politically oriented literary composition. In the preface to a 'loyal' poem (1877), he wrote that, in deference to the glory of the British, the natural impulse to express sentiments that had long been nursed in the heart must be restrained by humility and the meticulous observance of truth.[97] However, as he realized to his cost, caution could not always obviate the risk of an adverse official reading. He came under the cloud of official suspicion for what, according to him, the authorities had unreasonably interpreted as 'disloyal' writing in *Kavivachansudha*.[98] Pratapnarayan, in a poem addressed to the visiting Prince of Wales, showed himself taking the Prince away from the guided tours organized by officialdom, in order to show him, instead, the depressed conditions of the country. Pratapnarayan expressed the fear that he, the narrator, would be beaten up and not be permitted to cry out if the officials got wind of what he was saying.[99] The frequent use of asides by Bhatt to say harsh things about the British in his dialogue between Englandeshwari and Bharat-Janani seems to call for a similar discursive strategy.

Yet loyalty was more than a simple function of pragmatism born out of fear. As a young boy of twelve, Harishchandra could hardly have been moved by pragmatic considerations to write a poem on the death of the queen's spouse. Nor is it likely that Raja Rampal Singh 'danced with joy' on reading the song in *Bharat Saubhagya* that wished Queen Victoria a long life of 'a hundred thousand years'.[100] The question of loyalty received serious consideration from Govardhanram Tripathi. Having made a fetish of clarity, this cerebral analyst of Indian affairs sought to remain unswayed by despair or by wishful thinking in his examination of foreign domination and freedom, to which he turned time and again in his *Scrap Book*. On 22 November 1892 he noted:

> India is under foreign control and the foreigner is the kindliest of all foreigners available. To gel rid of the foreigner by force or fraud is an idea associated with all the incidents that remind us of his rule being foreign. The idea naturally haunts our uneducated instincts; to the educated instincts the idea is both foolish and fallacious. It is foolish because it is not practicable, and because any experiments founded upon it would send the country from the frying pan into the fire. It is a fallacious idea because the distinction between a native and a foreigner is only transient, and the distinction is not a guarantee of the native being a better ruler than the foreigner in such a mass of heterogeneous people as makes up my country. The proper problem is not the absolute eviction of the foreigner, but of his accommodation to the native element.[101]

In questioning the too readily accepted distinction between 'foreign' and 'native', Govardhanram was not positing an identity between them. He was warning against assuming a homogeneity of interests on the simplistic basis that these diverse people happened to live within the same territory. He was not unmindful of the opposition between foreign and native interests. The 'proper problem', as he elaborated it in the same entry in the *Scrap Book*, was:

> In India the sovereign is enlightened, and yet has an interest foreign to the country. Two things have to be done. This interest has to be made to cease to be foreign; and, while it is foreign, we want natives who will guard against the civic temptations to which the foreigner is exposed by his position, people who will enable native interests to grow and develop without any hindrance from the adverse interests of the rulers, who will in fact watch over the real interests and develop the future welfare of the country.

'And', Govardhanram added significantly, 'it is possible to do this both loyally and patriotically.' In the four volumes of his magnum opus, *Sarasvatichandra*, he tried to demonstrate the practicability of this exercise. Planning the novel as an epic in prose about his times, he combined realism and idealism to provide, in moving terms, a view of the present and a vision of the future. In the third volume, particularly, he took up the question of British domination. In what was perhaps the most daring and poignant treatment of 1857 in nineteenth-century creative or discursive Indian writing, he showed how British rule meant both the subjection of India and a potentially great phase in the country's history.[102]

When the third volume appeared in 1898, 'a strong rumour' was afloat in Ahmedabad that Govardhanram had been arrested in Bombay for sedition. The rumour set in motion a train of thought in Govardhanram's mind. For two days his wife, sister and mother agonized in Nadiad, until they got his letter and telegram saying he had not been arrested. It led Govardhanram to ask himself: 'Was it a mistake to have written a book which has so disturbed the peace and happiness of my family? What is my duty? To boldly write such a book for my people or secure the peace of my family against such contingency?'[103] In the midst of this anguished speculation there was, however, one point about which Govardhanram was perfectly clear. 'My book', he insisted, 'is not only loyal, but my innermost soul feels that it is written for and must tend to the welfare of both the rulers and the ruled. My heart is not burdened with care on that point.'[104]

If Govardhanram's *Scrap Book*, with its stern introspectiveness, offers any clue to contemporary educated Indian thinking on the subject, the notion of a necessary tutelage under the British was certainly more than merely a sentiment intended to placate the rulers. British rule was expected to revitalize a polity and civilization in decline. One extract from the *Scrap Book* entry of 22 November 1892 runs:

> The political sagacity and shrewdness, the moral unity and strength, the practical art and energy and activity, the physical stamina and virtues, etc., make the rulers a giant to the ruled pigmy. Yet, in the comparative conscience of British institutions and people, there is a real and most pregnant hope for the pigmy. It is also a question of turning the pigmies into beings with higher statures.

> I see the European and the Native, and what is great and little in either. The smallest European is a very powerful spark of fire: powerful for good and for evil, and more for the latter within the present generation in India. Some of the greater Natives that I could see were bloated semblances of a live coal without any real fire, except for their absorption with Europeans: flatterers, place-seekers, cowards, fools, rogues and spies, were these Natives. Others there are of a really admirable type — but a

Dadabhai is rare, and mostly there are those that have virtue and capacity without position, and it is generally a doubt whether the position, when reached, will not spoil both virtue and capacity rather than improve them.[105]

The high standards Govardhanram set for personal and public conduct may have made him sceptical of the actual capabilities of his fellow Indians. But his assessment was shared by most of his compatriots, including even militant ideologues of Indian nationalism like Bankimchandra Chatterji (1838–94).

Narmad was naive enough to believe that were a member of the British royal family sent out to govern India, the foreignness of the foreigner would disappear. 'Instead of the Mughals', he observed, 'the English would live here, and with that the country's morale, wealth and prosperity would blossom forth.' If Narmad anticipated a possible conflict with the British, it was in the distant future when, going against their better nature, they might refuse to give Indians their due. Should that happen, Indians would have to fight, and God would not disapprove of their action. In the meantime, however, all would be well with the permanent stationing in India of a member of the royal family.[106]

Similarly, despite his conviction that no conquering nation had ever done good to the conquered, Pratapnarayan Misra believed that one of the chief reasons for India's troubles lay in the transitory nature of Anglo-Indian officials in India. 'Without living together for long', he felt, 'mutual affection cannot develop; and without such affection one cannot be a well-wisher of the other.' For him, too, British royalty stationed permanently in India would help solve the problem. The royal touch would make India a home for the rulers, who would then treat its people with solicitude and love.[107] Radhakrishna Das did one better: he wanted the queen herself to settle in India and banish the poverty, ignorance and sorrow of the Indian people.[108]

Cynical resignation in the face of political power was condensed by Tulsidas and transmitted over the centuries as folk wisdom: 'Whoever be the king, what harm can it be to us.'[109] This, clearly, was unacceptable to educated Indians, who tended to devise more complex ideological constructs to come to terms with political subjection: a rationalization of their acceptance of subjection was necessary.

As summed up by Narmad, the dilemma facing Indians was: swaraj was the only *anukool sthiti* — agreeable state — but it was madness to even talk about it. Writing with a candour and clarity not usual for him and his times, he explained in a long essay entitled 'Aryotkarsha' (1882) that although swaraj was the only effective solution to India's problems, it was a goal towards which Indians, in their existing state of mind, were not inclined to work. It would not be possible to uproot the British, so systematically had they entrenched themselves in the country. It would, in fact, be foolish for Indians to make the kind of efforts made by Italians for the freedom and unification of their country.[110] The reference to swaraj occurs almost fleetingly. Narmad mentions it as a general ideal; its importance for India is confined to a tantalizingly brief footnote. In the main text he quickly moves on to stress the need for India to have a body of selfless, independent-minded, honest and discerning leaders who will act as intermediaries between the people and the government.

Narmad's attitude towards British rule was obviously influenced by pragmatism. But such pragmatism did not always operate at a conscious level. The realization of what seemed feasible in the foreseeable future tended to constrain people's very conception of what needed to be done. Imperceptibly, the feasible was inscribed into the normative. Thus was created the space for the writing of loyal poetry by Narmad, and by others like him who were serious and patriotic men of letters and not mercenary bards. Genuine faith and pragmatic considerations fused in the making of Indian loyalty.

Harishchandra's *Vishasya Vishamaushadham* is a fine specimen of this fusion. Betraying a range of tone not entirely intended by the playwright, it illustrates the amalgam of naivety, deep-rooted faith, petty personal calculations, and serious national considerations which collectively account for Indian loyalty. This is the play that ends with the six-line song simultaneously wishing for permanent British rule and the victory of India. Dealing with the deposition of Malharrao Gaekwad, it recapitulates how the British first came as traders and managed in the course of time to acquire a power by which they could treat Indian rulers like 'flies in the milk' and cast them off. The tone is clearly hostile to the British. Although the narration is given an apparently different turn when the British are praised for intelligence, power, and good governance, there are hints that this praise should not be believed. 'That which the king administers is justice', we are told; also that the king and God are alike; you can only see and suffer whatever they do; there is no room for dissent. Finally, we are treated to an anecdote involving a king and three flatterers. The king asks if they can flatter him. Two of them answer in the affirmative and, predictably, are disgraced. The third worms his way into royal favour by saying: 'Do I have the power to flatter you, great king!' We are also shown the petty calculations that lie behind such time-serving.[111]

All this pertains ostensibly to the court of Malharrao Gaekwad, but there is no doubt that it also applies to the British. There is, again, an oscillation between loyalism and patriotism: it is hoped in the *Vishasya Vishamaushadham* that the British will stay in the country so long as there is water in the Ganga and the Yamuna,[112] even as the title of the play means 'poison kills poison'.

One may see, in all this, the coming into being of a new myth which was required for different reasons by both the rulers and the ruled.[113] This myth rested on belief in a prolonged phase of anarchy from which the British had been divinely willed to rescue India. This was consistent with the faith in a divine teleology that formed an essential constituent of Hindu cosmology,[114] and also with the scheme of causation in traditional Indian historiography. The British throve on this myth, and it was reinforced by their account of the dark interregnum between the downfall of the Mughals and their own final triumph.[115] It was, however, the habit of explaining critical historical events in terms of divine will that made the acceptance of British rule easier for Indians.

Children in schools were fed on this sort of divinely directed history through textbooks like Shiv Prasad's *Itihasatimirnashak*. Written with official blessing and translated into English by M. Kempson, the Director of Public Instruction, it was widely used in the North West Provinces and Avadh. The following excerpts relating to the foundation of the Mughal empire are typical of the mode of historical explanation used in this book:

> Here he [Babar] found Ibrahim Lodi posted to receive him with an army of 1,00,000 horse and foot, and 1,000 elephants. Babar's troops were only 12,000 men in all; but victory and defeat are in the hands of God; and Ibrahim Lodi perished at Panipat....

And further about Babar and his dynasty:

> At one time he was in such a plight that he determined to go as a faqir to China; but God had willed that his grandson was to become the greatest and best sovereign that ever governed Hindustan, whose dynasty was to last till the coming of the English.[116]

> Then the Mughals fell on evil days and God willed the English to provide relief to the people of Hindustan. When the English troops reached Delhi, they found: "The Emperor was almost starving, and the people were in a miserable condition...."[117]

The British, with their golden touch, 'converted' India 'from a wilderness into a garden'. This happened during the rule of the East India Company. When the Company had accomplished what the 'Creator' had ordained, something better came India's way. The Crown took over the Indian empire, and 'even the black people became the subjects of Empress Victoria'. Readers of *Itihasatimirnashak* were advised to pray that a 'ryot-protecting ruler' like Victoria may 'forever remain above their heads'.[118]

Concomitant with the creation of a myth of divine dispensation was fostered the belief in British moral superiority and military invincibility, particularly after 1857. The world had seen many conquering races, but, continued Shiv Prasad's account, they had all lapsed into luxury and eventual doom. The British were a different kind of conqueror. With dramatic exaggeration, an essential element of effective myths, Shiv Prasad inspired his young readers with awe for their heaven-sent masters:

> Thus the nations beyond the Danube conquered the Romans; thus the Arabs conquered the Iranis, and the Tartars the Chinese; and thus at the present day the Farangis have conquered the whole world. Their power is now immense; but such is the currency of knowledge among them and such its increase day by day, that instead of falling into luxurious ease they even add to their military prestige; and if, by reason of their great wealth, they fall into habits of luxury, to the prejudice of their constitutional vigour, yet such is their scientific skill that they make cannon, guns, ships, and all sorts of novel machines, by the aid of which a single man becomes as powerful as hundreds, or thousands, or even ten thousands, of his fellows.[119]

The effect of such ideas on English-educated Indians is illustrated by the diary of young and adolescent B. K. Thakore (1869–1952), who rose to be an eminent Gujarati historian, critic and poet. As a young man of nineteen, studying in Bombay, he happened to read in *Mahratta* 'an extract from an article in the Contemporary Review by one Townsend'. The piece 'so absorbed' him that he 'determined to finish it carefully and so did not go to the Law class'. He was stunned by it. Thakore's account of the way he was affected offers a rare insight into the agony that informed the consciousness of men and women when they accepted the British superiority. In an entry dated 25 July 1888, the day he read Townsend, Thakore wrote:

> The effect it produced on me was prodigious and wholly unexperienced before. I can't say what it was like even metaphorically. I don't know whether I would feel so if my heart were bored through by a red hot iron bar. Perhaps I felt as I might feel if I heard someone relating with pride a long list of murders in cold blood of those most dear to him and perpetrated by himself.[120]

Thakore summarizes Townsend's argument in this way:

> We Asiatics do not and can never regard with anything but dislike a Government by law. What we most prize is the independence of our will to all law whatsoever. The power to dispense even life and death merely as the feat of our will, total irresponsibility, is and cannot but be our only ideal of political power. This every individual had a chance to attain to in all the past regimes of India.[121]

In Thakore's rendering of Townsend's argument, this ideal of political power is antithetical to everything the English stand for. Consequently:

> We, the English, can never offer them such a chance in the faintest degree, and so they can never be contented in our regime. This discontent was the real cause of the Sepoy mutiny; ... The vastly additional security to life and property, the infinitely greater convenience, the strictly impartial justice that the British can offer and must offer will be offered in vain; and so during the next three hundred years, though there is no chance of foreign aggression, England will have to leave India on account of one, two or three internal revolutions which at length she would not see the good of

crushing. And within 10 years after England has gone the country will be almost in the same state, the state loved by Asiatics, in which it was when she came. Thus the grand experiment Europe tries on Asia will inevitably end in failure; it is in the very nature of things that it should be so.[122]

The myth was, clearly, in full force. So, rattled to the core, poor Thakore wondered:

> Now what torments me most is that looking to our past history this theory cannot be 'exploded' as a too ingenious one. Are we then doomed forever? Can the past never be annihilated, nullified, revoked, modified — are the present and future mere beatings in the void! What has the present done — has it touched anything but big cities — and how lightly has it touched even these! . . . And what a gigantic past it has been! The study of Indian History has become a more imperious necessity. What do I know of the backbone of the Indian people — or can anything be known — has it any backbone? Or can it ever be created? — What a dreadfully long time it would take — and what chances are there for our success in improvement or creation. — At any rate religion and eloquence are the only means and even these, where are they — God!![123]

A similar current of feeling was voiced by Radhakrishna Das, who complained that most of the current histories of the country 'planted in young tender hearts the thought that they are worthless and meant to be slaves forever'.[124] There were others who understood the urgency of a reconstructed, new past. The rulers, whether Muslim or British, had provided histories of India in accordance with their own requirements, and it was incumbent on the subject people to seek freedom from this vision of their past. M. M. Kunte explained in the Preface to his *The Vicissitudes of Aryan Civilization in India* (1880) why he had felt driven to undertake this sort of work:

> As yet, Indians themselves have not undertaken seriously the investigation of important historical problems connected with their own country. But they have a stand-point of their own — a stand-point supported by overwhelming evidence, and a stand-point which at once encourages and gratifies patriotism. From this stand-point, the strange revolutions — through which India has passed during the thousands of years over which her history extends — have been reviewed . . . with that anxious care and accuracy which scientific history demands.[125]

The search for a counter-history was facilitated by the traditional absence of a distinction between mythology and history. So, both literary and quasi-historical classics of the past — the Ramayana, the Mahabharata and the Puranas, for example — came to be seen as more than repositories of the community's myths, wisdom and traditions; they were seen as containing a history and a meaning relevant in providing the raw materials for reconstructing India's past. They were histories.

The past, in myth, is part of a community's collective memory. A mythic past is felt, and lived, in the present. While one might establish a binary opposition in analyzing history and myth, within real-life situations there is never a sharp distinction between mythical and historical consciousness. In nineteenth-century India, though it was beginning to be made, the distinction between myth and history was minimal. It was natural even for the English-educated to consider, for example, Ram and Yudhishthir at par with Akbar and Ahalyabai in terms of their historicity. They could, with equal ease, date back the political history of India to solar and lunar dynasties from which, supposedly, the heroes of the Ramayana and the Mahabharata had emerged.

This consciousness produced the myth of a glorious past as a counterpoint to the myth of the white man's civilizing mission. The two myths together created a balance in which the Indians' sense of subjection, while continuing to be galling, ceased to be paralyzing. The myth of a glorious past was constructed not simply to get away from the humiliation of the present sensation of subjection, but also by the need to accept the present as divinely ordained; this alleviated the sense of impotence that Indians felt.

Eager to provide an alternative and inspiring narrative, Radhakrishna Das drew attention to political expansionism in ancient India. In a biographical series planned to highlight the greatness of yore, he included a vignette of Vijay Singh, scion of the Sinhabhumi dynasty that had ruled over Bengal 2500 years earlier. This was a striking inclusion because, unlike other celebrities in the series, Vijay Singh had a reprehensible character. But Radhakrishna Das was anxious to remove the misconception that Indians in general, and Bengalis in particular, had never achieved glory or conquest abroad. The inclusion of Vijay Singh, who had carved out for himself a kingdom in Sri Lanka, was meant to do this. More significantly, Das hoped that Vijay Singh's example would inspire young readers — tormented as he knew they were by a sense of worthlessness and the prospect of eternal slavery — with something of the 'exultation of foreign conquests', and imbue them with pride in the glory and might of their country.[126]

The assumption in much modern Indian historiography that the myth of an ancient Indian millennium was the creation of later-nineteenth-century socio-religious movements like the Arya Samaj — which are described as revivalistic — is not strictly true. The myth was integral to the mental stock of an educated Hindu.

We have seen that even the beneficiaries of a liberal education in English, including some who embraced Christianity, subscribed with pride to the idea of a glorious Indian past. A critical example relates to a neglected dimension of R. C. Dutt's (1848–1909) nationalism. Irrespective of ideological divisions within it, modern Indian historiography has enshrined Dutt, author of *The Economic History of India* (a classic two-volume *exposé* of the economic consequences of British rule), as one of the chief proponents of 'economic nationalism' in contradistinction to 'cultural nationalism'. In actual fact Dutt contributed to the growth of nationalism in both its economic and cultural aspects, because for him the material and the cultural were inseparable constituents of Indian nationalism.

The neglected dimension of Dutt's nationalism pertains to what he called his 'literary patriotism'. It prompted him to translate the Rig Veda, the Ramayana and the Mahabharata, and to write the *History of Civilization in Ancient India* as well as four historical and two social novels. His 'literary patriotism' reveals why this anglicized civilian viewed himself as a progressive conservative.[127] The translations and *Civilization in Ancient India* recall a glorious past. Elegiac in tone, the historical novels, in particular, lament the loss of this past. This lament is also implicitly an attempt to recover the past in order to make bearable the oppressive present.

Dutt's first historical novel appeared in 1874 and the last in 1879. During the course of these years he realized there were risks in recreating a past which overlooked the achievements of Indian Muslims. A period of introspection and a different kind of creative gestation then followed. When Dutt's first social novel, *Sansar*, came out seven years later, in 1886, there was a marked shift in his treatment of the past. Though he idealized a Hindu–Buddhist past in *Sansar*, Dutt avoided the anti-Muslim bias that had run through his historical novels. This was conceived as a realistic novel encapsulating the more salient socio-religious and political aspects of late nineteenth-century India. The novel seemed important enough for Dutt to translate it from Bengali into English as *The Lake of Palms* (1902).

The past is inserted as a basic and recurrent theme in this realistic novel. In terms of the structure of the narrative, the insertion remains unconvincing and mars the flow of the narrative. But so important is the idealization of the past in Dutt's scheme of things that, despite its parenthetical character, it occupies nearly as much space as do the more integral constituents of the narrative: the past figures compulsively as a personal and collective psychological necessity.

Being socially necessary to sustain the present, the past need not have figured extraneously. But Dutt lacked the stylistic innovativeness required in order to weave it into the fabric of his narrative. He only managed to insert the past in the form of authorial observation or dialogues on facts, both of which read like lessons in history. These lessons now appear more hortatory than stirring, though the contemporary Indian — shall we say Hindu? — response was probably the reverse. An example of Dutt's writing is:

> Ancient empires and ancient nations have passed away, and the antiquarian and the explorer trace their remains in Egypt and in Babylon. In India alone there is continuity between the past and the present, and the past with all its glory and splendour lives in the hearts and in the lives of the modern nation![128]

The authorial voice holds forth on this link by explicating the 'meaning' of Banaras:

> The modern traveller ... carries away with him the impression of a curious old town with strange superstitions and uncouth rites. The thoughtful enquirer sees in Benares a microcosm of the old Hindu world — with its ancient faith, its antique learning, its quaint methods of business, — a strange survival of an old-world prince. And as he stands by the cloisters of some temple where the Vedic Hymns are still chanted, or visits some old Swami who still teaches the lessons of the Vedanta, glimpses of times

like the early days of Greece come back to him for a moment amidst all the hurry and bustle of a steam-worked railway-girdled modern world. Men, living in humble huts amid squalid surroundings, still hand down to generations of modern Hindus those venerable systems of philosophy, faith and learning, to which Socrates must have given an utterance, and Alcibiades have heard.[129]

The Lake of Palms is divided into four 'books'. The third 'book', entitled 'The Temple', describes a journey from Raniganj to Jagannath Puri. Ailing for months, Jagat Kisor, a rich young zamindar, has not responded to treatment. Even the change from unhealthy Burdwan to the more salubrious climate of Raniganj has had no salutary effect. His mother, an intelligent and cultured old woman, is inspired by Lord Shiva in a dream to take her son to Puri. She is convinced that the pilgrimage will restore his health, as, indeed, it does. But neither the oneiric interlude nor the ultimate realization of its objective makes the journey integral to the main narrative: it remains a mere contrivance for Dutt to detail 'the past with all its glory and splendour'.

The journey from Raniganj to Puri is thus a long detour in terms of the novel's narrative. A further detour is devised in the course of this journey to bring about a visit to Bhubaneswar, then an abandoned city of caves and temples which did not fall on the route to Puri. This is intended to let the reader get a glimpse of this glorious specimen of the past and appreciate the authorial verdict: 'For the Hindu planned as a Titan and worked as a jeweller.'[130] It would have been too unrealistic to have put Jagat Kisor, the patient who provides the pretext for the pilgrimage, in to this detour. He stays on in Cuttack, as does his young wife. It is his mother and brother-in-law, Sarat — a bright and idealistic university student — who make the detour to Bhubaneswar upon the insistence of their generous host.

The pious old lady, by her very upbringing, is steeped in the past, in the culture the novelist seeks to romanticize and make available to his people. But she alone will not do, for the future of the nation lies with the young and the educated. They must together discover a national identity. So, in Bhubaneswar the old woman tells the young man: 'This is a city of temples ... surely they were gods who could build like this.' And the young man answers: "They had indeed more than human skill and human fervour, in the ancient days, to have covered this ancient city with such structures. They had an aim and purpose in life. . . .'[131]

For the woman, the divine is real in the sense of being perceptible in life and in things around her. For the young man it is a metaphor that he can translate into secular terms. And to the novelist the important thing is the rapport between the two with regard to their national culture. At one point the man says: 'we live listless and aimless these days.' And the old woman cheers up the young patriot:

> Aye, my son, you speak truly. Those who have faith can do much, and the gods assisted the kings who reared these temples of old. Strive, my children, ye who are young and strong, strive with faith and with a purpose, and ye, too, shall achieve something for your country, even in these days.[132]

Patriotism thus cements the cultural bond between the generations, represented here by Jagat's mother and Sarat.

In *The Lake of Palms* Dutt is not looking for a pristine past far removed from a superstitious present. He searches for a past that lives on in the present. This is not mere revivalism, because it is not enough that Sarat, symbolizing the culturally deracinated youth, should discover his heritage and, through it, his national identity. Dutt considers it important that he be able to relate this identity with the life and values of the older generation, from whom he has been estranged. It is in account of this kind of revivalism that, like his discovery of Bhubaneswar, Sarat comprehends the reality of Banaras in the company of a devout old woman. On this occasion the woman is his own mother. The old lady, having pined for years to be in the holy city, is 'entranced' at the cluster of temples and residential buildings in Banaras. She goes to the temple of Vishwanath, the Lord of the World: 'Thrice she prostrated herself at its gate, and then reverently entering its precincts, the world passed from her soul.'[133]

Sarat resists the spell of the city, but succeeds only for a while: 'Sarat, undergraduate of an English College, had not entered a temple, nor offered worship to a graven image. He waited for his mother outside, but the chanting of the ancient Mantra struck his ear, and the silent prostrations of the pious caught his eye, his heart too was moved to a silent prayer.'[134]

The scene seems to symbolize a historic moment in the life of the nation, and this is what *The Lake of Palms* celebrates. It is at the point of recording Sarat's change of heart that Dutt reports a larger change:

> The teachings of the missionary and the schoolmaster during the early years of the nineteenth century have unsettled the mind of the educated youth of India, and produced a reaction against the prevailing forms of worship. But a deeper education is teaching the later generations to enter beyond the mere forms of ceremonial, and to seek for light and religious consolation in those ancient scriptures which are the undying heritage of this great nation. Greek and Persian, Hun and Scythian, Moslem and Christian, have battled in vain against that ancient and deep-seated faith, that worship of the One Universal Soul, which is the creed of the modern Hindu, as it was the creed of the ancient Upanishads and the Vedanta. And every passing year of thought and study only brings the millions of Hindus closer to this cardinal faith of their forefathers.[135]

As unravelled in *The Lake of Palms*, 'the undying heritage of this great nation' — the cultural continuity between past and present — is steeped in religion. Social life and institutions have over the millennia been so intertextured with religion as to make culture indistinguishable from religion. It is this intertexture that makes it possible for the past, 'with all its glory and splendour', to live 'in the hearts and the lives of the modern nation'.

The historiography of modern India may have ignored the cultural dimension of Dutt's nationalism. In his own day, and for decades thereafter, it was as much a source of inspiration to Indians as was his exposure of material devastation. His novels reached different parts of the country through translations, while his *History of Civilization in Ancient India* commanded a country-wide readership because it was written in English. We have seen how, having been shattered, B. K. Thakore stumbled upon the 'imperious necessity' of studying Indian history. Soon it became crucial for him to know what had befallen 'a people once so Godlike ... of grand achievement and heroic confidence', and to be able to answer the question: 'How could such *swayambhu* power ever leave the earth it had ennobled by its self-manifestation?'[136] Early in 1890, following two years of torment, Thakore came across *Maharashtra Jivanprabhat* (1878), one of Dutt's historical novels. Thakore records its effect upon him: 'Jivanprabhat moved me for days and I could not rest until I beg [*sic*] a long review of it in Gujarati. I dashed off ten pages but the subject grew as I went on writing and the review proper is not begun yet.'[137] Two years later Thakore read the *History of Civilization in Ancient India* which gave his 'patriotic endeavour' an exceptional impetus:

> Finished Dutt's Ancient India. I remember the first time, 4 years back, that the reading of Macaulay first awakened me to Nationality and national progress.
>
> A procession of noble patriots holding aloft the sacred banner of a nation on the march — that is History.
>
> I first saw this while reading Macaulay's History of England: I was first able to recognise and name the complex surging up as one read on. . . .
>
> Have looked into not a few histories and philosophies and political books in these four years. . . . Each worthily written passage and chapter, each speculation that cast a beam on the mind, and indicated however dimly some of the forces against which, some of the laws in conformity with which a nation has attempted to advance, if but a step, towards the slowly attainable ideal, has touched me at once with that complex massive emotion impelling one more directly to the path of patriotic endeavour than, in my case at least, all the poetry and all the religion in the world put together. Dutt's is the first book by an Indian I have read capable of exciting in the sympathetic heart something like the same feeling.[138]

Because of his university education and wide reading of western thinkers and writers, Thakore shared with Dutt some similarity of intellectual exposure. But Dutt's influence need not be ascribed to this similarity, for its spread was much wider. As an example we may mention Maithilisharan Gupta (1886–1964) who, unlike Thakore, was very different from Dutt with regard to social background and formal education. Privileged with neither wealth nor proper education, Maithilisharan emerged from an orthodox Hindu mofussil background to be honoured as *rashtrakavi*, a national poet. The first poetical work that shot him to fame, and which remained throughout the struggle for freedom a source of inspiration to people of different ideological hues, was *Bharat-Bharati* (1912–13). Written in stirring cadenced stanzas, the work nostalgically recalls the awe-inspiring achievements of the ancient Aryans in all walks of life, recounts the pathetic and total degeneration of their progeny, and exhorts the latter to emulate their ancestors and dedicate themselves to the realization of a bright future.

In his 'Preface' to *Bharat-Bharati*, Maithilisharan reveals the patriotic impulse of this work. He is aware of the power of poetry to inspire, but this is tempered by the suspicion that his readers may write off his account of Aryan greatness as mere poetic fancy. So Maithilisharan decided to seek credibility for his account with evidence from authoritative discursive writings. Judging by the numerous footnotes in *Bharat-Bharati*, Dutt's *History of Civilization in Ancient India* seems to have been the most powerful single work influencing his reconstruction of the Aryan past. Dutt's influence, moreover, is not confined to *Civilization in Ancient India*; nor is it limited to footnotes. In a section dealing with the degenerate present, the sorry state of Indian fiction is bemoaned. Of the two novels mentioned as offering hope, one is Dutt's *Maharashtra Jivanprabhat*.[139]

Thus, though its forms varied, revivalism was an essential constituent of the structure of colonial consciousness. Past, tradition and history were terms that conjured up in the minds of the educated Indians a reality from the depths of which could be drawn the resources and reasons for believing in themselves. If Radhacharan Goswami, the Vaishnava priest from Vrindaban, and R. C. Dutt, the anglicized intruder within the heaven-born civil service, are seen as the two polar points of a wide spectrum, the myth of a glorious past reflects something common to their thought processes.

There was yet another way in which relief was sought from the oppressiveness of the present. Belief in an interregnum of anarchy, we know, was essential for the twin myths of divine dispensation and past glory. The Marathas were occasionally held responsible for this anarchy, but the interregnum was seen mainly as tyranny let loose by Muslim rulers. British rule, in this explanatory framework, was the nemesis visited upon the Muslims.

The celebration of this nemesis created the illusion of freedom. This was freedom from Muslim subjection. The illusion seems to have been nurtured through a dual approach to the question of subjection. It consisted of a fine distinction in the treatment of subjection during Muslim rule, and under the British. As if in response to some barely felt possibility of psychological relief, subjection under Muslim rulers was detailed in concrete terms. But British rule was mentioned more abstractly. In *Nil Devi*, for example, Harishchandra condemned Hindus who fought against their own coreligionists and on the side of alien Turks.[140] He called for the complete renunciation of hope for India because of such renegade Hindus. But nowhere in his vast corpus did he express such tortured anger against those who collaborated with the British. Instead, he discussed the problem of subjection under the British either in abstract terms, or in relation to a nostalgia for the past millennium. He never connected this subjection with his frequent wails against the numerous evils of the English *suraj*.

The abstraction of subjection in the context of British rule performed a double function. It permitted a feeling of release from a specific past subjection. At the same time, it facilitated rationalization of present subjection without obliterating the sense of subjection. That is how, in spite of its acknowledged absurdity — Pratapnarayan's 'horns of an ass' may be recalled — the idea of freedom as a gift of British rule could be seriously entertained.

Like faith in the British, the use of 'Muslim misrule' was a double-edged weapon: Muslim rule could be shown as the very picture of tyranny from which the British had provided deliverance, and also as one that was nothing as bad as its successor in its oppressiveness. There was one constant note, however. It was generally agreed that Muslim rulers had made India their home, with the fortunate consequence that the country's wealth remained within, while the outflow of wealth was inherent in the British refusal to settle in India. Harishchandra dramatized this difference when he likened Muslim rule to cholera and British rule to tuberculosis.[141] That both could be fatal was beside the point.

The unfavourable comparison of British with Muslim rule belonged to the category of the patriotic indictment of the former discussed in the first section of this chapter. It did not invalidate the loyalty felt for British rule. Critics, in fact, felt obliged to explain — indeed explain away — the evils for which they were condemning British rule. In normal circumstances, this function should have been discharged by the rulers and not by the ruled. But the irony was that in colonial India the subject people were saddled with this responsibility as well. The need to justify their acceptance of British rule and the simultaneous recognition by them of the fundamentally baneful character of this rule left them with no alternative. The job was done with varying degrees of sophistication. There was, however, a striking resemblance in the arguments and imagery employed for the purpose, just as there was in the expression of faith in the British.

In India the subject population were sometimes even held accountable for the failings of the alien rulers. Explaining why the British were not able to mitigate Indian grievances, the normally militant Pratapnarayan observed: 'Unless the boy in her lap cries, the mother cannot know that he is hungry.'[142] No less militant Bhatt employed the same metaphor: 'Even a mother does not offer milk to her child until it cries.' He added: 'If you speak out, your just government will certainly listen to you.'[143] Premghan multiplied the metaphors: 'Just as a child gets no milk without crying for it, a beggar no alms without begging, and the thirsty no water without asking for it, the ruled do not obtain justice from the ruler without petitioning and wailing.'[144] That this imagery was widespread is reflected in Dalpat's comment: 'A mother does not give her child food until it cries. Nothing will be achieved if you keep your thoughts and feelings locked within your chest.'[145]

Equally puerile, in retrospect, may seem the attempt that was made to harness fatalism in order to sustain faith in the British. Thus, in *Bharat-Janani*, Harishchandra makes Mother India say of her sleeping children: 'The time for their awakening is not yet. Any efforts made at present will be fruitless.' A sympathetic Englishman says in the play: 'Brother, what can one do in this matter? Everything depends on the Creator. Appeal to Him for He is the saviour of the whole world and of its suffering humanity. May He free you from the web of your difficulties.'[146] Elsewhere, Harishchandra says that God has turned His face away from India. Or, he wonders, has 'the merciful Keshava gone off to sleep?'[147] A frequent use of devotional songs to express, often despairingly, the country's plight, also suggests a common tendency to rationalize helplessness by attributing it to the inscrutable designs of God. This was a further aspect of the mentality that made possible the myth of divine dispensation.

Other explanations of why the British failed to provide relief to India were given. Raja Sir T. Madhav Rao (1828–91), for example, discounted the British suspicion that the educated Indians were disloyal. He said they saw British rule as 'The strongest and the most righteous and the best suited to India's diverse populations and diverse interests. ... It is the most capable of self-maintenance, of self-renovation and self-adjustment, in reference to the progressive advancement of the subject races.'[148]

Madhav Rao, the proud Maharashtrian Brahman who had been diwan of three Indian states and had twice declined to be a member of the supreme legislative council, knew that 'it must be contrary to human nature itself to expect that the British nation should undertake the heavy duty and responsibility of governing and defending India without any advantage to itself.' He was not opposed to some legitimate compensation being taken by the British for their pains. However, taking a political position as advanced as almost any during the later nineteenth century, he wanted Indians to make sure that the compensation did not exceed legitimate limits. This needed to be done, he explained, because 'human nature is so constituted that the most exalted political virtues have an inherent tendency to deteriorate unless public opinion acts as a constant corrective'; and also because the British Indian government was liable to lapse from its 'high ideals' as a result of its 'temptation to prefer English to Indian interests'.[149]

In the public pronouncements of Madhav Rao, as in the introspective domain of Govardhanram's *Scrap Book*, could be discerned refined versions of the proverb that even a mother would not feed her young unless the infant cried.

III

Faith in the British carried profound implications for Indian civilization. It marked the real triumph of what we found summed up in the phrase 'English poetry'. Individual Britishers well disposed to India may have seemed futile, but it was believed that British rule would, in general, help India's regeneration. This belief was the thin end of a wedge, for with it the British were able to exercise the sort of dominance that Macaulay, one of their most articulate ideologues, enunciated as early as the 1830s. This was a dominance that was expected to survive colonialism itself, bringing the highest glory to the British nation.[150]

More than the rulers, the ruled needed to nurse this dream. Thus, having witnessed the 'uncertain and painful' state into which the 'politics of the country' had been plunged during Curzon's viceroyalty as a result of that Viceroy's 'conceit, highhandedness and utter disregard for the opinions of those who, as educated Indians, have a more permanent function in Indian politics . . . than any single Viceroy possesses or can possess',[151] Govardhanram could do no better than conclude in his *Scrap Book*: 'But, all the same, the political follies and wickedness of British Officers, when unblushing and acute, are to be seriously deplored as unseemly features of a picture that has excellent beauties elsewhere.'[152]

Govardhanram wrote this between January and May in 1906. He died on 4 January the following year. Compared to 1891, when he justified the Indian National Congress only 'because of our confidence in Hume and Wedderburn',[153] and 1892, when he suspected that the 'virtue and capacity' possessed by a few of his countrymen might be spoiled by 'position', it was an impressive advance to view educated Indians as the real arbiters of the country's destiny. It was not time yet, however, for a comprehensive disavowal of British rule. The West was recognized as the repository of all that was modern, and British rule as the instrument of change along the desired lines.

Govardhanram put it neatly in his *Scrap Book* when, elaborating his plan of intellectual self-training in the service of his country, he wrote with regard to the Upanishads: 'I think there is some meaning in all this, which must be translated into the language of modern ideas before I could accept or reject it.' We can savour something of this translation within the same entry of the *Scrap Book*: 'Nirguna and Nishkarma do not mean more than what Mill would have called "Not manifested through visible sensations".'[154]

For Govardhanram an educated Indian — Hindu — was one who could 'enjoy Shakespeare and Kalidasa' equally.[155] The general acceptance of this ideal is confirmed by the increasing number of translations and adaptations of both Shakespeare and Kalidasa in different Indian languages during the second half of the nineteenth century. Govardhanram was using the two great dramatists emblematically, in order to lay stress on a familiarity with both indigenous and western modes of knowledge as an essential requirement of Indian education. Conversant as he was with the Vedanta and Positivism, the Gita and Utilitarianism, Buddhism and western atheism, Govardhanram could well have defined the educated Indian in his own image. But he was not atypical in this respect. What made him extraordinary was not so much his intellectual repertory as the quality of his mind. The scales, in this conception of the model educated Indian, were weighted against Kalidasa: he could not be at par with Shakespeare. For, although great names of Sanskrit poetics like Bharat and Anandavardhana had lost little lustre, Kalidasa had of necessity to be translated into the language of western literary theory. And Bharatendu too, in a long essay entitled 'Natak' (1883), argued for adapting indigenous dramatic forms in the light of western dramatic forms and principles.[156]

Govardhanram does not seem to have realized the grave politico-cultural implications of a situation that made him translate his own traditions into the language of 'modern' ideas. To the end of his life, he remained seriously engaged in assessing the value and relevance of traditional Indian philosophy and science in the light of western knowledge.[157] The naturalness with which a thinker like him could carry on this sifting operation, without being aware of the fact that it implied an admission of the inferiority of his own knowledge system and world-view, is an index of the effectiveness of imperialist discourse.

Bankim, unlike Govardhanram and the majority of his educated countrymen, was aware of this hegemony. In the course of a controversy with William Hastie (1842–1908) of the Church of Scotland, sparked off in 1882 by a grand *shraddha* (the Hindu last-rite ceremony) in Calcutta, Bankim refused to go along with European scholars because 'no knowledge to them is true knowledge unless it has passed through the sieve of European criticism'.[158] This struck at the root of western supremacy; yet Bankim himself could not do without the European sieve. For example, despite being immersed in the Indian aesthetic theory of *rasa*, he sought to countenance it with western poetics.[159] Similarly, in his discussion of ancient Indian epistemology, he drew upon western philosophy to uphold the traditional Indian position(s) with regard to the question of 'proof'. It mattered little that in conclusion he felt that European philosophy was veering round to the verities of ancient Indian philosophy, and argued that the empiricism of Bacon and Mill resembled Charwak, and that Comte's refutation of this empiricism paralleled Vedanta.[160] Again, in an otherwise scintillating essay on Sankhya, a philosophical system he admired immensely, Bankim did not hesitate to enlist contemporary western psychology and atheism in support of Kapil, the founder of Sankhya.[161]

Perhaps the most sustained attempt to translate indigenous traditions into the language of 'modern' ideas was made in *The Lake of Palms*. The achievements of ancient India are often set forth in this novel against the backdrop of ancient Greece and Rome, the fountainheads of western culture. Thus, an old Swami who teaches Vedanta in modern Banaras brings to mind 'those venerable systems of philosophy, faith and learning, to which Socrates must have given an utterance'. The novel always seeks to unravel in simple, rational terms the mystique of the undying Hindu–Buddhist culture. The oneiric interlude mentioned earlier, in which Lord Shiva commands Jagat Kisor's mother to take her ailing son on the long pilgrimage to Jagannath Puri, is translated into secular and rational terms through the mediation of a European civil surgeon.[162]

It mattered little, then, whether the indigenous past was used to find analogues — and on their strength to claim precedence — for the ideas and institutions that the British prided for themselves, or, alternatively, to glean from this past the traditional alternatives for reshaping Indian society. The point is that the final framework of validation came from the West. The way out of this was to reappropriate an Indian past from the British and rewrite history. But, given the primacy of the rulers' framework of validation, the history of the ruled — both as reconstruction of the past and as the unfolding of a future — could not transcend imperialist discourse. The generations which produced Dalpat and Bankim or Harishchandra and Govardhanram had not entirely lost their traditional moorings, and their writings reveal many ways in which the traditional and the modern mixed in their mental make-up. But a rupture with traditional life had also set in, which kept widening with every succeeding generation. Hence the paradox that the nearer Indians came to political freedom, and the more they felt driven towards their own history and traditions, the surer became the hold upon them of imperialist discourse. The fate of Gandhi's *Hind Swaraj* most fully embodies this paradox.

2

Tradition

Orthodox and Heretical

♠

In *The Lake of Palms*, R. C. Dutt constructs an attractive past and offers the illusion that there is no need to look back towards it. The 'undying heritage' of the nation is shown to exist in the everyday lives of people. This sort of response was difficult to sustain, and one to which Dutt himself could not consistently adhere. Generally, the need to relate to tradition by recovering it from the past rested on the admission of a breach with it, an unfortunate breach to which could be attributed the country's degeneration and subjection. There were differences about what constituted tradition and about the ways of reclaiming it, but there were virtually none with regard to the idea of tradition as the most effective counterpoint to the cultural aggression of colonialism. It was an idea that, in consonance with the requirements of social and cultural cohesion, could serve as a reservoir of orthodoxy and also as a spring-board for radical innovation.

Into these efforts at the recovery of tradition was built, ironically, the acknowledgement that it was also somehow irretrievably lost. Perceived as a counterpoint to the West, it also thus came to be viewed increasingly in the image of the adversary culture: even when the West was apparently rejected, tradition was upheld rather as an improvement upon than an alternative to the West. In this sense tradition, as the answer to western culture, was also a capitulation to it and was doomed to an endless and progressively unequal dialogue with the West. Though not always visible, the West became a persistent factor for the colonized within their attempt to recover their tradition or selfhood. The earlier autonomy of Indian thought was no longer possible.

This drive to recover tradition reflected the aspirations, fears, tensions and ambiguities, both existential and social, of a whole culture. Here we turn to the tension that existed in the search for tradition — *apunapau* as Bharatendu Harishchandra described it — especially in regard to the question of social regeneration.

I

Scholars of social change in modern India are familiar with the dichotomy between belief and action that characterized the behaviour of educated people during the later nineteenth century. There was frequently a divergence between profession and practice within advocates of social reform. This dichotomy, at a deeper level, reflects an unresolved tension within the structure of the prevailing beliefs.

Here are two well-known instances. When, towards the end of 1873, Mahadev Govind Ranade lost his first wife, speculation was rife that, being a prominent member of the Widow Remarriage Association of western India, he would live by his reformist principles and, despite an orthodox father, take a widow as his spouse. Letters started pouring in from like-minded friends — 'This is the time when you must tell your father that you will not marry a young girl. You must announce to him that you will marry a widow'.[1] This is precisely what Ranade did not do. To his friends' consternation, and within a month of his first wife's death, this thirty-one-year-old bright star of the social reform movement married a minor less than half his age; she was chosen by his father.

The second instance relates to Gopalrao Hari Deshmukh (1823–92), who was president of the same Widow Remarriage Association. A judge by profession and popularly known as 'Lokahitawadi' — the advocate of people's interests — he had been concerned since the 1840s with the ills besetting his society. In June 1869 a widow's marriage was solemnized under the auspices of his association. Invitations to the wedding were sent out by seven people, including Deshmukh and Ranade. After a fruitless attempt by the organized Hindu orthodoxy of the area to have some of these 'rebels' falsely implicated in a criminal charge, all seven were 'excommunicated'. In March 1870 a debate was arranged by the Shankaracharya in Poona to settle the issue of the *shastric* validity or otherwise of the remarriage of Hindu widows. Vishnu Shastri Pandit (1825–76), hailed as the 'Vidyasagar of western India' because of his passionate championing of the widows' cause, led the reformers' side in the debate. He was assisted by Ranade. The two sides named five arbiters each, and there was an umpire to vote in the event of a tie. The debate lasted nine days. In the end, only three arbiters of the reform party voted for remarriage; the other two were either cowed down by threats of ostracization or lured away by pecuniary promises. But the denouement was the *prayaschitta* — penance — undergone by Gopalrao Hari Deshmukh for his part in the 1869 remarriage that had set in motion this tangled sequence of events.[2]

These examples show how, when it came to the crunch, even leading social reformers often failed the acid test of matching precept with practice. There was, clearly, a hiatus between belief and practice.

The hiatus may be located within the context of traditional unities like caste and religion, which continued to be the centre of the social universe. Thus, Deshmukh had a daughter whose mother-in-law threatened to turn her out of her house if Deshmukh resisted orthodox pressure. The happiness of his daughter, as he confessed in a letter to Vishnu Shastri Pandit, obliged him to seek readmission to his caste and suffer the ignominy of *prayaschitta*.[3] As for Ranade, according to the testimony of his second wife he was 'in deep agony' on the day of his marriage. He ate nothing, spoke to no one, went to his own room and locked himself in. The agony, it seems, never left him; he felt as if he had 'flung away his self-respect and the esteem arising from it'. Yet he courted this shame and agony because he could neither 'go against the wishes of his father' nor 'disturb the peace and well-being of his family'.[4]

At this distance in time, with joint and extended families having substantially given way to more nuclear units, it may still be possible to appreciate Deshmukh's predicament; but Ranade's reasons certainly make one sceptical. Considering the pattern of nineteenth-century familial relationships, however, the emotional and moral pressures on Ranade were scarcely less binding than they were on Deshmukh.

This is shown by another incident involving a choice between familial compulsions and reformist commitments. Two years after Ranade's agonizing failure to live up to his reformism, Vishnu Shastri showed the courage of his convictions by marrying a widow. Soon thereafter he happened to visit Poona, where Ranade was then posted. As a gesture of respect for the older reformer, and of continuing concern for the cause, Ranade invited him to dinner along with a few other friends. Ranade's father, who was then staying with him, was beside himself with rage — he could not live in a house to which an apostate was invited. However, he avoided a confrontation with the son. Instructing his wife to stay in — it being customary for the women of the family to serve guests — he himself disappeared from the house, leaving word that he would return late, and ate nothing when he came back. He had made up his mind to leave for Kolhapur the following morning.

Pained by this turn of events, Ranade spent a restless night and stood by his father early in the morning. The old man took no notice of him. A whole hour went by without a word being uttered. At last *Mamanji* — that is how the old man was addressed — asked his son to sit down. The latter neither budged nor spoke. When, after a while, the instruction to sit down was repeated, the son said: 'I shall sit down when you assure me that your intention of going . . . is given up. If you are all going . . . what is it that will hold me back here? I shall also come with you. I had no idea that last night's affair would offend you so much. Otherwise I would not have thought of it.' *Mamanji* remained unmoved. Hours passed, and it was time for Ranade to leave for the courts. Finally, with a great deal of effort (he was not given to sentimental outbursts) and without directly addressing his father, he said, 'I know I was orphaned the day my mother died,' and rushed off upstairs. Soon after, he sent word to his father that he had made up his mind to resign his judgeship and would accompany the family to Kolhapur. At this point the father relented. 'Never again', says Mrs Ranade at the end of her account of this incident, 'did the son give occasion for a similar situation to arise.'[5]

Such filial devotion was not peculiar to Ranade. Even the apprehension of such a clash could bring filial compulsions to the fore. This is illustrated by a critical juncture in the life of Ishvarchandra Vidyasagar (1820–1901), the man who made the most outstanding single contribution to the cause of widows and to the passing of the Widow Re-marriage Act (1856). After Vidyasagar had completed the manuscript that demonstrated the *shastric* validity of remarriage for

Hindu widows, he felt it necessary to obtain, severally, the permission of his father and mother to have this published. When his father asked what he would do if he was denied permission, Vidyasagar replied: 'In that case, I won't publish it so long as you are in this world. After your demise, I will do with it as seems to be best.'[6] Luckily, Vidyasagar was not required to defer publication.

The best among the social reformers, then, could falter in the face of organized orthodoxy. In other cases, the reasons for failing to live up to professed ideals were not always so compelling. Practical considerations of lesser magnitude, plain hypocrisy or pusillanimity, too, could cause a split between thought and action.

II

Without denying the role of pragmatic considerations in shaping people's public conduct, it should be possible to question the basic assumption that there was an internally consistent belief structure, a system from which specific actions are seen as being deviant. When looked at in this way, the very structure of belief appears to comprise opposing elements. Having earlier noticed the way organized orthodoxy utilized joint-family ties to maintain conformity, we can trace a similar normative ambivalence in the structure of beliefs, especially with regard to the institution of the joint family itself. This was an institution which proved a common site for the interpenetration of the historical/sociological and the biographical/individual.

In an essay entitled 'The State of the Hindu Society in the Bombay Presidency' (1873), written when he was studying for his BA at the Elphinstone College, Govardhanram Tripathi offered the following advice: 'The moment you get married, start living separately from your parents....' Intended to avoid domestic acrimony following the inevitable differences 'between the two women' (mother-in-law and daughter-in-law), this advice was also prompted by an awareness of the importance of women for realizing happiness among men; 'Women are the very source of human happiness, one of the principal means of the improvement of society, the centre of our domestic bliss and the easy delight of the human heart.'[7] Govardhanram was married when he wrote this — his first wife died the following year — and he had not broken away from his parental family. If his advice regarding post-nuptial separation from one's parents is taken as illustrative of a definite and internally consistent position with regard to the joint-family system, here is yet another example of the dichotomy between belief and action.

However, a 'finished' and relatively unambiguous text containing a public pronouncement, like the essay presented by Govardhanram in 1873, gives the misleading impression of finality. As against the essay, in which he felt constrained to take an unequivocal position, in the *Scrap Book*, where he was engaged in an endless dialogue with and against himself, his response to the joint family vacillated between two extremes. He discusses here, with complete frankness, his own family — there was 'an average of 14 people in the house throughout' — and says on one occasion that he felt 'frozen' as he read what he had written about his aged parents.[8] Nevertheless, he reverted to his domestic predicament with an almost embarrassing frequency. Caught in what he calls the 'prison-house' of the joint family, but not blind for that reason to the larger social dimensions of the problem, he penned long notes in the hope of being able to pronounce a final judgment on the desirability or otherwise of the joint family in the changing circumstances of the country. Yet he never really worked his way out of the 'conflicting voices, views and desires' that found expression in his *Scrap Book*.[9]

Writing on 28 May 1892, Govardhanram described the joint family as 'a joint nuisance' and explained how it could, instead, be productive of peace and harmony:

> A joint family would be a joint nuisance, unless you could steer through it with ungrudging and all-sided sacrifice, taking care at the same time that the other members of the family do not tyrannize each other, which they are sure to do if left to their own uncompromising and blind procedures; and, what is more, if you wish the sacrifice to have its good effects, viz. peace and harmony, never boast or complain that you are sacrificing anything; it is sufficient that the silent sacrifice bears an audible fruit — Peace and Harmony in a family.[10]

Judging by subsequent observations in the *Scrap Book*, Govardhanram himself did not take long to realize the near impossibility of his prescription. Although he quietly made the requisite sacrifices, he could not save his family from being a 'joint nuisance'. A week later he betrays an impulse to be relieved of the futile burden of a family: 'the drones [i.e. his family] ... though of course not [deserving to be] killed, should ... not be pushed off, like some beggars? Then, again, if it is a virtue or duty to be consumed by them, is it not equally a virtue to be eaten up by bugs and tigers and bears and serpents, and to supply them for the only food they can have?'[11]

Articulated through such questions, this dilemma entailed a *reductio ad absurdum* for the 'philosophy of consumption' by which Govardhanram had vowed to regulate his life. Being his version of *Advaita*, the philosophy required the individual will to consume itself — the consumption being its own *raison d'etre* — in the discharge of its duty to the Great Will. He had to explain or admit the *reductio ad absurdum*, and on whether he explained or admitted it depended the way he was to behave towards his dependants. Pressed, on this occasion, for time, he ended this entry in the *Scrap Book* with a resolve that he 'must at leisure solve both these questions'.[12]

Govardhanram turned frequently to the substance of these questions, but could not stick to any one answer. Believing he possessed a greater capacity for making 'silent' sacrifices than did common people, he stated a year and a half later: 'all have not my mind and temper, and 99 out of 100 individuals will be baked or burnt on the frying pan or fire of the gall or the torture.' He added: 'My crucifixion in my own family must direct me to rise from this grave and try to relieve my countrymen from the troubles from which I could not relieve myself.'[13] Thus, 'My lesson from all this, as a student of Sociology, is a confirmation of my views against a Joint Family System ....' But if ending the system was not possible, he felt there must be a means of minimizing its problems, as might happen, for example, 'when one son serves in Bombay, the other in Karachi, and the father's house is at Surat'.[14] Individualism as an alternative principle of social cohesion appealed to him particularly, because he saw in it the prospect of greater emancipation for women. He wanted the practice of early marriage to disappear along with the joint-family system:

> The joint family system and early marriages must go to the wall, and man must be manly and woman must be herself — not the girl-daughter-in-law of the joint family, mother-in-law at 25, nor wife at 12, nor the powerless and clashing fraction of an exclusive unit of worms, but a self-subsisting unit of society by herself. Bring that day for the country if you can.[15]

Yet this was not Govardhanram's only verdict on the subject. In the *Scrap Book* he expresses himself equally categorically in *favour* of the joint family. But this is barely characteristic, for he was, more often than not, uncertain and hesitant, considering always the pros and cons of the system, and, consequently, feeling pulled in opposite directions. Even while proposing an end to joint families, he appreciated their functional viability as the key unit of social organization. With a slight shift in stress, moreover, this acceptance of functional viability could be transformed into the assertion of a cultural superiority vis-à-vis the West, the nursery of individualism.

The assertion of cultural superiority on the strength of the joint-family system on the one hand, and its thorough denunciation on the other, could mean the logical development of two separate ways of reacting to the system. Operating within a single person's attitude, these represent ambivalence and a state of shifting balance. If, thus, the balance was disturbed by the feeling that the joint family was a 'joint nuisance', it was restored by the following modification in the original proposition: 'A joint family is a joint blessing and a joint nuisance, according to the circumstances.'[16]

Even as he felt weighed down by his own experiences within the joint family and condemned the system as a drain on the vitality of the nation, Govardhanram was driven to devise ways that would ensure its smooth functioning. The call for silent sacrifice was a counsel of despair that may have occurred impulsively to one who derived an almost masochistic pleasure in the pursuit of his philosophy of consumption. But, influenced by Utilitarianism, Govardhanram also came up with a less taxing and apparently more practical maxim for 'domestic management'. This was enunciated in the *Scrap Book* on 6 April 1891: 'While everybody is to have his or her liberties in my family, the liberties of no one are to go to the extent of clipping the necessary liberties and moral rights of other members, including even minors.'[17] He hoped to introduce through this a balance between enlarged familial obligations and personal growth. Two years later there is a different emphasis: 'I allow you your liberty and I shall have mine.'[18] There seems now a positive assertion of personal rights. A year later we find him wondering if the principle was 'consistent with the joint family', and asking himself 'which of the two must yield if the inconsistency is great?'[19]

Though it was responsible for 'our bad healths and early deaths', as it was for the continuing enslavement of our womankind and the very ruin of the country, there was also the 'brightest side of the joint family': it was 'protective'.[20]

A long note in the *Scrap Book* also discusses the distinction between Indian and Western modes of social organization. Using the then current terms — of the two modes, respectively, as tribal and territorial — Govardhanram writes: 'Territorialism spends its force in raising up individualism; tribalism revels in destroying individualism.' As one proposing to promote individual growth without destroying the joint-family ethos, Govardhanram could well have felt divided about the relative merits of these two modes of social organization. Instead, he waxes eloquent about the superiority of tribalism:

> Tribalism, while it suppresses individualism and individuals, offers its whole strength to protect the integrity and existence of its system and members whom it feeds and clothes and saves from the inclemency of all elements outside the hearth. ... The whole family keeps a jealous watch over individual vagaries or notions. At the same time this system carries within itself the elements of an Insurance Society built on affections and family ties, unviolated by the lawyer's gaze and unwilling to introduce selfishness. ... Take for instance my own family. When my father's firm failed and he became a great and bankrupt debtor who turned lunatic at the idea of his fall and inability to pay his great debts, where would the poor man have been if there had not been in all that darkness one gleam of light and hope in the idea that his son would assist him one day with heart and soul?

Support to the joint family acquires here a higher purpose, serving to idealize the Hindu vis-à-vis Western culture. Having romanticized his own example by a valorization of tribalism, Govardhanram reads in personal experience larger cultural meanings and nearly obliterates the distinction between the personal and the collective when he asks: 'Could I have left them in the cold, myself enjoying the warmth of my means? No, not for the world, so long as I was myself — a Hindu and not a European.' As a Hindu, he believed, it was not open to him to act differently.

Of this he had reason to be proud. For, representing tribalism par excellence, the joint family did more than symbolize just the values that were different from, or superior to, those which characterized Western social organization. The joint family demonstrated the relative backwardness of the West even in terms of its own cherished ideals:

> ... the merit of the Joint Family is that it provides the fatherless with fathers, the motherless with mothers, the sonless with sons, and the daughterless with daughters; paupers with maintenance, the homeless with homes, the sick with nurses, and the decrepit and the old with a helping hand to lean on for support ... It prevents and checks all untoward propensities, not only by its moral force and prestige, but also by lending to all proceedings the weight of its inquisitorial power....

But the survival of this institution, 'so holy and so invulnerable till now', was threatened by 'the aggressive influences' of 'the territorial nations who now rule us'. The 'wise Hindu', therefore, owed it to himself and to 'the love-borne secret of our protected Home and Family' to 'pause, observe, wait, study himself and others, and find out whether he is not better where he is, or whether he should move to a stage from which others are trying to recoil.' Govardhanram refers, at this stage in the note, to the seamy side of the joint family. But even this serves only to glorify the system by bringing into sharp relief the loving acceptance by individual members of the sacrifices demanded by life in the joint family. The 'evils of the system' were 'in some matters a natural outcome of its advantages.' At the end of this long note Govardhanram took a more realistic view of the joint family, but without giving up its claims to remain the basis of social organization: 'When we look to the evils of both, the question seems to be not what is better, but what is not worse.' Modifications, which might include occasional partitions within families like his own, seemed acceptable, but for the nation as a whole he would allow 'no quackery[sic] medicine to the ignorant masses who are protected by their own old, naturally-selected and instinctively-moulded ways of living, except by slow and well-judged alterations.'[21] Thus ends this enigmatic entry, dated 25 April 1894, in the course of which Govardhanram shows the joint family as both anachronistic and invaluable.

In the remaining thirteen years of his life, Govardhanrarm's *Scrap Book* did not grapple with the joint family with similar concentration.

There is only an abiding resentment against members of his family.[22]

In fact, Govardhanram never fully accepted the normative or moral superiority of the joint family as a social institution. As late as January 1902, shocked by the death of his eldest daughter Lilavati — whom he had fondly brought up and trained as a model Hindu woman and who he believed had died a martyr at the altar of the joint family — he wrote: 'I doubt whether it would not have been wiser and more moral for Hinduism to have left the responsibility and risk of choosing husbands to the girls themselves rather than to their father.'[23]

He did not face the sequel to this thought: how consistent was such individual freedom with the ethos and requirements of the joint family, and which was to be preferred in case of a conflict? As regards his own life, despite his problems with the joint family and the tragic death of his favourite child, he tended to be softer than ever before towards the joint-family system.

Within the nineteenth-century Indian colonial context, the satisfaction of feeling the superiority of 'tribal' socio-cultural organization was powerful enough to subordinate many a personal frustration and tragedy. Faith in the normative value of the joint family could be made part of its lived reality. For example, Govardhanram could recall with pride all that he suffered for his father, a man who could 'plough up living minds with knives in the belief that he was using pen and ink on paper, not knives and blood on bodies'.[24] Here, clearly, belief in one's cultural superiority over the West reveals an elation that marks the idealization of tribalism.

Beginning with the 1873 essay and down to the last entries on this subject in the *Scrap Book*, Govardhanram's treatment of the joint family covered a wide spectrum of responses that ranged from condemnation to romanticization. No specific point on this spectrum represents his real attitude; the whole spectrum, with its tension, ambiguities and contradictions, collectively indicates an attitude. In this attitude were fused the elation of idealization, a faith in the functional viability of the institution, and an acknowledgement of the limitations of the joint family. Ultimately, Govardharnam looked upon himself as a dutiful son and as a model head of his joint family. Few among those who knew him would have seriously questioned his self-image; nor can we dismiss this, despite knowing almost the worst that he thought about his family.²⁵ Govardhanram seems to have been as devoted a joint-family man as were Vidyasagar, Gopalrao Hari Deshmukh, Ranade, and others of that time.

Govardhanram's fiction may be seen to mirror the ways in which people like Deshmukh and Ranade felt about the joint family. Here, again, the tyrannical hold of the joint family upon the individual is clear; yet the lasting impact made by *Sarasvatichandra* on the general reader is one in favour of the joint-family system. 'Chuni the Suttee' (1902), a longish short story which appeared a year after the completion of Govardhanram's four-volume magnum opus, similarly valorizes traditional Hindu social life.²⁶

Read against the *Scrap Book*, *Sarasvatichandra* yields meanings that might otherwise strain credulity. At one level, the novel may be seen as a massive elaboration of the enigmatic *Scrap Book* entry of 25 April 1894: the note betrays a range of responses that seem mutually irreconcilable, and so does *Sarasvatichandra*. But whereas the *Scrap Book* reflects ambivalence, in the novel we tend to discover a dominant position and attribute it to the author. We need to see how the *Scrap Book* suggests a more complex reading of the novel.

In the last volume of *Sarasvatichandra*, Uddhatlal and Chandrakant embody two discrete positions with regard to the joint family. Uddhatlal adopts the kind of radical abolitionist stance that Govardhanram had taken when suggesting the need to do away with the joint family. His name suggests the idea of impudence (*uddhat*). On the other hand, Chandrakant, who as an intimate friend of Sarasvatichandra (the wise protagonist) has better credentials, provides an impassioned defence of the joint family. The defence runs along the lines of the 25 April entry in the *Scrap Book*.

Replying to Uddhatlal's trenchant criticism of the joint family, Chandrakant begins by conceding the truth of his criticism, but argues for a brighter side which completes the picture of the joint family. There follows an inspiring account of the insurance made possible by joint families, and of the way it fulfills socialist aspirations. He argues that European solutions to the familial stranglehold solve nothing, and larger national considerations, too, require the preservation of the age-old Indian system for it inspires patriotism.

Chandrakant even lapses from Gujarati into English to reiterate the substance of his rhetoric:

> The Hindu ideal is eminently *socialistic* in life and practice, ... The main feature of our Hindu Socialism is that it is *protective*. It protects the purity of the sex from outside influences which operate elsewhere and are always at the mercy of accidents and intrigues. It protects the weak, the infants, the women, and the aged from starvation and its consequential crimes. It protects family wealth from the whims and follies of profligates and imbeciles at home and from the operations of rogues abroad, by a domestic organization of people who can watch like dogs and guard like sentinels. It protects and protects.[27]

Having appropriated socialism as part of the brighter side of the joint family, Chandrakant argues for a system that incorporates the best within the European alternative:

> ... though I am no socialist in aspirations, I feel it a duty to give fair scope to the free operation of that ideal, side by side with the forces of Western *Individualism* which are stirring our souls, so that both may by the laws of natural selection adjust themselves to each other....[28]

Ostensibly, Chandrakant and Uddhatlal represent opposing positions, but viewed from the vantage point of the *Scrap Book* they appear two complementary halves of a single complex attitude. Pieced together as one composite character, they yield, with one difference, an uncanny resemblance with Govardhanram, their creator. The difference makes the resemblance even more marked. In the real-life situation of the *Scrap Book*, Govardhanram is aware of the problems in reconciling the need for family and the need for personal space. In the novel, on the other hand, Chandrakant is confident that such a fusion will not take much more than a generation to materialize. This difference represents the visionary in Govardhanram.

Even enthusiastic martyrs to the cause of the joint family thus betray towards it an attitude that is ambivalent. Govardhanram in the *Scrap Book* and Chandrakant in *Sarasvatichandra* are ambivalent because there was no easy solution to this central social problem confronting the articulate individual in colonial India.

The joint-family problem exemplifies the fact that tradition could be the basis simultaneously of orthodoxy as well as of a radical departure from it. The depth of the ambivalence is underscored by the absence of any sense of oddness while legitimizing tradition in terms which draw upon contemporary western intellectual and philosophical trends. Thus, Govardhanram posits a survival and reinvigoration of the joint-family system in society's 'own old, naturally-selected, instinctively-moulded ways'. He summons Burkean conservatism, evolutionism and positivism, as also utilitarianism and socialism, to justify the continuation of something he considered integral to tradition.

Such ambivalence was pervasive. Confined neither to Govardhanram as a person or writer, nor to the joint family as an issue, it informed the very perception of tradition as the bedrock of social reconstruction through much of this transitional phase, when two civilizations confronted each other.

III

Bharatendu Harishchandra, a devout Vaishnava who extolled his faith and observed all its rituals, employed the idea of tradition to suggest a number of social reforms which were potentially subversive of some of the basic beliefs, practices and institutions of his society. For example, taking stock of the decay that had set in within Hindu society, he traced the rot to the imposition of 'superior' and 'inferior' social categories, and to the proliferation of castes. This unfortunate development, he felt, forced division and deprived people of the possibilities of love and understanding. Worse still, it brought in its train the idea of untouchability, further deepening social divisions.[29] The multiplicity of caste loyalty cut at the root of social unity.[30]

Because Harishchandra believed in a glorious past and attributed its loss chiefly to the institutionalization of social inequality through caste, by his logic the elimination of such inequality was not a deviation from, but rather a reassertion of, tradition. As a beginning, he found it prudent to plead for the alleviation of the harshness of the caste system and laid special stress on greater consideration for the lower castes.[31] This was pragmatic and far from radical.

What appears much more indefensible is the delight with which, elsewhere, Harishchandra supported the caste system. He supported it virtually as it then existed, with all its harshness. He was much upset by the efforts increasingly made by a number of intermediate and lower castes, during the later nineteenth century, to acquire a superior ascriptive status. This entailed a process with which we are now familiar. While the final legitimizing point in the process was the recognition accorded by the government to a particular claim — through a favourable judicial decision or through higher grading in the census reports — it was preceded by the preparation of an elaborate case, through pundits and genealogists, supporting the caste's upward placement in the *varna* hierarchy.

Harishchandra disapproved of attempts to disturb the existing social and moral order. In *Andher Nagari*, a dhobi is pronounced, for a mere farthing, a Brahman, and vice versa.[32] Harishchandra's penchant for invective appears the more vitriolic in two farces written on this same theme, 'Sabai Jati Gopal Ki' (1873) and 'Jnati Vivekini Sabha' (1876), being especially unsparing in his attack on Kayasthas who attempted to move up in the *varna* ranking.[33] Deep down he was scandalized that low castes like *Chamars*, *Dhobis* and *Doms* had the cheek to aspire to a higher ascriptive status. The worst of his rather vicious sarcasm is directed against Brahmans who lent, for petty material consideration, *shastric* credibility to lower-caste pretensions. Harishchandra used expressions like 'mean' and 'lowly' with a brazenness that scarcely squares with his realization of the ill consequences of caste discrimination.

Some of the other reforms that Harishchandra considered necessary were the promotion of widow marriage, the abolition of child marriage, the avoidance of matching horoscopes when selecting a spouse, removal of the ban on sea voyages, the encouragement of foreign travel (especially to the West for educational and mercantile purposes), the promotion of female education, and the elimination of both *kulinism* and ordinary polygamy.[34] Wide-ranging as they were, these reforms were proposed as part of an integrated view of national progress that involved changes in all walks of life, social and religious as well as political and economic.

Though he believed that religion was the basis of all reforms, Harishchandra realized that, in India, religion and social institutions were inextricably mixed. However difficult the exercise, these needed to be perceived as separate for social reform. Unless this happened, corrupt social institutions would be perpetuated in the name of religion.[35] He believed that the essence of religion had been lost — it has 'become so effete and thin that mere touch or a palmful of water can destroy it. It is, alas, weak like an ant or a piece of rotten yarn!'[36] He argued for resuscitating customs and practices that lay buried in the *Dharma shastras*.[37]

But extracting from these venerable texts alternatives for changing times was hardly in keeping with the rationale behind the distinction between religion and social institutions. As repositories of traditional wisdom and the source of every social reform, the *Dharma shastras* were credited with containing the unchanging truth by which society was to be moulded. Theoretically at least, the possibility of *real* change, in the sense of something new and unprovided for in these texts, was wished away; and yet, paradoxically, there persisted a belief in the desirability and possibility of change. This was, perhaps, a subtle resolution of the tension between accepting the need for change and the attachment to tradition.

The tension was not always resolved thus. Like his attitude towards caste, Harishchandra's espousal of social reforms in general was informed with resistance to them. In two of his burlesque compositions — 'Panchave (Choosa) Paighambar' (1873) and 'Angrez Stotra' (c. 1882) — he made fun of precisely those reforms of which he was in favour. In 'Angrez Stotra' (In Praise of the English) — which, with the exception of a short prologue in Sanskrit, is a nearly literal translation of Bankim's 'Ingrej Stotra' — Harishchandra had a dig at sham reformists who ingratiated themselves with their English masters. These Indians pray:

> We shall cast away our own language and speak yours, renounce our ancestral religion and embrace Brahmoism.... We shall marry our widows, destroy the caste of *kulins*, and abolish the caste system — because if we do so you will give us a good name. So that you may be pleased with us, O Englishmen! we salute you.[38]

'Panchave Paighambar' purports to be a medley of the commandments of a spurious prophet. The prophet exhorts his followers to encourage female education, do away with early marriages, reduce marriage expenses, promote widow marriages, abolish the caste system, and ruin *kulin* families. These exhortations are interspersed with others that call upon the followers to partake of alcoholic drinks, learn to fall in love, play cricket, wear tight clothes, eat out in hotels, frequent ball-rooms and the theatre, speak their own language with an anglicized accent, and the like.[39]

Clearly, given the tone of the two compositions, the fun made of social reform and reformers in 'Panchave Paighambar' and 'Angrez Stotra' cannot be seen as a categorical denunciation of reform. Nor can it be dismissed as mere lampoon signifying nothing serious. About 'Angrez Stotra' it is arguable that what the prose ridicules is not reforms *per se*, but those who feigned a commitment to reform in the hope of currying favour with the British. Similarly, the medley of commandments in 'Panchave Paighambar' corresponds to the stereotypical image that recurs in later-nineteenth-century Indian literature of the senselessly westernized recipient of English education who finds nothing worthwhile in his own culture. About the only significant omission in this medley is the habit of urinating while standing; this, brutish as it seemed in terms of conventional Indian etiquette, provided an interesting human detail to the stereotypical representation of the anglicized buffoon.[40]

There is more to the mentality that inspired the parodying of social reform and reformers than merely an anxiety over the spuriousness of reformist impulses. Part of such reviling was directed against genuine reformers as well. For example, the Brahmos are reviled in *Vaidiki Himsa Himsa Na Bhavati* with a savagery that, by comparison, makes the reference to them in 'Angrez Stotra' look like friendly banter.[41] No distinction is made in the play on the basis of genuine or false motivation among Brahmos. Read with *Vaidiki Himsa*, 'Angrez Stotra' cannot be seen as denouncing only those Brahmos whose sole motivation was to please the English. Similarly, in a bilingually-titled essay, 'A Wonderful Dream Ek Adbhut Apurva Swapna' (1874), Harishchandra adopts a tone that, despite being satirical, conveys quite unequivocally his opposition to social reform. Besides resenting their attack on 'idol-worship' — expected of a Vaishnava *bhakta* like him — he castigates those who favour widow marriage and the marriage of middle-aged women, and those who feel unhappy about the *varna* system, about the custom of eating within the ritually purified space of the *chowka*, about those who follow no restrictions on inter-dining and the practice of matching horoscopes before arranging marriages.[42]

Those attacked in 'A Wonderful Dream' are not the culturally deracinated and sham reformers. This delightfully written essay sucks within the orbit of its condemnation men like its own author — the very Harishchandra who promoted most of the reforms assailed in the essay!

Burlesques like 'Panchave Paighambar' and 'Angrez Stotra' provide an understanding of the apparent contradiction between the insistence on and the recoil from social reform. Generally, in Harishchandra's work, it is a serious patriotic text like *Bharat Durdasha* or a public statement like his celebrated Ballia lecture that advocates social reform *unequivocally* as a prerequisite of national progress. As against this, in writings where the humour is more unrestrained the attack on social reform is much more strident.

This suggests a certain pattern in the contradiction: the more serious and earnest a writing on the state of the country, the greater and clearer its espousal of social reform; the more humorous the work, the greater its tendency to make fun of social reform and reformers. In the latter category, humour is employed with an abandon that creates the impression of absurdity and permits the writer a measure of freedom from the normal constraints of logical consistency and moral responsibility. Explicitly, however, Harishchandra denied himself this freedom. Sharing the contemporary concern with the social function of literature — in that he upheld it as an instrument for national regeneration — he was socially motivated even in the writing of the *Stotra Pancharatna*. In his preface to these five *Stotras* (1882) he hoped that the discerning readers would 'cull from these humorous pieces many a lesson' that would help them work to save their country from ruin.[43] The missionary in Harishchandra could rest only when he was creating literature of a strictly conventional kind, for then it involved little risk of a social fall-out.

Despite his moral earnestness and social commitment, Harishchandra permitted himself the luxury of not feeling wholly bound by the demands that followed from his recognition of a correlation between social reform and national regeneration. Both in 'Panchave Paighambar' and 'Angrez Stotra' he presents a supposedly comic assortment of traits: these range from the advocacy of widow marriage to female education to reduction of marriage expenses and to a raising of the age for marriage — reforms that, in a different mood, he would have approved — to vogues such as the fondness for ball-rooms and liquor; these latter representing things that he would have disapproved.

'Panchave Paighambar' and 'Angrez Stotra' may not elicit a smile today, but they seem to have regaled contemporary readers. A publisher found it worth his investment to bring together these five *stotras* in book form and to reissue them four years later (in 1886). We also know that Harishchandra translated Bankim's 'Ingrej Stotra' and palmed it off as his own; these facts point to the popularity of the humour that characterizes these texts. This humour depended for effect on titillating the orthodox moral sensibility of the Hindu reader. Harishchandra did this with a relish that only increased as the risk of his appearing to pander to orthodoxy diminished. Hence the difference in the intensity with which he reviled social reform and reformers in 'A Wonderful Dream' (with its temperate sarcasm), and in 'Panchave Paighambar' and 'Angrez Stotra' (with unrestrained parody). As regards caste and social reform, Harishchandra thus used various hues of humour, which permitted varying degrees of freedom from the moral and logical constraints of his belief in social change.

There were, however, other strategies, even subtler, manifest for instance in his writings on women. The *Kavivachansudha* carried on its mast a verse that summed up in four lines Harishchandra's dreams about what should happen in the country: 'May women be like men.'[44] Again, when in 1874 he started the *Bala-bodhini*, a monthly devoted to the upliftment of women, it carried couplets that summarized the desired character and status of women in the country, stating axiomatically what *Kavivachansudha* expressed as a hope: 'That women are the same as men is beyond dispute.'[45]

This seems an amazingly radical postulate, more so in the context of late-nineteenth-century India. But the radicalism is swiftly negated, for, after asserting the equality of women and men, *Bala-bodhini* holds up the ideal of *satis* like Sita, Anusuya and Arundhati. If only India's women accept these ideals they may shed their sense of inferiority and become truly the controllers of their own lives, and the 'begetters of the brave'. Modesty and humility are also prescribed to India's oppressed women. *Bala-bodhini* seems mostly designed to promote these 'womanly' virtues.

This point is further illustrated by Harishchandra's preface to *Nil Devi*. Written on Christmas day, 1881, its preface begins with a description of colourfully clothed and slender-waisted English ladies in artificial jewellery and wigs, moving joyously about with their husbands. This is a spectacle that reminds the author of the pathetic state of the simple women of his own country, and greatly distresses him. There is a stress on 'freedom' in this description of Englishwomen, with the additional information that they are moving about with their husbands. This contrasts with the all too common Indian portrayal of the easy virtue of white women in ball-rooms. However, Harishchandra hastens to warn his readers not to misunderstand his 'envy' of the English. Not even in his dreams, he clarifies, would he want Indian women to set aside their 'sense of shame' and freely flaunt themselves with their husbands. It is in altogether other respects that he wants the women of his country to resemble Englishwomen: they should be vigilant, educated, proficient in domestic management, capable of bringing up their children, aware of their duties towards their country and able to discharge these. He wants them to be conscious of their own existence as human beings, and not waste away their lives as domestic slaves.

Having clarified the qualities to be cultivated by Indian women, the idealization swiftly shifts to a glorious Aryan past. *Nil Devi* is intended to remove the misconception that the prevailing miserable condition of women in India has always been thus. Harishchandra here aims to weed out degenerate local customs and revive the 'true' Indian ideal of womanhood by locating it in Aryan times.[46]

However viewed, Harishchandra's explication of his views about women significantly dilutes the radicalism of his assertion about the equality of women with men. But it cannot be construed as antireformist. Sentiments that can be so construed were expressed essentially in farcical compositions like 'Qanoon Tazirat Shohar' (1884; this borrowed heavily from Bankim's 'Dampatya Dandavidhir Ain', that is, The Matrimonial Penal Code) and 'Stree Seva Paddhati' (The Mode of Wife-Worship).[47] This kind of writing reflects a mentality that felt, at the same time, repelled from and drawn towards social reform.

This mentality was not unique.[48] It characterized the contemporary intelligentsia. Thus, if in social matters Harishchandra appears to have been more a non-conformist who remained deeply attached to his society as it was, Balkrishna Bhatt was, in comparison, more an orthodox Brahman who felt a strong urge to reform some of the institutions that cast their powerful spell on him. In an article dealing with the 'Methods for the Improvement of the Hindus' (1878), Bhatt began by directing sardonic aggression against the orthodoxy. Taunting his 'Hindu brethren', he wrote:

> ... the *Kali Purana* contains some fine prescriptions which may or may not benefit you. But there is not a shred of doubt that if you follow them your total ruin will be quickly effected. The first prescription is: On the fifth day after her birth you must give away your daughter in marriage, lest she remain unmarried until her pubescence, for that will spell the end of *dharma* and twenty-one generations of your forebears will keep wailing in hell. Further, make a fortune by observing the most meticulous miserliness, and squander it at the time of your sons' weddings.
>
> This will bring you glory and name. Your elders are adept in this. Learn from them. Lock yourself within the innermost chambers of your homes. You will lose caste the moment you step out. There is yet another risk entailed in stepping out. You may contract thereby the 'air' of civilized, foreign people. Leave your limbs loose, stay idle and stick fast to your faith in the great unseen, so that the very purpose of human existence — *purushartha* — may remain cast aside.... 'One who sleeps never falls'. Adhere to this principle, cover your eyes and keep sleeping. Don't open them for otherwise you may start seeing.... Don't take the burden of indolence off your head.[49]

Bhatt was thirty-four and no callow idealist when he wrote this. His commitment to social reform did not wane with advancing years. He presented, almost two decades later, in 1896, a stronger plea for such social changes as would bring India at par with Europe, which then 'occupied the apex of civilization'. 'When Indians are sacrificing themselves in the name of their forebears, and the mere mention of change betokens sin', he asked, 'where is the hope that they will ever rise?' The Hindu dharma, customs and practices had become detestable because they had lost their novelty. The Brahmans of old, who had acted as legislators, were undoubtedly selfish and avaricious. But they possessed the sense to present with a new facade those religious principles, social practices and customs that had ceased to interest people. This is what occasioned new digests, commentaries and modern *puranas*. But the foolish Brahmans of his day, Bhatt complained, lacked the intelligence to realize that existing Hindu customs were too detestable to attract civilized people. Even if some Brahmans noticed this alarming trend, they would not reverse it for fear of a temporary setback to their personal interests, or out of sheer mischief. Hence the true and patriotic principles enunciated by Swami Dayananda were not permitted to gain ground.[50]

Consistency was not a strong point within Bhatt's criticism of the Brahmans. Having accused them of precipitating Hindu decline by failing to see people's lack of interest in socio-religious principles and practices, he charged them with cunning on the grounds that they passed off as *sanatan* anything that happened to interest the people.[51]

Finding it 'filled with all the evil and vulgarity of the world', Bhatt was irked by *sanatan* dharma: 'It seems to us that India cannot progress so long as that foundation of vanity and hypocrisy, the *sanatan* dharma, survives, and any of its votaries remain ... everything that will help us progress is opposed to this *sanatan*.' Bhatt was radical enough to observe:

> Inter-dining, marriage of girls when they are fifteen or sixteen, sexual relations — *yonik sambandha* — and marriage across the *varnas*, foreign travel, and all those measures that are beneficial for us have been tabooed by the *sanatan* dharma. We are not permitted the slightest movement away from its tight control. Why, then, should we wish its welfare?[52]

If he could commend social change with such fervour, it is not surprising that in a farce he serialized in the October and November 1878 issues of his *Hindi Pradip*, Bhatt wrote with passion in favour of women's education.[53] A month later in the December issue of *Pradip*, he described caste as 'a device to keep Indians confined to a dark room'.[54] But the very piece in *Hindi Pradip* which so succinctly bares the viciousness of caste strikes a discordant note when, in apparently lighter vein, it offers the following definition of women's freedom: 'Increase in licentiousness: quintessence of English civilization.'[55] Here, once again, is the characteristic tension of contemporary social consciousness.

This article appeared only a month after the farce supporting the education and elevation of women. Humour was being harnessed for very different, indeed conflicting, ends.

This essay, in which Bhatt defines caste on the one hand and women's freedom on the other in such a manner as to make both 'orthodox' and 'enlightened' the butt of his ridicule, is not singular in his oeuvre. Even 'Methods for the Improvement of the Hindus' did not exhaust its savage sarcasm on the 'orthodox'; it shot at the 'enlightened' as well. After advising the orthodox not to unburden themselves of their sloth and foolishness, it addressed the 'enlightened' thus:

> Learn a few things from western civilization, too, for they may prove handy in your hour of need. The first thing is to loosen the hold on your mind of the restrictions that relate to commensality. Eight Brahmans will either have nine hearths or eat just about anything. Don't think of the *hukka* at all. A cigar, according to the new fashion, is the essence of civilization.... *Bhang* alone will not do, drink brandy and champagne as well....[56]

In yet other writings, Bhatt stands enthusiastically by the orthodox. In his 'Kaliraj ki Sabha' (1873–4, serialized in *Harishchandra's Magazine*) — adopting the then popular form of fantasy, employing expressions and images that occur in Bankim's 'Ingrej Stotra' and in its plagiarization by Harishchandra — Bhatt writes with unmistakable relish against those whom he describes in his Hindi text as the 'educated' and the 'enlightened'. Other English words, too, are liberally employed in the Hindi text as a device to make the sarcasm more forceful and to caricature the educated and the enlightened more effectively. In the following translated excerpts from this text, the italicized English words indicate that they occur in the original.

Bhatt reminds the readers of 'Kaliraj ki Sabha' that they live in the nineteenth century:

> Lord of Degeneration! In the Bengal that not long ago was pauperized, now obtains, thanks to *liberal education*, a dreadful civilization which surpasses even that which prevailed during the diabolical rule of Ravan ... a rule the *narration* of which it is hard to provide, and the *duration* of which will match that of your own dispensation. Inspired by Bengal and taught by the same guru, even the inhabitants of the North-West, devoid as they are of confidence in their own intelligence, have started becoming *enlightened* ... were that not so, why would the Hindus, consequent on acquiring a smattering of English, lose their own faith, a faith that

embodies the real essence ... why would they fancy themselves more presentable in coat and boots, why would they choose to become lame by carrying a walking-stick and blind by wearing spectacles; why would they use spoons and forks and eat off tables and in hotels everyday; ... why would the *kulins* forego their caste; ... why would they so readily agree to renounce idol worship; ... why would they frequent the theatre and please the English ladies by shaking hands with them and greeting them with '*How do you do*'; why would they open schools for women and corrupt their daughters and daughters-in-law by sending them there; why would they reckon it to be a sign of wisdom to piss while standing; ... and, above all, instead of *agni hotra*, why would they recite the *angrez stotra* every morning and hope thereby to attain salvation which they think consists in receiving the kindness of Englishmen.[57]

Despite its humour, 'Kaliraj ki Sabha' is fairly serious and categorical in its criticism of social reformism; reformism *per se*, not just its dangerous excesses, is the object of this criticism. It represents one unambiguous position characteristic of a part of Bhatt's work. This is matched by another, of which the farce on women in the October and November 1878 issues of *Hindi Pradip* is representative. The 'enlightened' are assailed in the former, the 'orthodox' in the latter. Taken together, these define an attitude towards social reform.

It is possible to argue that 'Methods for the Improvement of the Hindus' is not an internally contrary text. What Bhatt does in the essay, according to this argument, is to expose to ridicule both the orthodox and the enlightened for their excesses. As such he is not torn between advocacy of and resistance to social reform. Yet one does not need to dismiss this reading to argue that it does not go far enough. For, apart from the perspective set for it by Bhatt's work as a whole, this essay itself carries tonal nuances that point to something more than the articulation of a well-thought-out position on reforming society.

The existence of a similar sort of textual ambivalence occurs strikingly in Radhacharan Goswami's *Yamalok ki Yatra*, mentioned earlier. Despite his orthodox upbringing, Radhacharan was convinced of the need to reform Hindu society. Writing in 1883, he bemoaned the backwardness of the North West Provinces as compared to Bengal and berated reactionary pundits who resisted progress. For such people, anyone who sought to acquire English education was a

'Christian' or an 'atheist' and, therefore, destined to the worst kind of hell. To educate women, in the view of such pundits, was to train them for prostitution. If they could, these pundits would pull out the tongues of those who favoured widow marriages, sea voyages, and the abolition of the caste system.[58]

Two years later, in a remarkably lucid plea for reforming Hindu society, Radhacharan wrote:

> It is because of blind tradition that Hindu society today is so abysmally degenerate! Widow marriage is conducive to the progress of our community, but we do not adopt it for fear of blind tradition! Caste divisions are productive of envy, jealousy and revolt among us Hindus, but we do not remove them simply because we fear blind tradition! ... Brothers! Stop being preoccupied with this senseless jigsaw puzzle, do not worship indolence in the name of religion! We, too, are like the English. Muster up courage so that we can progress as they have. Get out of the well, race out into the fields! Cut the web and soar up to the sky! You still have some breath left in you![59]

Radhacharan was here taking a bold stance on social reform. Harishchandra, who was prepared to go only as far as to call for the alleviation of the harsh rigour of the caste system, felt anxious on account of his young admirer and counselled discretion. Whether as a result of his mentor's advice or on his own, Radhacharan was pragmatic enough to propose a compromise between what he termed 'our *enlightened* and our *oldfool*' (using the two italicized English expressions as collective nouns in his Hindi text). The 'enlightened', according to the terms of this compromise, were to accept idol worship, the *Vedas* and the *Puranas*. The 'oldfool', on their part, were expected to accept widow marriages, sea voyages, and admission within the Hindu fold of converts from other religions.[60]

This was not a compromise at the expense of reformism. In any case, before writing *Yamalok ki Yatra* (1880) Radhacharan had not suggested any compromise. Appropriately enough, therefore, the fantasy begins with a clear expression of commitment to social reform. A victim of mistaken identity, the young 'enlightened' narrator of the fantasy is being carried to the kingdom of Yama. Lamenting his premature demise so early within this century of progress, he regrets his failure to witness the popularization of widow marriages, the removal of the ban on sea voyages, and the extermination of caste divisions. This was the position that obliged Harishchandra to counsel Radhacharan to be temperate.

As the fantasy develops and the 'enlightened' youth is taken around *Yamalok*, the text leaves its initial radical position. Besides heaven, and a court over which the Lord of Death presides, the kingdom shown here is divided into twenty-eight main hells. To these are consigned individuals in accordance with the sins committed by them. Most of these sins are caused by the violation of some religious or social code — though, going by the reformist professions at the beginning of the text, those guilty of these violations should have been assured a place in heaven. The seventh hell, for example, is shown as a particularly crowded place; it has as its chief denizens 'many enlightened gentlemen of the day'. The punishment given specifically offers instances of those who have violated regulations relating to caste: no less than four hells are reserved for transgressions against caste.

As we move along with the narrator in the bizarre world governed by Yama, visiting one excremental hell after another, we look in vain for the young man who, at the start of this journey, was sorry to be dead before having seen the last of caste squabbles. After describing a particularly nauseous hell — hell no. 15 — the narrator informs us that it is reserved for those Brahmans who cohabit with or marry *Shudra* women. He also adds (not unexpectedly, and using the italicized English term for the purpose) that 'many *educated* Indians also are mired' within the faeces, urine, etc. of which this hell is made.

This may be seen as a faithful record of the working of a moral order in which caste is an essential constituent and over which, despite questioning it, the young narrator has no control. But the tone of the narrative indicates some satisfaction in this being so, and there also occur other tell-tale comments from the narrator. For instance, after describing hell no. 15 in which are mired Brahmans guilty of sexual intimacy with *Shudra* women, he wonders how much more harrowing must be the fate of those *Shudras* who marry Brahman women and of those Brahman women who accept *Shudras* as husbands. Similarly, in the course of his encounter with Chitragupta, the records officer in Yama's court, the narrator is upset by the efforts made by *Kayasthas* to pose as Kshatriyas, and, he fears, to aspire eventually for the highest placement in the *varna* hierarchy. He is relieved to discover that Chitragupta is waiting to mete out proper punishment to these pretenders when it is their turn to appear before him.[61]

Yamatok ki Yatra is designed to be humorous, but it is not a farce. All along it maintains an obvious seriousness of purpose. The expression of commitment to social reform with which it begins is transparently earnest. The reforms that the departing narrator wishes he had seen effected are enumerated along with such other unfulfilled desires as the termination of the second Anglo–Afghan war, the repeal of the hated Vernacular Press and Licence Acts, unobstructed entry and promotion of Indians in the civil service, the victory of the Liberals in the British general elections, and, equally importantly, the spread of Hindi over the length and breadth of the country. The seriousness of these desires cannot be questioned. Humour comes into play as the narrator's peregrination in the land of Yama begins, and it gets directed against social reformers. But it is not exaggerated enough to permit freedom from the moral and logical implications of the earlier reformist position.[62] There is no suggestion of disapproval for the way Yama thinks fit to punish social reformers. Nor does it seem that any distinction is being made in this text between genuine and spurious reformism. If anything, there seems some sadism in the depiction of the ordeal to which the 'enlightened' and the 'educated' are subjected in this abominably putrid world.

Yamalok ki Yatra provides, perhaps, a wider spectrum of internal ambivalence than is betrayed in the works of Harishchandra and most of his contemporaries. On the one hand, in its support to social reform, the *Yatra* goes farther than many writings of the period; on the other, it remains unsurpassed in its almost gleeful portrayal of the brutality with which, in Yama's world, social reformers are treated for their pains to make their world more humane.

It is possible that more than most of his peers, Radhacharan tended to be carried away by the impulse of the moment. He could write with passion and unintended exaggeration about whatever it was that happened to engross him, unmindful of whether it agreed with what had preceded and what would follow. As one who knew him well and who followed his writings closely, Pratapnarayan Misra once said with irritation that Radhacharan expressed opinions on the spur of the moment without bothering about the overall consistency of his position. Inconsistency got the better of Radhacharan, especially when there was a chance to be humorous.[63]

This proclivity of its author may well have been what lent an extra measure of ambivalence to *Yamalok ki Yalra*. But that does not make it an aberrant text. Radhacharan may not have realized the moral and psychological implications of his clearly non-disapproving depiction of the plight of social reformers in *Yamalok*. But insofar as he could unselfconsciously use this as an entertaining scenario, one that with his uncanny sense as a writer he expected his readers to enjoy, *Yamalok ki Yatra* reveals the scale of the ambivalence that we are seeking to understand. It shows that with the concern for reform was fused a deep resistance to it.

Pratapnarayan Misra was naturally alert to similar inconsistencies and lapses on his own part. In his response to the problems of his society, he endeavoured to achieve a coherence that places his work among the least ambivalent of his times. He was a true conservative. He would not, therefore, resist change *per se*.[64] Once he was convinced of the need for change, he would look for ways to plan it in keeping with what he called *sanatani maryada* — the traditional moral framework of the Hindus.[65]

This framework, he argued, had been so designed by the ancient sages as to be in harmony with the climate and nature of India. 'Our welfare is dependent on the pursuit of our own tradition.... We should preserve our selfhood and attempt to remove the deficiencies in it. Therein alone lies the possibility of our progress, as also the welfare of others through us.'[66]

The moral autarky implicit in the pursuit of tradition did not imply the adoption of an insular attitude towards alien influence. He was alive, in an inquisitive and friendly spirit, to people of different religions and countries: 'Nowhere in our moral code is it laid down that we should follow the opposite of what followers of other sects or religions practise. Why should we, then, give up the good things held by others?'[67] He was not unaware of the massive scale at which social refashioning was required. His *Kali Kautuk Rupak* (1885), a realistic portrayal of contemporary urban life, admits that a variety of corruption and evils had gripped the Hindu society.[68] But Pratapnarayan believed that, if suitably revitalized, tradition was capable of sustaining this vast and urgent cleansing operation. His *Bharat Durdasha*

Rupak, as we shall see, illustrates the way in which this revitalization needed to be done.

However, even Pratapnarayan was subject to the underlying ambivalence of contemporary social consciousness, and we shall attempt to understand the working of this ambivalence within the context of a single issue: widow marriage.

IV

Once the practice of *sati* was abolished in 1829, it seemed logical that widows should be permitted to remarry. More so because, given the prevalence of child marriages and the fairly common practice of old men marrying girls, many of these widows used to be virgins whose marriages had not been consummated. Their life was one of grim austerity, lacking even the basic requirements of physical survival. Sexual relations were taboo for them, whereas the sexual exploitation of widows was endemic.

In 1856, the remarriage of Hindu widows was legally sanctioned. The man who contributed most significantly to the creation of public and official opinion in favour of this legislation was Ishvarchandra Vidyasagar. Two pamphlets that he wrote in January and October 1855, establishing the *shastric* validity of widow marriage, prepared a viable case for the legislation. More than that, they forced, and set the lines for, a debate that raged within Hindu society for many decades. Ostensibly, the debate was confined to the question of whether, despite the 'enabling' legislation of 1856, it was desirable for upper-caste widows to remarry. Actually, it involved larger issues on which hinged the position of women in society.

Inevitably, the question of widow marriage figured in later-nineteenth-century Indian literature in diverse forms — fiction, drama, poetry and the essay. Besides works which dealt with them parenthetically or partially, whole works were produced with widows as their pivotal concern. In fact, within a year of the passage of the Widow Marriage Act was published *Yamuna Paryatan*, a novel by Baba Padmanji (1831–1906) which detailed the typical hardships and miseries to which widows were subjected. Like most contemporary writings on the subject, it was well-intentioned rather than well-formed.

Among the leading Hindi writers of the period, many took up this question in stray pieces or as part of works dealing with the state of society in general. Radhacharan Goswami and Pratapnarayan Misra wrote separate works to promote widow marriage. Moved by the efforts of a Kayastha doctor from Agra to have his ten-year-old widowed daughter remarried, Radhacharan wrote a small treatise in 1888 to demonstrate the validity of widow marriage. The treatise made him, for several months, the target of a vicious agitation, and even his credentials as a Vaishnava *acharya* seemed threatened for a while. But he remained unmoved in his conviction that widow marriage, as he put it, was 'in accordance with the authority of Reason, Shastras and Law'.[69]

Even before he helped the Kayastha doctor arrange the marriage of his widowed daughter, Radhacharan had supported the cause of widows to the extent of suggesting that, in the case of minor 'virgin widows', the enabling legislation should be made obligatory. Referring to Section 7 of the Act, which provided that the marriage of a minor widow would be considered void without the permission of her parents or guardian, Radhacharan proposed this amendment in 1883:

> If the widow is a minor and has not slept with her first husband, her parents or near relations should within three months arrange her second marriage. Those acting contrary to this injunction will be liable to be punished with imprisonment for a year, or fine, or both.

Radhacharan regretted that though this Act had been passed twenty-seven years earlier, it had not been adequately broadcast and people were not aware of its existence. He therefore reproduced the Act in his *Bharatendu*, hoping that members of various widow marriage associations would take advantage of its provisions.[70]

Radhacharan's treatise, except for its preface, seems laboured, and his amendment to the Widow Marriage Act no more than rash. Yet his support to the cause is not devoid of feeling. Apart from discursive writings, he wrote poetry and what he called a 'novel' on the plight of widows.[71] In a single sentence review of a book called *Hit Prabodh*, he said: 'Everything else is fine [in the book] except that it does not dare support widow marriage.'[72]

Just when Radhacharan's writings were discharging his duty towards his society and its helpless widows, in 'Kaliyuga Raj ka Circular' (1883) he assumed a diametrically different stance on widow marriage. Using the popular metaphor of *Kaliyuga* (symbolizing all-round degeneration), the 'Circular' is intended to expose how Hindus are kept within their degenerate state. The Lord of Kaliyuga is worried because, after years of exertion, Ishvarchandra Vidyasagar and the movement for widow marriage have suffered a setback. He directs his officials to forcibly introduce the practice of widow marriage among all the upper castes. They must also ensure that every woman takes eleven husbands, and that people feel free to be married temporarily.[73] The traditional upper-caste mode of marriage, including the prohibition of widow marriage, is seen as essential for the survival and regeneration of Hindus. Humour, in 'Kaliyuga Raj ka Circular', is enlisted in the service of orthodoxy. And this is done precisely when, in most of his serious writings, Radhacharan is playing the social reformer, and when his strongest sympathies seem reserved for the unhappy state of the Hindu widow.

As for Pratapnarayan Misra, he wrote a full-length play which offers *shastric* defence of widow marriage. It depicts the marriage of a beautiful young widow to the man she had loved before her first marriage. The play, *Bharat Durdasha Rupak*,[74] begins with Sarup, a handsome young barrister, developing a liking for Lakshmi. He wants to marry her and she seems willing. The lovers belong to the same endogamous community, making the match eminently desirable. But Lakshmi's father thinks otherwise, and she is married instead to a profligate. After a brief experience of marital misery, she is widowed. Meanwhile Sarup, as a widower, has lost none of his old ardour for Lakshmi. The situation is designed to end with their marriage. Before showing the desired end, the author counters existing prejudices against widow marriage. This is done by introducing a sadhu who discourses on *sanatani maryada*. Driven by social obloquy to attempt suicide, Lakshmi is rescued by the sadhu and, following an elaborate *shastric* exposition upon the validity of widow marriage, is persuaded to marry Sarup. As in Radhacharan's treatise, the *shastric* testimony employed by the sadhu is the same as was marshalled by Vidyasagar. This testimony seems to have become the common property of all those who supported widow marriage.[75]

Bharat Durdasha Rupak is a remarkably radical text. Most advocates of widow marriage were concerned with virgin widows; in contemporary parlance, with widows who had an *akshat yoni*. It is a measure of Pratapnarayan's boldness that he showed Lakshmi's first marriage as having been consummated.

While *Bharat Durdasha Rupak* is contrived and propagandist, the poems Pratapnarayan wrote on the subject are simple and unembellished. Written occasionally in conventional forms like the *bhajan* or *lavani*, they appeal straight to the heart and leave no doubt about the intensity of the poet's feelings. For example, in a long poem describing the reactions of different kinds of people to the question 'when is life fulfilled?', he imagines widows as saying, 'When either the government permits us to commit *sati* or the pundits let us remarry.'[76] In another poem, describing with great despondency the state of the country, he remarks that not a soul appears to be happy, and adds that, given the curses of innocent child-widows, the country cannot but remain thus.[77] He laments the lack of dedicated people who could rescue suffering widows by ensuring they remarry.[78]

Pratapnarayan's support to widow marriage was within the framework of *sanatani maryada*. Though he had developed a satisfactory theoretical position which ruled out contradictions between tradition and reform, in practice he found situations in which his theory was put to severe strain. One such arose when he was scandalized by some of the resolutions passed by the National Social Conference at its fourth annual session in 1890, especially one that proposed fourteen years as the age of consent. It proposed penal action by the government if the legislation was violated. Considering the violent passions aroused by the Age of Consent Bill, one can appreciate the sharpness of Pratapnarayan's reaction against the Social Conference for proposing a measure that sought state intrusion into private life. 'How many homes', remarked Pratapnarayan agitatedly, 'will the government bring under police surveillance?'[79]

Pratapnarayan also saw in the other resolutions of the Conference a confirmation of its humiliating reliance on the government, and its lack of will to effect change on its own. Two of these other resolutions related to widows. One demanded that no widow be tonsured against her will; with this Pratapnarayan had no quarrel. But it also added that the widow's willingness should be expressed in the presence of a magistrate, and this seemed yet another reflection of the reformers' inability to manage the affairs of their own society. The other resolution proposed that the Widow Marriage Act of 1856 be amended to entitle the remarrying widow to a share in her deceased husband's property.

Pratapnarayan was annoyed enough to sound almost an anti-reformist. For example, brushing aside the proposal to amend the Widow Marriage Act, he wrote dismissively about the proponents of widow marriage: 'Decent Hindus and Musalmans are still not in favour of widow marriage. The few that are, enjoy no respect in society.' On the substance of the proposed amendment, he envisaged nothing but moral degradation: 'The truth is that to rely on the government to help a widow — after she has *gone to another man* — get her dead husband's property is tantamount to aiding licentiousness in the country.' (Italics mine.) In this sense, it seems clear that Pratapnarayan too deviated from his concern for widows, and from his commitment to their marital cause. The deviation was subtle, and more in terms of the implications and resonances of what he said. Given his keenness on consistency, he does not show the kind of ambivalence he himself saw and denounced in Radhacharan Goswami. At the same time, he did not perfectly comprehend the circumstances which gave contemporary social consciousness its specific tensions and ambiguities.

V

Though later-nineteenth-century Hindi writers turned time and again to the question of widow marriage, none of them, Radhacharan and Pratapnarayan included, wrote a major work on the subject. It was Bankimchandra Chatterjee and Govardhanram Tripathi, two outstanding intellectual-litterateurs of the period, who produced masterpieces with widows as their theme. Bankim was the foremost Indian novelist of the century. His works began to be translated and plagiarized in his own lifetime, and he excelled in depicting the plight of widows. Govardhanram dealt with the question of widow marriage at a scale unparalleled in nineteenth-century Indian fiction.

In two of his fifteen novels — *Vishabriksha* (1872–3) and *Krishnakanter Will* (1878) — Bankim's central concern is widowhood.

His discursive writings, similarly, show the same concern. So seminal and continuous was the influence of his fictional portrayal of widows that no subsequent Bengali novelist of note, including Rabindranath Tagore (1861–1941) and Sharatchandra Chatterjee (1876–1938), felt free of its weight. In *Chokher Bali* (1902), which is perhaps the first work after Bankim's writings in which we encounter a rich and subtle portrayal of widows, Tagore alludes to *Vishabriksha* more than once as an aid to his own characterizations. He uses it symbolically to denote, and in the course of the narrative to neutralize, a particular attitude towards widows. *Chokher Bali* was merely the first in a series of serious creative attempts to combat this attitude. It suggests the later writers' anxiety to right a wrong suffered by widows in Bankim's fiction.[80] Bankim's treatment was not a caricature or condemnation of widows. Had it been, it would not have troubled writers in the way it did. It drew attention later precisely because underlying the condemnation there lay a sympathy for the tragic destiny of widows and an understanding of their emotional world. But it also evoked a feeling of disquiet, and still does.

The tension in Bankim's attitude towards widows accounts for his impact. He seems to have been torn between the urges of a sensitive artist and a stern moralist; both operated in a colonial milieu that affected the directions of social change. From this uncertainty he sought release by tilting the balance in favour of a moralist position. He worried that the creative writer within him would get the better of his moral position and create a social impact damaging to the social fabric. Thus, *Vishabriksha* (Poison Tree) is so titled to pre-empt readers being carried away by descriptions of the cheerless existence of widows. The effect of the moralistic title is deepened in the first three chapters, which build up an atmosphere of impending doom with the help of ominous occurrences like a storm, a death and a dream that encapsulates the imminent tragedy.

The story of *Vishabriksha* moves along a sort of triangle. It comprises Nagendra, a handsome young zamindar who owns large estates; Suryamukhi, his charming and devoted wife; and Kunda, a beautiful young widow of great innocence. Nagendra and Kunda are drawn into a bond of attraction that, naturally, Suryamukhi cannot bear. But, as a self-sacrificing Hindu wife, she arranges to have them married and quietly slips out of the house. This shocks Nagendra out of his passion for Kunda. He leaves her and sets off in search of Suryamukhi. Kunda languishes, wondering what she did to deserve this fate. Finally, Suryamukhi and Nagendra are united. Kunda poisons herself, leaving Nagendra and Suryamukhi to mourn her death.

Kunda is portrayed with great tenderness. Orphaned as a young girl and widowed at eighteen after five years of marriage to a nondescript schoolmaster, she knows little of the ways of the world and barely comprehends the turmoil inside her. She lacks even the will to seek her own welfare. The pace and pattern of events are always decided for her. All she does is submit and suffer. Her sole initiative comes at the end, when she kills herself to clear the way for Nagendra and Suryamukhi; her only gain is a posthumous restoration of love to which she vainly aspired as Nagendra's wife.

This may seem sentimental now, but is completely characteristic of Bankim, as of much nineteenth-century Indian fiction that derives from certain sorts of English fiction. What is striking about *Vishabriksha* is the sympathy with which the sadness of an innocent widow's life is depicted, despite the moral relentlessness that runs through the novel. Equally striking is Bankim's boldness (for reasons earlier noticed in Pratapnarayan's *Bharat Durdasha Rupak*) in showing the remarriage of a woman who, having been widowed at eighteen, was no longer a virgin.

Vishabriksha permits an alternative reading. Kunda's tragedy is the result of opposing emotions in which no moral stigma attaches to any of the three protagonists. It could be seen, in this reading, either as the tale of a happy couple with the 'other' inevitably entering the scene, or as a social novel directed against the evil of polygamy. But this reading would treat as inconsequential the crucial detail of Kunda's widowhood. As a co-wife and the cause of Suryamukhi's ordeal, Kunda need not have been cast as a widow. The extra complication caused by this detail can, by no stretch of the imagination, be ignored as fortuitous or purposeless. The novel is undoubtedly most significant as a work about widows and their fate, and it is here that it becomes an ambiguous text.

Assuming that the widowhood of the 'other' woman has a function in *Vishabriksha*, then its moral tone seems directed against widows *qua* widows. Besides the relationship between Nagendra and Kunda, there is another 'poison tree' in the novel. This, too, involves a widow.

Her name is Hira Dasi. A vivacious and attractive woman, she belongs to the same caste as Nagendra, and it is in his household that she is employed as chief maidservant. Unlike Kunda, she knows what assails her. For long she spurns all temptation, but finally succumbs to passion. However, when she deviates from the path of virtue, it is in the belief that the man she is sleeping with is in love with her. She does not know that he, a handsome and lecherous zamindar, is a proficient seducer. This entitles her to no sympathy from the author, who condemns her as a 'sinning woman', though a stronger epithet is reserved for the seducer who is called a 'sinning animal'.[81] The two meet their nemesis and die in excruciating pain.

This confirms one's conviction that the choice of widows in *Vishabriksha* is designed, and that it is against them that the novel's moral wrath is directed. Except for providing a more credible object for this wrath, the fall of Hira Dasi is not integral to the narrative. Not that the tenderness with which Kunda is portrayed exempts her from the author's moral reprobation. But the novelist seems unwilling to take chances. Hence the extraneous moralism which mars the aesthetic structure of the novel.

Five years later, in *Krishnakanter Will*, Bankim comes back to the Hindu widow. Once again she is the 'other' woman in a triangle. This time the widow, Rohini, is more self-conscious, assertive and strong-willed. Not prepared to be wafted along, she seeks to optimize the little manoeuvrability she has as a widow. In her, for the first time in modern Indian fiction, the widow struggles to stand up as a person. This is what brings about her doom. Her doom does not lie in her desire to go beyond the social boundaries of widowhood. It stems, rather, from the novelist's unease with respect to her insistence on satisfying her inner passions.

Rohini lives in straitened circumstances with an old uncle, and is first introduced as a prepossessing young woman with considerable strength of mind and character. Even the scheming, disinherited son of the affluent local zamindar cannot fool her. He wants her help in stealing his father's will in order to replace it with a counterfeit entitling him to a substantial share in the family property at the expense of his first cousin, Govindalal. The bait he offers Rohini is marriage. This is more than the widow, desirous of a full life, can resist. But she refuses to touch the money offered as a reward. Later, when the job is done and she discovers she has been inveigled by false promises, she more than matches the crafty son. She knows her price and will not accept anything less.

While understandably tempted by married life, Rohini is a person of great integrity. She is troubled by the thought of Govindalal being cheated of his inheritance. She must restore the genuine will. This time she is caught and disgraced. As a sequel, she and Govindalal, for whose sake she had dared the attempt, come emotionally close to each other.

Tongues wag as their mutual attraction grows. Exaggerated accounts start reaching Bhramar, Govindalal's wife. Soon the triangle is in full operation. Tired of the endless complications and stung by a message from Bhramar, Rohini tries to end her life. This only brings her and Govindalal closer. They steal away from the village and start living together. Then follows the denouement. Suddenly and inexplicably — that is, in terms of her characterization in the novel — Rohini surfaces as an ungrateful degenerate who, while attempting infidelity, is killed by Govindalal. Back in the village, her health corroded by her husband's desertion, Bhramar prays for an early death. Her prayers are answered — answered along conventional Hindu lines. She dies in the presence of her husband, who appears in time for the dying wife to take the dust off his feet and seek his pardon.

In its attitude towards widows *Krishnakanter Will* resembles *Vishabriksha*. There is some compassion for widows, but also considerable unease about them. Obtrusive enough in *Vishabriksha*, moralism becomes particularly strident in *Krishnakanter Will*. The less a widow acquiesces to the demands made upon her by society, the sharper her condemnation in these novels. Hira Dasi, described very favourably so long as she remains above temptations, is condemned as a sinner the moment she seeks sensuous gratification with the man she loves. Rohini, determined to stake her claim for life, receives the most pitiless reprobation. She is treated sympathetically only until her elopement. The description of her despair following the failure of her attempted suicide is particularly moving. Thereafter, when despair gives way to desire for life, she is metamorphosed into the very picture of evil. Despite having remained loyal to Govindalal, she is shown falling for the first man she sets her eyes on in the course of her isolating existence with Govindalal.

However unconvincing, Rohini's post-elopement metamorphosis is sociologically important. In living incognito with her, Govindalal observes an exemplary fidelity, behaving better with her than with his wife. It enrages him, therefore, to find that she has betrayed him, the very man who, having forsaken wealth, wife, *dharma* and character, has for her sake courted exile and overwhelmed her with love and devotion.[82]

What is implicit in the contrast between Govindalal's constancy and Rohini's infidelity must have been explicit to Bankim's contemporary readership, with its caste Hindu sensibility — of which his aggressive moralism was a manifestation. Bankim's position is implicitly an attack on a major reformist premise, first articulated by Vidyasagar, that widows be permitted the option to remarry.[83] Bankim had the good sense to leave this implicit; it was more often luridly explicit in other contemporary writings on the subject. Moral hygiene was, for many, a decisive reason to permit widow marriages. They barely acquiesced in the reform and were by no means enthusiastic about liberal alternatives to the prevailing social coerciveness. A character in Harishchandra's *Vaidiki Himsa Himsa Na Bhavati* puts it pretty bluntly. Even remarriage, he argues, is powerless to prevent widows indulging their lascivious urges. To a readership that believed this, and much more, Rohini's metamorphosis and the moral tag must have appeared crystal clear and convincing.[84]

Both *Vishabriksha* and *Krishnakanter Will* throw into sharp relief the tension that underlay Bankim's attitude towards widows. A similar tension is also reflected in his non-fiction, though with a difference. Rationalized almost beyond recognition, moralism here assumes the form of a grudging acceptance of certain constraints. This is on the grounds that no social reform can really be effected, for the time being, by transgressing these constraints; and that, in the immediate context, caution seems essential for commitment. There is deep sympathy for widows, and the case for their remarriage is admitted. But doubts are raised about the immediate practicability of the measure, and the doubts are philosophized in such a way as to justify pragmatism in matters of social change.

In *Kamalakanter Patra* (1875), a volume made up of bantering but penetrating essays on the state of the country, Bankim makes a passing reference to widows. This loses none of its poignancy by occurring parenthetically in a sentence which makes a political point. Employing powerful traditional similes in the hortatory vein characteristic of this work, he brings out the pathos of a widow's existence by likening her desire for the love of a husband to the desire of the mute to talk intelligently, of the blind to enjoy painting, and of the cripple to walk briskly.[85]

Two years later, writing in his own monthly, *Bangadarshan*, Bankim mentioned widows as part of a broader argument about the causes of human suffering. Referring to such socially caused sufferings as temporary and removable, he says: 'The contention, in this country, that widows cannot marry is a social evil, a social suffering; it is not natural.' This suffering, he observes, may be eliminated by changing the direction in which society is moving: 'Hindu society is different; other societies do not have this suffering.'[86] In 1885, in an essay on religion and literature, Bankim made a trenchant attack on prohibitions to widow marriage:

> An eight-year old girl is widowed. She knows not what *brahmacharya* — celibacy — means. Upon her is inflicted the pain of a *brahmacharya* which even an old man of sixty would find hard to practise. She is made to cry; we ourselves cry, other members of her family cry. Otherwise dharma is lost.[87]

In its angry irony against hideous social demands — the effect is only feebly conveyed in translation — this passage vies with the best that Vidyasagar wrote on the subject. But there the resemblance ends, for whereas this awareness prompted Vidyasagar to defy social authority, Bankim argued for a retreat that would uphold social authority. He did this in two related ways, one less brazen than the other.

The less brazen way was worked out largely in the *Bangadarshan* article which concedes that the suffering of widows needed removal. This entailed converting a minority attitude into a broader social belief. Hope lay in the persuasive effect of education; by this the majority would ultimately come round to the existing minority view in favour of reform.[88] Till such time as this Fabian liberalism began to work, widows must remain oppressed.

In Bankim's more brazen retreat from a passionate indictment of society to an abject defence of orthodoxy, the relationship between a reformist minority and an orthodox majority was reversed: it was now the majority that had to be saved from the cruelty of the minority. With one quick shift of logic, the call for kindness was now countered by the idea of justice. Bankim's *Bangadarshan*, in its issue of June 1880, contains this:

> But we do not think that the hardships of the widows are intolerable. Suppose they are intolerable, but, at the same time, highly beneficial to society, what necessity is there to remove them? Hearts that weep for only a few people ought to break down for the thousands of others who are needy in our society ... If it is a cruelty not to relieve the miseries of a handful of widows, then it must be a barbarous inhumanity that causes mischief to thousands of individuals by inaugurating widow-remarriage; it is no piety to gift a pair of shoes after killing a cow.... We are of a gentle temperament, and have therefore learned only to be kind; we cannot bear to see the severe form of justice. As a consequence, we cannot keep justice in view; we keep in view only our emotions, and express our opinions accordingly. This is exactly what Spencer calls 'emotional bias'.[89]

This is the nearest Bankim came to betraying in non-fiction the moralism characteristic of *Vishabriksha* and *Krishnakanter Will*. Though emotionally charged, the formulation is couched in impassive and seemingly rational terms. It is, at the same time, modulated to cover its flawed logic — by shifting the focus from intellect to emotion. The emotive reference to cow killing was an effective narrative strategy, in particular for a Hindu readership. Little wonder, then, that Subal Chandra Mitra, who wrote the first full-length biography of Vidyasagar in English, found it 'a most reasonable article against re-marriage of widows'.[90]

VI

Unlike Bankim, Govardhanram Tripathi was inspired by a reformist impulse in his conception of *Sarasvatichandra*, a novel which he wrote over a period of fourteen years (1887–1901). Originally, Govardhanram had planned to write a series of essays on the state of his society and the ways of reforming it. On second thought, however, he 'discovered that the reading classes in Gujarat were, for various reasons, difficult to reach through abstruse or discursive matter.' He realized, he tells us in the English preface to his Gujarati novel, that 'flesh and blood under the guise of fiction can supply the ordinary reader with subtler moulds and finer cast for the formation of his inner self than abstract discussions.' Hence his four-volume venture to 'induce reality under fiction'. The fictionalization was to attempt integrating the real with the ideal.[91]

The narrative in *Sarasvatichandra* moves along the tragic axis of love between Sarasvatichandra and Kumud. It provides long discourses on aspects of Indian national life that the didactic and patriotically-minded novelist considered important. He succumbs — especially in the last volume — to a discursiveness which results in a grand scale and a mazy structure that constitute both the strength and the chief failing of this masterpiece.

Govardhanram saw the lives of individual men and women as integrally related to society, the desired transformation of which he aspired to help bring about as a writer.[92] For this reason his novel delves into larger social issues, even at the cost of digressing. But the novelist's interest in the vicissitudes of the fate of his protagonists never flags. Indeed, the fictional world of *Sarasvatichandra* began to acquire a reality that often resonated in his personal life.[93] Kumud, especially, seems to have become like a daughter to him, the bond being intensified by events in his own domestic world. For example, when he gave way to his mother's pressure to betroth his youngest daughter, Jayanti, while still young, he cursed himself and remembered how Kumud had been similarly let down by her father:

> Curious coincidence! Jayanti betrothed on the 25th, and I get the first proof of the second part of my novel on the 26th. The betrothal pinches me, and I compare myself to Vidya Chatura, who accepting in haste a woman's arguments, betrothed Kumud to Pramad, and dropped all talk of Sarasvatichandra.[94]

This incident in the novel gives a critical turn to Kumud's life, which henceforth proceeds irreversibly along a tragic course.

With all its digressions, the question of widow marriage remains central to *Sarasvatichandra*. On that hinges, in fact, the final determination of the complicated twists to which the love of Sarasvatichandra and Kumud is subjected. True to his original reformist impulse,

Govardhanram leads the narrative towards a climax in which widow marriage is not implausible.

Though betrothed traditionally, without their consent and as an upshot of an arrangement between the two families, Sarasvatichandra and Kumud fall in love with each other before they are married. A sensitive young man, ever restless owing to his unchannelized patriotic stirrings, Sarasvatichandra suddenly disappears from his affluent home after a misunderstanding with his father. Kumud is disconsolate. Her father, the *dewan* of an Indian state, marries her off to Pramadadhan, the good-for-nothing son of the *dewan* of another state. Kumud is self-effacing, cultured and dignified. She acquiesces in the ill-fated match. Meanwhile, wandering pseudonymously as Navinchandra in search of peace and purpose, Sarasvatichandra finds himself unwittingly in Kumud's family and becomes someone her father-in-law begins to trust and turn to for advice. As the delicacy of the situation dawns upon him Sarasvatichandra withdraws from the scene, but not before Kumud's husband has sensed their earlier relationship. It matters little to the husband that she has remained chaste physically. However, he disappears mysteriously and is given up as dead. About the same time, while on her way to her father's place, Kumud is supposedly drowned.

Most of these developments are contrived by the novelist as a possible preparation for the final resolution of the love between Sarasvatichandra and Kumud. Thus, both of them find refuge in the same hermitage, where the bond of feeling between them is discovered. Serious efforts are made, at the behest of the chief of the *ashram*, to persuade them to get married. The two families, too, come to know the whereabouts of the lovers and agree to their marriage. Family and religious authority concur in this way on the widowed Kumud's marriage to Sarasvatichandra.

But the resolution of their love takes a different course. Kumud stays on in the *ashram* as an anchorite. Sarasvatichandra marries her younger sister, Kusum, with everyone's consent. Blessed, at long last, with peace of mind, clarity of purpose and enormous wealth, the restless wanderer becomes a householder in order that he fulfil his mission of national regeneration.

This unexpected denouement is not wholly unconvincing. At a philosophical as well as pragmatic plane, the narrative takes a turn towards the end of the novel which makes the conclusion acceptable. This is achieved by idealizing Sarasvatichandra and Kumud to the point of making them transcend common human desires and passions. The body is voluntarily valorized by them in favour of the spirit. The subtle (*sukshma*) sets aside the gross (*sthula*). A sense of duty becomes their dominant, almost their sole, passion.

Govardhanram knows that such sublimation is not easy to achieve, and suggests that bodily desire is not entirely destroyed; it keeps awaiting an opportunity to assail the supremacy of the spiritual. He makes this point by using dreams: in their dreams Sarasvatichandra and Kumud enjoy a physical ecstasy.

It is clear from the endless soliloquies in his *Scrap Book* that, during the fourteen years it took him to complete the four volumes of *Sarasvatichandra*, Govardhanram was being progressively possessed by his philosophy of consumption. The conclusion of his novel is in consonance with this philosophy. Yet it does not imply a negation of the original reformist impulse that had set in motion this elaborate and prolonged exercise. In Govardhanram's fusion of the real with the ideal — which he considered necessary for inspiring 'a people who must be made, and not simply left, to read' — the ideal tended over the years to dominate the real. By the time the exercise neared completion, the highest ideal this writer could visualize for his protagonists was asceticism and a willing self-effacement.

But why should this ascetic ideal of duty have militated against the marriage of Sarasvatichandra and Kumud? In this conception of duty, marriage is not taboo. After all, it was with Kusum as his spouse that Sarasvatichandra had embarked upon his mission. Indeed, the logic of the narrative made his marriage a precondition for the success of his mission. He might well, then, have married Kumud, more so because nowhere in the novel is widow marriage questioned in principle.

It seems that the question of duty move away from philosophy into pragmatic considerations. Pragmatism and duty work against Kumud's marriage. This, precisely, is in striking contrast to the fact that neither in the novel nor in the *Scrap Book* is pragmatism philosophically acceptable to Govardhanram if it violates dharma, for it is in dharma that his notion of duty is ultimately anchored.

One verdict on this problem comes from a character called Chandrakant. Having left home to follow his runaway friend Sarasvatichandra, Chandrakant tracks the lovers down to the *ashram*. Unable to decide what they ought to do, they tell him about their feelings for each other — confessing also their dreams — so that he may counsel right action. Chandrakant's spontaneous reaction is that their relationship is beautiful and should not be opposed. However, he then remembers the state of his society — Arya *samsar* — which disallows ideal relationships such as theirs. It is clear to him that social ostracism and the failure of higher ideals will flow from their marriage.[95]

Vidya Chatur, Kumud's father, provides another attitude. The news that reaches him of the disappearance of his daughter is uncertain: is she dead or alive? He is plagued by the fear that Kumud, though not dead, is widowed. The thought is insufferable. He asks himself, significantly, in English: 'But as a practical man can I not see my remedy for a disease which threatens to be a fact?' The answer he dejectedly offers resonates like one out of Bankim: 'Other nations have it — mine bars it.'

The possibility of an escape for his widowed daughter makes the father wonder if Sarasvatichandra has the courage to marry a widow. But the moment he feels Sarasvatichandra may prove equal to the challenge, Vidya Chatur is filled with fear. The thought of widow marriage seems too subversive for sanity. He attributes it to his paternal frenzy born of a father's bereavement. But the thought, having flashed across his mind, does not leave him. He works out the costs involved: his parents and uncle are unlikely to welcome the idea; social opprobrium will mean an end to his *dewanship*. He is undeterred by these considerations. His earlier frenzy now becomes duty's call.[96]

Vidya Chatur's resolve is firm and honourable. He rejects his worldly-wise old father's stratagem to have the couple married quietly in order to ward off the social fall-out. Instead, he makes a public declaration of his determination to help his world-weary daughter, whom even death has betrayed, eke out whatever little joy she can by fair means. Recalling the cruel wrong done to her by Sarasvatichandra's impetuous disappearance, he defies Sarasvatichandra to marry her openly and face the hostile social reaction.[97]

Making a distinction critical within the contemporary debate on social reform, Kumud's father stresses the subordination of *lokachar* — common practice or popular custom — to *dharma*, arguing that widow marriage is opposed merely to *lokachar* masquerading as *dharma*.[98] Considering that Govardhanram's personal values and beliefs intrude excessively in the last volume of the novel, it is more than merely aesthetically relevant that here he effectively develops a point of view that defies social authority.

Sarasvatichandra thus reflects the contemporary ambivalence on this major social question. It offers, on the one hand, a powerful argument on behalf of widows and a poignant portrayal of a very human situation. On the other, the effect of this exposition is substantially mitigated by the ultimate subordination of the option of remarriage to a glorified ideal of asceticism and renunciation.

The final, unexpected, turn in the fictive world of *Sarasvatichandra* has its parallel in the actual day-to-day world of the *Scrap Book*. In an entry dated 27 February 1906, referring to the death of the wife of a young relative named Shivalal, Govardhanram writes: 'Of course a new substitute will be sought for the one that is gone. When a husband dies, the widow cannot get similar relief.' This could well be the prelude to a denunciation of the prevailing iniquity; but in what follows the key shifts suddenly from the anguished expression of personal anger to a generalized sympathy for the social reformer's view of the case: 'Our reformers complain of this injustice to her. The complaint is as right and the sympathy for her as well deserved as the custom against her is successful in keeping her down.' This does not obliterate indignation at social injustice, so that we are unprepared for the anti-climactic rationalization with which the entry in the *Scrap Book* ends:

> But this is not a mere question of rights *v.* might. The custom is based upon joint family exigencies, and the castes that have it not admit divorce, too, on easier terms than the law can afford. New circumstances will probably bring about some happier compromise. In the meanwhile, orthodoxy, with nature's gift of instinctive self-preservation, must hold its own as an iron wall, and reformers grow wiser and less sorrowful with their frequent knocking of heads against the wall, until the wall begins to crumble and the heads grow stronger by frequent exercise in knocking and breaking;

and a new scheme of reciprocal adaptation between Family, Caste and Justice sparks out of the friction. But I won't lecture here.[99]

The morality of justice, in the final analysis, is neutralized by the need for a social equilibrium. Judging by the evidence of both the novel and the *Scrap Book*, Govardhanram clearly supports widow marriage. But, equally clearly, he wants to defer the issue. He hesitates at the level of action as well as belief, using the notion of a higher ideal in the novel to transcend a problem which was both central to society and personal life, as well as one which evoked such varying configurations of ambivalence.

VII

Tension within later-nineteenth-century Hindu attitudes towards widows was manifest in a variety of ways, perhaps most critically at the emotional plane. The sight of eight-year-old widows condemned to a celibacy impossible for sixty-year-old men was disturbing; the masquerade of *lokachar* as dharma was frustrating. Despite its articulation in rational terms, the concern for social stability was an emotional need, more so with regard to widow marriage. Conservatism, as a system of authority, deterred deviation from time-honoured norms; it also inculcated among individuals varying degrees of resistance to change. It was this that made possible the expression of both a sympathy for the plight of widows as well as hostility towards them in a work like *Krishnakanter Will*.

Some of this can be understood by locating the attitude towards widows and remarriage within the larger context of the dominant Hindu ideal of womanhood. Bankim, for example, waxed eloquent on the ideals of Hindu womanhood. And he did this in a different part of the same work in which he had drawn upon venerable similes to highlight the tragedy of the widow's desire for the love of a husband. Though responses to his description will very likely be far removed from what he intended, it is stirring enough:

> When I think of elevated sections of women, the vision that rises is of the sati, determined to be cremated along with her dead husband. I picture the burning pyre and, in the midst of rising flames, the virtuous woman lovingly holding to her bosom her husband's feet. Opening out slowly, the

fire embraces one portion of her body and moves towards the other. The fire-gripped woman thinks of her master's feet, and, in between, exhorts the assemblage to chant the name of Hari. She betrays no trace of physical pain. Her face is joyous. Gradually, the sacred flame flies up, life is left behind, and the body reduced to ashes. Blessed is her tolerance! Blessed her love! Blessed her devotion!

When I think that, until a while back, the delicate women of my country could court death in this manner, a new hope courses through my mind. I am convinced that the seeds of greatness are inherent in us. Shall we not be able to witness this greatness tomorrow?[100]

This seemingly bizarre ideal was deeply and widely shared. In *Nil Devi*, Harishchandra scanned the centuries between the ancient *satis* of Hindu mythology and their successors, valorous Rajput women who wielded arms and burnt themselves *en masse* for honour and chastity, as the occasion demanded. Harishchandra was inspired to undertake such writings as part of his mission to bring about national regeneration.[101]

Similarly, in *Sarasvatichandra*, Govardhanram provided idealized pictures of women in the Gujarat of his times in order to remind his readers of the glories of Aryan womanhood. His task was complicated by the nature of his tale: under no circumstance could the love between Sarasvatichandra and Kumud be demeaned; at the same time, having been married to someone else, Kumud would fall from the ideal of Hindu wifehood if she were (even mentally) unfaithful to her husband. She keeps singing: 'Pramadadhan is my true and dear lord! Everything besides him is untrue! To everything besides him I am unattached! Nothing, besides him, is dear to me!'[102] She cannot help feeling guilty at the thought of marrying a second time. The ideal of the husband as supreme lord also explains why Bhramar, in *Krishnakanter Will*, dies peacefully only after she has sought pardon of a husband who, having given her unmerited pain, should have been begging forgiveness of her.

The role of pragmatic considerations in determining the denouement in *Sarasvatichandra* reveals the strength of the ideal of *sati*, and the attendant revulsion at the idea of widow marriage. Despite the purity of her love for Sarasvatichandra, Kumud could not be his wife because, among other reasons, as a remarried widow she was bound to be looked down upon by the very people for whose welfare

Sarasvatichandra had decided to dedicate his life. Neither in the *Scrap Book* nor in the novel does Govardhanram seem dissatisfied with the way pragmatic considerations intrude into the lovers' lives. It seems reasonable to assume that he too resisted remarriage for a woman he envisaged as the very picture of Aryan womanhood. Govardhanram's celebration of transcendence and Bankim's criticism of 'indulgence' spring from the same source: an acceptance of the popular ideal of *sati*. Both these novelists, like several of their peers in colonial India, believed in the writer's didactic social role. Govardhanram had declared his social purpose in the first volume of his magnum opus. Bankim finished *Vishabriksha* with a two-sentence epilogue that has since become famous: The tale of the 'poison tree' having been told, he concluded sanguinely, every home would now enjoy the blessings of an elixir.[103]

The feeling that widow marriage represented a fall from a lofty ideal is corroborated, incongruously, by Vidyasagar's plea for such marriages. He stressed 'the irresistible stream of vice which overflows the country', — widows' inability to curb physical urges — implying thereby an unfortunate departure from the tradition of *sati*. The term *sati*, in his context, meant not so much one who mounted the dead husband's funeral pyre, but one who remained ever virtuous and devoted to his memory. Further, in his enunciation of the *shastric* validity of the proposed reform, Vidyasagar assigned special weight to the *Parashar Samhita* on the grounds that this was the scripture for Kaliyuga, the degenerate last stage in the cycle of creation prior to annihilation.[104] He was genuinely worried by vices like adultery and foeticide which followed upon the ban on widow marriage. Left to himself, he may have made a simple rational and humanitarian case in favour of widow marriage. But he knew that a scriptural defence was necessary to satisfy Hindu society. He himself did not subscribe to the specious mythological glory of women burning on funeral pyres, but was interested in devising a narrative that would bring about social change.

The same could hardly be said of those who, in support of widow marriage, employed Vidyasagar's erudite and moving arguments: most of them merely believed that the *Parashar Samhita* represented a necessary but lamentable departure from a great Hindu ideal. A roguish priest in Harishchandra's *Vaidiki Himsa* lashes out against widows, arguing that marriage does nothing to curb their lascivious propensities: 'So far as immoral sexual gratification is concerned, women who desire it have it even when they are married.' When he reaches the climax of his outburst against female promiscuity, the assembly he is addressing breaks into a roar of approval.[105] Rationalized as moralism, the same anger takes over *Vishabriksha* and *Krishnakanter Will*. In *Sarasvatichandra*, this anger is sublimated. At another plane, all these manifestations of anger are intellectualized as a concern for, or a submission to, social stability.

This pattern of ambivalence notwithstanding, the general historical trend was inclined in favour of widows. At the beginning of this century, Tagore's *Chokher Bali* (1902) is a pointer. The struggling Hindu widow in *Krishnakanter Will* had been scotched by the moralist in Bankim. In Tagore's *Chokher Bali* she is, for the first time, a person in her own right. She fails to marry the man she loves, indicating again the relative strength of the anger, as against the sympathy, with which she was viewed by society.[106] But at least her author stands by her. Refusing to either condemn or idealize, Tagore depicts Binodini, the widow in *Chokher Bali*, with care and respect. But even Binodini, gifted, self-assured and determined to have her due, has to wilt under the variety of pressure, moral and emotional, exerted by her society.[107]

The fact that Tagore stood by Binodini while Rohini was 'betrayed' by Bankim and Kumud by Govardhanram may not, in itself, indicate much of a change. But then only about twenty-five years separate Tagore's work from *Krishnakanter Will*, while the last part of *Sarasvatichandra* appeared as late as 1901. The pace of change, though slow, seems visible. Moreover, in a matter involving dark psychic forces owing to its ineluctable connection with the vagina — *kshat* and *akshat yoni* — the change was bound to be slower and more painful than in other areas.

Whether it related to caste, the joint family, or widow marriage, tradition was fluid and subsumed within it varying shades of orthodoxy and heresy. As orthodoxy and heresy, it evoked both fascination and revulsion and became a discursive site accommodating contradictory feelings. Caste could mean conforming to tradition as easily as betraying it. The joint family could be invested with traits associated with territorialism, and yet not lose its distinctiveness.

Widow marriage could mean reverting to traditions severed by the advent of the Muslims, and also mean something that no decent Hindu or Musalman would support. Looked at in tandem, however, tradition and its subversion both helped hold together a society which was in frontal confrontation with the alien culture of British colonialism.

♣

3
Defining the Nation

♠

One section of the Hindu intelligentsia in the nineteenth century traced the general decline of the country to the beginning of Muslim rule. As it fulfilled certain collective needs, this belief was not dependent on historical evidence. It possessed sufficient vitality to defy the facts that undermined it. Associated with this belief structure was a way of defining those who belonged to the country, of who constituted the nation, as distinct from those who did not. Hindus, in this view, formed Hindustan, while Muslims, specifically, were seen as alien. It was to these 'non-Indians' that 'Indians' had lost their freedom a 'thousand years ago'. Prithviraj Chauhan and Jayachand were represented as the symbols, respectively, of an abortive bravery and a successful treachery that marked this sad turn in the country's history.

Implicit in such a historical construction was a narrowing of the conception of the Indian nation. However, this conception operated along with a larger notion of the nation that rose above divisions of religion, region and language. Muslims also were defined, in this conception, as part of the Indian nation. Since the term 'Hindu' was used, within the narrower conception of 'nation', as including Buddhists, Jains, Sikhs, and tribals, what seriously upset the larger notion of 'nation' was the chauvinistic tendency to treat Muslims as alien. Correspondingly, the most determined attempt to include non-Hindus within the national fold tended to be addressed principally to Muslims.

There was yet another, narrower, conception of nation — an ensemble of nations — that characterized social consciousness in the period under study. Resting on such principles of socio-cultural cohesion as language and region, this conception consisted of what may be described as regional nationalism. Regional consciousness was, in many parts of the country, projected as nationalism in its own right.

The tensions in these conceptions of the nation are the subject of this chapter.

I

In his celebrated Ballia lecture, 'How Can India Progress?' (1878), Harishchandra referred to the fallen state of the country and stressed the need for forging unity among its people. While he advised the Hindus to do away with sectarian strife — such as the quarrels that kept the Vaishnavas and Shaktas at loggerheads — he was especially concerned about the integration of Muslims into the national community. He invited them to join Hindus in the race for progress, and he contrasted the natural advantages bestowed upon Muslims by their religion with their plight within daily life. He said they were neither riven by caste nor held back by restrictive dietary rituals or by bans on foreign travel, yet they had done little to improve their lot. They wallowed in a nostalgic pride about political supremacy, now irretrievably lost. 'Since they have settled in Hindustan', he said, 'it is proper for our Muslim brethren to stop looking down upon Hindus. They should treat Hindus like their brothers and desist from acts that pain the latter. When a house is on fire, domestic discord must be set aside and all energies directed to dealing with the fire.'[1]

It is clear in articulations such as this that Hindus, unlike Muslims, are constructed as a category that 'always' belonged to the country. In this statement by Harishchandra are fused the narrow as well as the grand conceptions of the Indian nation.

Even before the Ballia lecture, Harishchandra had consistently argued that the progress of both Hindus and Muslims was necessary for national regeneration. Besides making appeals for unity between the two communities, he also contributed towards a better understanding of Muslims by Hindus. For example, he translated parts of the *Koran* into Hindi (1875) and wrote biographical sketches of Prophet Muhammad, Fatima, Ali, and Hussain and Hassan (1884) with a view to inspiring respect for Islam.[2] In a long hagiographic poem on Vaishnava saints (1876–77), Harishchandra remembered with great reverence Muslim Vaishnava saints like Kabir, Rasakhan,

Tansen and Pirzadi Bibi. 'Crores of Hindus,' he wrote in a line that has since become a *locus classicus*, 'may be sacrificed for these Mussalman saints.'[3]

The remembrance of Hindu–Muslim unity in the past was informed by, and induced, an awareness of the damaging effect of communally-oriented presentations of Indian history. Early in 1874 Harishchandra carried in his *Magazine* a review in English of *Itihasatimirnashak*, the textbook by Shiv Prasad which had been prescribed for schools all over the North West Provinces and Avadh. The review was written by 'An Orthodox Hindoo of Kasi'. Harishchandra may well have been the 'Orthodox Hindoo'. Even if he was not, in giving it a place in his *Magazine*, Harishchandra was indicating a degree of sympathy with the views expressed in this review. Articulating the need for Hindu–Muslim unity, the reviewer here draws attention to the dubiousness of Shiv Prasad's chapter on the Muslims by showing that it is 'an epitome of the four volumes of Elliot's *Historians of India*'. The reliance on Elliot makes it 'a dreadful catalogue of the violence and oppression practiced by Delhi kings on their subjects'. Arguing that 'a historian ought to give both sides of the question', the reviewer cites the authority of those 'European critics and historians' who are 'unanimous in placing the names of Acbur, Jehangeer and Shah Jehan among the benefactors of the human race'. But Shiv Prasad 'sees nothing but faults in these'. The reviewer presses the point further, comparing these rulers favourably with their European counterparts:

> History tells us they have done all that could have been expected from the civilization and the form of government of that period, much better than the rulers of Europe of those days. They proclaimed toleration in matters of religion when it was unknown in civilized Europe.

There were 'wrongs' that 'the Mohammedans did to the Hindoos', but 'we do not want to remind tender children' of those horrors, 'as they are likely to produce a spirit of revenge and a natural hatred between the two principal sections of the Indian population'. 'It is time,' the 'Orthodox Hindoo' continues, when 'we should be co-operating with each other and making common cause, as natives of the same country, to make advances in civilization, to try to ameliorate our conditions, and to cultivate the useful arts of peace, under the beneficence of British rule.'[4]

There was an alternative view, in which these 'wrongs' did not need to be righted. As Balkrishna Bhatt put it, Hindus, subjugated by Muslims for a thousand years after Prithviraj's defeat, and the Muslims, the erstwhile proud rulers, were 'now bound together by ties of mutual sympathy in accordance with the principles of polities'. 'There no longer exists,' he added, 'any difference between the Mussalman victors and the Hindu vanquished.' This was a view that did not depend on a denial of the evils of Muslim despotism. It presented a picture of Hindus and Muslims living together within a common homeland even under 'Muslim' rule. Bhatt further observed: 'Consequently, Hindus and Muslims were united, as if they were one body, in such a way that some of them developed for one another the love that binds real brothers, while many habits, customs and rituals began to be more or less shared by the two communities.'[5] He also emphasized the absence, during this period, of discrimination between Hindus and Muslims with regard to employment.[6]

Radhacharan Goswami went a step further. In his play, *Budhe Munha Munhase*, he drew attention to the existence of Hindu–Muslim unity in the society of his own day, even though the unity seemed confined to poorer sections in the countryside. He portrayed the Hindu and the Muslim rural poor living in amity, and capable of concerted action in the face of an exploitation that did not exclude the sexual abuse of their women, and which transcended religious or sectarian affiliations.[7]

Among Hindi writers of the period, it is Pratapnarayan Misra, even more than Harishchandra, who reflects the most profound sense of urgency about grappling with the Hindu–Muslim problem. His writings abound in powerful and impassioned pleas for co-operation and understanding between the two communities. For example, in 1889, at the end of one of his numerous pleas, he says:

> Hindus and Mussalmans are the two arms of Mother India. Neither of them can exist without the other. They should, therefore, help each other as a matter of social duty. In this lies the welfare of both. No person can be happy by chopping off the left arm with the right or the right arm with the left.[8]

Whether he was considering the demands made by the Indian National Congress — which he was convinced was a truly national forum — or suggesting ways to improve the general state of Indian society, Pratapnarayan made it his recurring theme that Hindus and Muslims were indissolubly linked.[9]

This urgent need to bring about Hindu–Muslim unity was felt largely within the context of organized national efforts to deal with political subjection. Here arose a paradox, namely that a serious threat to the desired unity was posed by the very people who believed in the indispensability of national unity. Even as Harishchandra, Bhatt, Radhacharan and Pratapnarayan clearly grasped the correlation between Hindu–Muslim unity and the country's destiny, they could be perfectly venomous against Muslims, cutting at the root of their own efforts.

In a poem welcoming the Prince of Wales to India in 1875, Harishchandra hailed the supplanting of Muslim rule by the British as a termination of centuries of oppression. The memory of this rule, according to this poem, rankled in Hindu hearts, and was perpetuated by still existing reminders of Muslim misrule. One such reminder, in this poem, is the mosque beside the sacred temple of Vishwanath in Banaras.[10]

As a faithful Hindu from this ancient city, one who daily passed by this mosque, Harishchandra may have felt with special pain the sense of injury he describes in the poem. But a similar chord was also struck by Bholanath Chandra (1822–1910), an eminent Bengali writer, when he visited Banaras a decade and a half before Harishchandra wrote this poem. The sight of temples desecrated by Muslims made Bholanath think of 'the Hindoos of the day'. The desecration 'must have sorely plagued' their feelings. His own feelings were no less sorely plagued: with this difference, that he could rejoice over the nemesis that had overtaken the defilers of Hindu temples:

> How the sacrilege has been avenged with a tenfold vengeance by the overthrow of the Mogul empire! In the last days of his life Aurangzeb must have been haunted, a Hindoo poet would have imagined, with visitations of the god Vishnu, and filled with forebodings of the rising storm of the Mahratta power, the "sea of troubles" in which the vessel of state was to be tossed, its inevitable wreck and annihilation and the ultimate end of his posterity in exile on a foreign shore.[11]

Here was a mentality that could overlook the differences among individual rulers — which in a different context it would readily invoke — and conjure up a stereotype of Muslim rule characterized by violence and oppression against Hindus. It viewed the entire Muslim community as the 'other'.

A poem written by Harishchandra in 1877 further outlines this pattern of remembering Muslim rule. Beginning with the defeat of Prithviraj, the Muslim rulers, with their powerful hordes, harassed the Hindus in various ways, in the process destroying their religion and ravaging their country. After Prithviraj the Hindus were never happy. Though Muslims settled in the country over which they ruled, the Hindu community could never accept them. Akbar, out of pragmatism, dispelled some suspicion of the Hindus. But after the defeat of Dara Shikoh by Aurangzeb, who persecuted Hindus, the dominant anti-Hindu trend continued.[12]

In another poem, written the following year, Harishchandra talked of Muslims — not just rulers — as having taken away the religion, women and wealth of Hindus.[13] This picture was even more sharply drawn in his *Badashahadarpan* (1884), which contained brief accounts of 'those mad elephants' (the Muslims rulers) who had 'trampled to destruction the nourishing lotus-garden of India'. Along with Mahmud, Alauddin and Aurangzeb, Akbar was listed among those elephants. Realizing that his 'dear simple Hindu brothers' would be taken aback by this bracketing of Akbar with Mahmud and others, Harishchandra proceeded to disabuse them of their 'innocence':

> He [Akbar] was such an intelligent enemy that, as a result of his cunning, you regard him to this day as a friend. But that is not so. His policy was deep like that of the English. Aurangzeb was a fool not to have understood him. Else the whole of Hindustan would today have been Muslim. Hindus and Mussalmans would long ago have started inter-marriage and inter-dining. Something that even the English could not think of, Akbar did.[14]

Published in the year before Harishchandra's death, *Badashahadarpan* was no isolated text on Akbar's craftiness. In an article written sometime between 1872 and 1874, Harishchandra had lamented that Hindus had got so carried away by the shrewd Mughal's measures that they thought him an incarnation of God. Harishchandra tried to unravel the dark motives of Akbar's benevolence.[15] We also have the testimony of his cousin, Radhakrishna Das, that Harishchandra planned to write a play on Rana Pratap in order to further expose the 'true policy' of Akbar. Because Harishchandra did not ultimately carry out this *exposé*, Radhakrishna Das undertook the task as a labour of love and national service, and wrote a historical play entitled *Rajasthan-Keshari Athava Pratapsinha* (1891).[16]

Harishchandra does not seem to have succeeded much in his attempt to change Akbar's image. However, his anxiety to undeceive his credulous Hindu brothers reflects the extra hold on him of the mentality that construed the Muslim as the 'other'. This stereotype of Muslim *rule*, which became imperceptibly the stereotype of the *Muslim*, logically needed to resist an account of Indian history in which Akbar, a Muslim ruler, stood for a tradition of political and cultural catholicity. Nor could it cancel that part of the larger Hindu consciousness which treated Akbar as the acme of a political philosophy that put his contemporary European rulers to shame. Harishchandra, on occasion, elevated Akbar to the same level as the legendary Yudhishthira, Vikramaditya, Bhoj and Kalidas, saying that with the departure of such personages had disappeared the glory of India.[17]

In Harishchandra's perception of Akbar as, simultaneously, a villain and near-mythical figure are reflected, with a touch of drama, two opposed views which together constituted the educated Hindus' attitude towards Muslims. Harishchandra's contemporaries may not have been as divided about Akbar as he was. Generally, they admitted the pragmatism behind the great Mughal's benevolence, but without attributing to him the design of forever enslaving the Hindus. This did not, however, dispel their belief about the oppression let loose upon the Hindus by the Muslim rulers.

In a short play, entitled *Bharat Mein Yavan Raj* (1879) and adapted from a Bengali work, Radhacharan Goswami presented Muslim rule in India as a chronicle of the rape and abduction of women, the slaughter of sacred cows, the defilement of temples, the killing of children, and the unprecedented robbing of people. He called the Muslims *mlechchha* — a thoroughly derogatory term — and employed the kind of unrestrained language normal for such writings. At the same time, anxious for Hindu–Muslim unity, he assured Muslims, at the beginning of the play, that it was not meant to offend them! The play, he said, only brought out the bravery of Muslims as contradistinguished from the cowardliness of Hindus.[18]

This assertion of Muslim oppression by Radhacharan is only an elaboration of Harishchandra's lament over the loss of 'religion, women and wealth' to which Hindus had supposedly been subjected: even the details of this are paralleled in Harishchandra's corpus.[19] In terms of its basic thrust as well as in the mode of its articulation, the similarity between Harishchandra and Radhacharan is, in fact, a symptom of a wide identity of views. Such views extended into Bengal, from where Radhacharan had got the model for his *Bharat Mein Yavan Raj*; and the choice of this subject is not attributable to literary influence alone.[20] When Premghan referred to the 'resolve' of the Muslim rulers to 'deprive the Hindus of their women, wealth, and religion',[21] he wrote a line that is virtually indistinguishable from the one written by Harishchandra. Similarly, if Pratapnarayan Misra remembered 'Hindu princesses in their palanquins' being carried to the 'houses of the Turks',[22] Premghan recalled the 'many Hindu princesses' who had been 'kept' by Muslims in their 'palaces'.[23]

Irrespective of the order of enumeration, women, religion and wealth defined deprivation, as this was perceived in Hindu minds. This deprivation was a source of deep humiliation and is a major refrain in the Hindu literati's remembrance of Muslim rule.

What was there *now* that could still be taken away? The stress on *now* in this rhetorical question, posed *ad nauseum*, embodied a subtle shift from Muslim rulers of the past to the Muslim community of the present. Ironically, the shift is reflected in Radhacharan's assurance to the Muslims of his own day that there was nothing for them to mind in his characteristically intemperate description of Muslim rule. The 'bravery' that had made possible the persecution of Hindus in earlier centuries was the dubious virtue which nineteenth century Indian Muslims, as a community, were supposed to have inherited. By the same token, the 'cowardliness' that had led Hindus to suffer these 'wrongs' was one that Radhacharan and his co-religionists had to own and feel ashamed of in their own day. A further insight into this barely perceptible shift is provided in the three-line stanza by Pratapnarayan that bemoans the taking of Hindu princesses by Muslim rulers. Using the present tense in a way that obliterates, and also demarcates, the distinction between past and present, Pratapnarayan writes:

> Where the princesses in their palanquins are carried to the houses of the Turks,
> What else can happen that will make these people blush?
> Can these eunuchs be good for anything![24]

The 'eunuchs' are none other than the Hindus of his own day who are being asked to avenge past humiliation, recover courage, and become warriors of a proud Hindu identity. There is in Pratapnarayan, as in his Hindu contemporaries, a new kind of militancy which refuses to grant cultural and political legitimacy to Indian Muslims. The challenge is implicitly to disinherit the living inheritors of the Turks of old. It is directed against the poet's Muslim contemporaries. The lines of identification, Hindus vis-à-vis Muslims, are thus deepened, and the notion of the Muslim as 'alien' is thereby shaped. Encapsulating a 'thousand years' of Indian history in terms of oppression for Hindus and domination by Muslims, the inheritances manifested the causal relationship between the present and a past by which all Muslims became aliens within India. This view found expression, with varying degrees of awareness, both as assumption and as explicit formulation. For instance, Pratapnarayan wonders how, despite their numerical and educational inferiority, Muslims could kill cows, call the Hindu gods and *rishis* names, and prevent Hindus from taking their gods out in procession. These sentiments occur in an article that impresses upon Indians — 'Hindustanis' and *Bharatiya bhratrigan* and not just Hindus — the need to get united for the sake of defending their rights.[25]

In Radhacharan's work, Vamdev (a character in *Bharat Mein Yavan Raj*) is shown thanking the British for saving the 'Aryas' from the clutches of Muslims. He tells the Englishman: 'Victory to *Huzoor*! *Huzoor* has saved us Hindustanis from the jaws of death. These Mussalmans have for centuries given us no respite. Today, the uprooting of their raj has given us great happiness. May God perpetuate your raj.'[26] In Balkrishna Bhatt's work there appears this comment on the evolution of the Urdu language: 'Who says that Urdu is something alien? To tell the truth, Urdu is a different version of Hindi.

When *we* Hindus disgraced and abandoned it, the Mussalmans took pity on it and, embellishing it with the attires and jewels of *their own* country, named it Urdu.'[27] Commenting on the appointment of Syed Mahmud as a judge of the Avadh court, Bhatt wrote in 1879: 'In fact, if you ask for the truth, Syed Mahmud's appointment does not provide what the Hindus of this country have for years been seeking; because as a Mussalman Syed Saheb would be considered an alien. However, we thank the government for having at least opened the way....'[28]

Pratapnarayan's pleas for Hindu–Muslim unity seldom lost their fervour. But he readily asserted that it was the Hindus to whom the country belonged. 'Nay', he declared, 'they are the country.' Writing about Shri Bharat Dharma Mahamandala, an organization founded to bring together and revitalize the Hindus, he said in 1891: 'Hindustan is ours because we are Hindus.... Our progress or decline was, is and shall be the progress or decline of Bharat.... Hindustan can be made or marred depending upon whether Hindus are made or marred.' Hindus, as 'the chief inhabitants of the country', accounted for more than three-fourths of its total population. The decisive argument, though, remained emotional–cultural rather than demographic: 'Although Mussalmans, Christians and Parsis, all live here, they are called Hindustanis, and that is an appellation which is derived from our name.... We are Hindus and the country is our land. All the others are called Bharatiya in a secondary sense.'[29]

Harishchandra, too, equated the Hindus/Aryas with India. Anxious to save the country from 'the fire that raged all around', he saw in Vaishnavism the basis of true solidarity; it was the 'natural' religion of the country. Consequently, in an essay entitled 'Vaishnavism and India', he called for unity among the Vaishnavas, Shaivas, Shaktas, Sikhs, Bramhos, and other Hindu sects like the Kabir Panthis. Muslims, Christians and Parsis, in his view, tended to corner all the administrative positions that were available to Indians. 'The country is on fire as a result of poverty. Whatever jobs are left from the English are being taken up by the followers of alien religions like the Mussalmans, etc.... Your supreme dharma now is to ensure unity among the Aryas.'[30] This was a mode of perception in which — their internal differences notwithstanding — the Hindus or Aryas constituted the country: it was *their* poverty that set the entire country ablaze and brought into being a 'most terrifying age'.³¹ The alleviation of the country's poverty meant the alleviation of Hindu poverty.

Pratapnarayan remained oblivious to the implications of his identification of Hindus and Hindustan; Harishchandra's reaction to these implications was to argue them away. In his Ballia lecture, for example, he enlarged the meaning of the term 'Hindu' so as to cleanse it of its narrower communitarian connotations: 'Whatever be his colour or caste, he who inhabits Hindustan is a Hindu. Help the Hindu. Bengali, Maratha, Panjabi, Madrasi, Vedic, Jain, Bramho, Mussulman, all should join hand in hand.'³² 'Hindustan is ours because we are Hindus', and 'He who inhabits Hindustan is a Hindu', were two ways in which Hindu and India(n) were made synonymous. Moving one way, Harishchandra used the term Hindu and insisted that it meant all Indians. Moving another way, Pratapnarayan argued that Hindus constituted the real India, and clearly stated that it was by virtue of their association with Hindus that non-Hindu inhabitants qualified to be Indians.

Whichever way one moved along this semantic circle — and the same person could move both ways — at its centre lay an implicit communal assumption. Thus, despite his well-intentioned expansion of the term Hindu, Harishchandra continued to think of Indians as Hindus, to the exclusion of Muslims, and did so even in contexts in which his concern was with foreign domination and the need for liberation. In his *Bharat Durdasha*, the cruel, sword-wielding character who symbolizes India's fallen state and is, fittingly enough, named Bharat Durdaiva, is shown attired as 'half Christian and half Muslim'.³³ In this, his most important political play, Harishchandra displays no awareness of the incongruity between his concern for national unity and his visual representation of the country's fall through a figure like Bharat Durdaiva. He identifies Hindu with India quite unselfconsciously.

The more unselfconscious this communal mentality, the more powerful and persistent was its hold upon the writer. It allowed an easy and spontaneous switch-over from Indian to Hindu and back, as if these were interchangeable terms. And, in proportion as it was unselfconscious, this view prevented or enfeebled awareness of the fact that non-Hindus, especially Muslims, were left out when the terms employed were 'Indian', 'Hindustani' or 'people'. *Bharatmitra*, the well-known Hindi weekly from Calcutta, said in 1884:

> On what is based the rule of a handful of Englishmen over 25 crores of Hindustanis? Why do these handful of Englishmen not heed the call of these 25 crore *people*? Because Englishmen are endowed with moral strength, and *Hindus* are not. That is why in spite of being 25 crore in number the *Hindustanis* are not even one, and a lakh of Englishmen have surpassed these crores. Therefore, if the *Hindus* want to progress, they should stop depending on the government and work for their own betterment...[34]

Deep down, it would appear, India was believed by Hindus to belong naturally to them. Usually it was only within the context of specific issues that demanded unity — across what Harishchandra called differences of colour and caste — that a larger conception of national unity was explicitly articulated.

As we have seen, the position that 'Hindustan is ours because we are Hindus' sometimes prompted the explanation 'He who inhabits Hindustan is a Hindu'. This nationalist notion came about imperceptibly, in response to a growing appreciation of the need for broad-based unity. Nonetheless, this was not a notion that could be held unproblematically, and this helps explain why the equation between Hindu and Indian was betrayed every now and again even in the writings and utterances of those who had devoted themselves to the promotion of an Indian nationalism that transcended narrower loyalties. This tension was, in varying degrees, a component within the psychological make-up of Hindus.

The examples we have given so far, including Harmukund Shastri, the editor of *Bharatmitra* in 1884, relate without exception to people who can be described as orthodox Hindus. But even a liberal and westernized 'moderate' statesman like Gopal Krishna Gokhale (1866–1915) was not uninfluenced by this mentality. At one level, he too assumed the underlying logic of Hindu/Indian. Explaining his opposition to the Seditious Meetings Bill and demanding its withdrawal by the government, Gokhale told the supreme legislative council on 18 October 1907:

> I know the question is now complicated by the fact that the Mahomedan population of East Bengal expects certain educational and other advantages

to accrue to them from partition. No real well-wisher of India can desire that any of these advantages should be withdrawn from them, for the more the Mahomedan community progresses, the better for the whole country. But surely it cannot be beyond the resources of statesmanship to devise a scheme whereby, while the expected advantages are fully secured to the Mahomedans, the people of Bengal may also have their great grievance removed.[35]

Gokhale was far from being conscious of the implications of the distinction he made between the *Mahomedans* on the one hand and the *people* of Bengal on the other. And yet this was the familiar position by which Muslims were edged out of 'people'.

Since R.C. Dutt belongs to the same political class as Gokhale, we may consider some of the concerns in his historical novels that are pertinent here. After producing no less than four historical novels during the 1870s — *Banga Vijeta* (1874), *Madhavi Kankan* (1877), *Maharashtra Jivanprabhat* (1878) and *Rajput Jivansandhya* (1879) — Dutt realized the divisive potential of such fiction. Having an insider's view of the levelling effect of colonial exploitation on all the Indian communities alike, and feeling the pain of being a 'native' intruder into the magic circle of the covenanted civil service, Dutt was quick to appreciate the need for a different kind of fiction. Thus, seven years after the appearance of *Rajput Jivansandhya*, he published *Sansar* and, after eight more years, its sequel, *Samaj*.

Was there something in Dutt's historical fiction that obliged him never to return to it after the 1870s despite its countrywide popularity? It is unmarred by sanguinary details of butchered children, abducted women and Hindus forcibly converted to Islam. It mentions, in general terms, the persecution of Hindus, but is very restrained and cites little evidence, apart from *jaziya* and the mosque that was built upon the original temple of Vishvanath in Banaras. It avoids the stereotyped portrayal of Muslims as innately wicked and bloodthirsty. Several Muslims figure in his work as tolerant, friendly and fighting on the side of the Hindus; not permitting a uniformly reprehensible picture of Muslims *qua* Muslims.

Nevertheless, a strong sense of a separate Hindu identity runs through Dutt's novels. This appears as a recollection of the loss, with its many humiliating repercussions, of Hindu independence following the advent of Muslim rule, and as a hope for the reassertion of

Hindu supremacy over the whole country. The picture of Muslims as alien emerges just as sharply. Though Akbar, the sagacious emperor of *Bharatbhumi*, receives fulsome praise in *Banga Vijeta* and *Rajput Jivansandhya* (this despite the description of Rana Pratap's heroic struggle for Hindu independence), Muslims are described in the manner of foreigners. They are the enemies of 'our' country and of 'our' religion. Even Jaisingh, the wise and uncompromisingly loyal Rajput general of Aurangzeb who wins Shivaji over to the Mughal side for a while, admits that, by persecuting Hindus, Muslim rule has invited upon itself the curses of the Hindus. Combined with the Muslim fondness for luxurious living, these curses will spell the end of Muslim rule. The rise of Maharashtra under Shivaji foreshadows the restoration of Hindu supremacy.[36]

Dutt borrows greatly from Bankim. Yet his descriptions are markedly different from the usual nineteenth century Hindu picture of Muslim oppression; a picture in the drawing of which Bankim, perhaps, provided the boldest strokes. What Dutt shares with the rest is an admission of the polarity of Hindu and Muslim identities, at least during the centuries that he takes up in his historical novels. Here was an author who discerned the danger inherent in the portrayal of this divide; that is what took him away in the end from historical fiction. However, given his understanding of national awakening, where the will to safeguard the nation's material interests and the impulse for cultural assertion must necessarily be fused, it was imperative for him to portray a past that was worthy of the nation's pride and was related to its present. The new stress on the country's ancient — Hindu–Buddhist — past seemed to suggest an escape from the divisiveness of the historical novels. Hence, the elaborate discourse on Banaras as an embodiment of the country's cultural continuum and the long journey from Raniganj to Jagannath Puri in *The Lake of Palms*.

Despite his characteristic restraint, and the relative innocuousness of the theme of *The Lake of Palms*, Dull betrays in this novel, too, the tendency to see the Hindu as Indian and the Muslim as not quite 'one of us':

> The Moslem rule of six centuries might sweep over this hoary town — ay, and demolish its towers and temples — but the faith of a nation lies not between the hands of an Iconoclast, and the Benares of today is as quick

as when thirty centuries ago its buildings crowned the triumph of Hindu religion and learning.[37]

For the rest, the identification between nation and Hindu courses more quietly through the novel.

Unlike Harishchandra, Dutt is not led by Banaras to think of old wounds at the sight of a mosque beside the Vishvanath temple. Nor does he rejoice in the nemesis that Bholanath Chandra's imaginary 'Hindoo poet' sees visited upon defilers of Hindu temples. This is an important difference. It reflects a degree of success in the struggle against the Hindu view in which Muslims figured as alien and Hindus constituted the nation. At the same time, even if muted and disguised, the continuing hold of this view on the likes of Dutt and Gokhale provides an index of its underlying strength.

Partly, the view drew its sustenance from, and in turn sustained, the belief that Indian 'decline' began with the coming of the Muslims. They 'repeatedly destroyed', as Harishchandra put it, 'the intelligence, strength, education and wealth' of the country.[38] Writing in 1856, Narmad had delineated an idealized India that possessed peace, plenty and perfection before it was destroyed by repeated Muslim attacks.[39] The words used by Narmad and Harishchandra are *varamvarna* in Gujarati and *bahu bari* in Hindi respectively. Both mean 'repeatedly'. The use of similar expressions reflects the current of feeling that persisted over the years.

According to this communally-oriented construction of the past, specific social evils emerged in the country as a consequence of Muslim rule. For instance, the practice of *sati*, in keeping with the ascription of nearly every social evil to Muslim rule, was explained as a consequence of the lecherous nature of Muslims. Considering that the tradition could be traced to periods before the Muslims came to India, this was quite an achievement. Since the process of achieving this was no less important than the fact of the achievement, it is instructive to follow the process in one instance. In *Bharat Durdasha Rupak*, when the sadhu has provided the *shastric* exegesis that clears the ground for the marriage of widowed Lakshmi with Sarup, her old lover, the widow is assailed by doubt. She wonders how, in olden times, there could ever have been occasion for widow marriage or *niyoga*, since widows had to die as *satis* at the funeral pyre of their dead husbands. This is a leading question, and the answer to it is unsatisfactory, for *sati* was not prescribed as an imperative; nor, empirically, was it universally enforced. 'You are mistaken', the sadhu tells Lakshmi, and explains why:

> The practice of sati began with the advent of the *Yavanas*. Their character was not good, and the practice of sati was devised as a measure of escape from them by the brave Kshatriya women of Rajputana. Now in the English raj there is no need for this; at that time there was.[40]

The sadhu advances this sweeping explanation of the genesis of *sati* after he has referred to the *niyoga* by Kunti, in the *Mahabharata*, which resulted in the birth of Yudhishthira, Bhim and Arjun. He does not mention the *niyoga* by which Madari, the second wife of Pandu, gave birth to Nakul and Sahadeva, the twins who complete the quintet of Pandava brothers. Madari committed *sati* when Pandu died, leaving Kunti, the elder wife, to look after their five sons. Neither the sadhu nor Lakshmi could possibly have been ignorant of this, and of other instances of *sati* before the coming of the Muslims. But the fiction is maintained. The sadhu says *sati* was unknown in pre-Muslim India, and Lakshmi trusts him. The reader is supposed to do likewise.

Any mention of Madari might have made so much more brazen the silence about the fact that she committed *sati*. It is possible, therefore, that in *Bharat Durdasha Rupak* Pratapnarayan prudently chose not to refer to her. However, insofar as it formed part of a broad belief that, in all respects, the country had fallen on evil days because of the Muslims, it was practically impossible to refute the false attribution of a social evil to Muslim rule.

Given the role of repression and make-believe in memory, the belief was unlikely to be diluted either by the glaring selectivity of the facts that supported it, or by the soundness of the evidence against it: a collective amnesia seems to have marked Hindu social psychology. There was also an attempt to construct a Hindu ideology which would not be subject to attacks from the viewpoint of European Enlightenment or Christian ethic. This could then be linked to a past that appeared as wise and enlightened in its original impulses, these being later corrupted by the pressure of alien invasion.[41]

If it could be argued that Hindu widows preferred *sati* to Muslim lust, it could be further argued that *purdah* came into being to reduce the risk of such exposure.[42] For much the same reason, it was maintained, child marriages came into being. Muslims would forcibly take away beautiful Hindu girls; the only solution was to marry girls when they were very young. But there was a snag in this theory. If lustful Muslims were so disdainful of Hindu social norms, why did they spare married Hindu women? This was brushed aside with the answer that Muslims were 'bound' not to take a woman who 'already belonged to someone as a matter of right'.[43]

If facts were used as pliant instruments to relate *sati* to Muslim rule, logic was treated similarly to advance the same explanation for the beginnings of early marriages. In either case, the explanation was too transparent to satisfy, but it served those who were determined, for other reasons, to believe it. Thus, strikingly, the putative respect of Muslims for married women confirmed, instead of militating against, their putative lechery to make more convincing, instead of weakening, a stereotype of Muslim character and aggression.

The common factor here, for *sati*, *purdah* and child marriage, is lechery. But the pollution with which Muslims supposedly threatened 'Indian' society was seen as being wider, obliging the 'people' to forge larger institutional mechanisms for cultural survival. One of these was, supposedly, the creation of the caste system, which helped Hindus erect a protective wall for women and the community. Thus, Munshiram (1857–1926), the Arya Samajist leader who later became famous in nationalist politics as Swami Shraddhananda, wrote in a pamphlet entitled *Varnavyavastha* (1891): 'There was no trace of the present caste system during the puranic age. It is a direct outcome of the advent of Muslim rule in India.'[44] This was undoubtedly an extreme position, not taken even by Dayananda, whose theories on caste and class Munshiram had set out to explain in this pamphlet.

Alongside liberal opposition to caste, there existed a powerful *Sanatanist* view in which caste had taken the Aryans to the pinnacle of glory in ancient India. As the caste system weakened, decline set in. Such a view was eloquently advanced by Pandit Durgaprasad Misra (1859–1910), one of the moving spirits behind the Bharat Dharma Mahamandala and the *Bharatmitra* of Calcutta. In his *Shribharat*

Dharmma (1901), an important though neglected work that carried a preface by Balmukund Gupta, Durgaprasad spelt out the orthodox Hindu worldview. Believing that the hereditary caste system — in the sense of *jati* and not just *varna* — was the only scientific basis for social organization, he wrote:

> Today we are left with not many people who can so much as comprehend the noble ideas that prompted the Aryas to make caste restrictions rigid. So long as those restrictions lasted, the Hindus were happy. Now that these restrictions are slackening, unhappiness prevails.[45]

Durgaprasad, and Sanatanists like him, could not have ascribed social evils to Muslim rule because, in their view, these were no social evils. This, however, did not weaken their opposition to Islam. Durgaprasad, in *Shribharat Dharmma*, is characteristically virulent:

> Hindus were subjected to immense humiliation under *Yavan* rule. Beautiful temples that had cost crores of rupees were destroyed. The result, alas, is that our viceroy, Lord Curzon, can find in this ancient land no building that dates back more than a couple of thousand years. Far from finding remnants of temples that had domes that conversed with the sky, we find no one who even remembers them. Pilgrim centres were desecrated and their venerable symbols erased ... pilgrims and sadhus dwelling in forests were cruelly butchered. Libraries were demolished and baths heated with precious books. We are, consequently, left with very few old classics. Lakhs of Hindus were forced into Islam at the point of a sword. The sacred threads of Brahmans were slashed with knives with which cows had been slain, and the sacred marks on their foreheads were licked away.... Married women and unmarried girls were taken away to palaces by force. Thousands of men and women were turned into slaves. Lakhs of Hindus were despatched to mountains and slaughtered there. Unweaned children were snatched off the laps of their parents and dashed against rocks. This demoniacal play continued for long in the country, especially along the banks of the Ganga and Yamuna.

This inhuman oppression was said to have continued for seven to eight hundred years, and to have completely demoralized the people. The only glimmer of hope during these dark centuries lay in people sticking to their religion and organizing stray resistance to this oppression at great sacrifice to themselves.[46]

This belief in the relation between Muslim rule and Hindu decline was almost axiomatic. The correlation was projected even in situations where blaming Muslims strained the limits of plausibility. For example, writing in 1874 about the importance of good taste, Vishnu Krishna Chiplunkar argued, in the second issue of the *Nibandhamala*, that good taste was what distinguished an 'advanced nation' from an 'unadvanced nation'. Good taste inevitably led to the development of learning, arts and cultured behaviour. There was a time when 'we', too, possessed these characteristics. But they disappeared following the 'stabilization of the rule of foreigners here'. That 'foreigners' meant only 'Muslims' is clear from the next sentence: 'But there are real possibilities of these characteristics being revived during the reign of the existing liberal and wise government.'[47]

If Chiplunkar could relate something so nebulous as loss of good taste to Muslim rule, it is understandable that he also associated the denial of the freedom of thought and expression to Muslim rule. Before the British restored it, people had supposedly enjoyed this freedom under the Hindu raj. In 'Amachya Deshachi Sthiti', Chiplunkar illustrates this notion by saying Aurangzeb had Sambhaji's tongue chopped off for criticizing Prophet Muhammad; and, further, that two thousand Vaishnavas were forced to commit suicide following persecutions by Tipu Sultan.[48]

From this view of Muslim rule derived the notion of a dark interregnum in the country's history. This facilitated the myth that British rule was divinely ordained and helped to make the present subjection bearable. It also buttressed faith in the countervailing myth of a glorious past, and this was done with some ingenuity. The villainy of Muslim rulers accounted for Hindu lapses from former high ideals. Thus *sati*, besides being a cruel practice unknown among the great Aryas, simultaneously became a stirring symbol of Rajput women's readiness to court death for the sake of honour.

This representation of *sati* reflects the underlying ambivalence within the social consciousness that has been the central theme of this book. In varying measure, the same could be said with regard to caste and *purdah*. Thus, Hindus could simultaneously work for the alleviation or elimination of social evils, as well as hold them up as manifestations of the community's ability to evolve new modes of cultural resistance and survival.

The violence that marked the communally-inspired depiction of Muslim rule appeared also in the Hindu discourse on Muslims in contemporary India without, however, wiping out those aspects of the discourse which emphasized Hindu–Muslim unity. The stereotype of the cruel Muslim meant that the average nineteenth-century Muslim citizen could be invested with the malign characteristics of sinister Muslim conquerors. A family resemblance could be asserted between the commoner and the tyrant, stressing centuries of Hindu helplessness. Radhacharan Goswami drew, in 1883, the following contrast between Hindus and Muslims:

> Whether today or eight hundred years ago, the Hindus never fought the Mussalmans without being provoked. It was Mussalmans like Mahmud Ghazanavi, Muhammad Ghori, Aurangzeb, Nadir Shah and others who harassed Hindus endlessly in earlier times. And to this day the grandchildren and great-grandchildren of these very Mussalmans are carrying on their hereditary enmity.[49]

In the year the Indian National Congress was founded, Goswami shifted his attention away from ancestors to focus exclusively on contemporary Muslims. The violence of his language had not decreased:

> That the Muslim community is aggressive and strife-loving all over the world is hidden from no one. Mischief-making runs through their every vein. Quarrelling, rioting, causing harm unto others are, for them, normal acts, and oppressing the oppressed and persecuting the poor constitute their daily routine.... Mussalmans are extremely incensed with Hindus on account of the fact that whereas Hindus were once their shoe-bearers, they are now holding positions equal or even superior to those held by Mussalmans.[50]

Conversely the peace-loving Hindus, with their backs up against the wall, hit back only in self-defense. Goswami then addresses the strife-loving Muslims:

> You were baptized with blood, and we with milk. Discord is the seed of your religion, and ours is rooted in peace. We, therefore, never offer the first provocation. When you nettle us needlessly, our policy, too, is: "Do evil unto evil".... Be that as it may, in the end we implore Mussalmans once again to give up their Nadirshahi temperaments.

Such tyranny and obduracy will not last long! The government has seen your character through and through. The rest is upto you.[51]

In a small poem written at the end of 1883, two months after Goswami emphasized the congenital cruelty of Muslims, Pratapnarayan implored God to rescue Hindus from 'the infinite excesses of the Turks'. Specifying the excesses, he wrote: 'These murderers destroy our temples, vex the Brahmans, and kill the cows.'[52] In yet another poem he complained to God that the British, who had been willed by Him to govern India, were doing precious little to protect Hindus, and 'the *Yavanas* are behaving like nawabs under the rule of Englishmen'. Already smarting under 'the extreme humiliation they have caused us during the festivals', Pratapnarayan was afraid that 'our lives will not be safe at the time of the *tazia* processions during Muharram'. He concluded the poem (written in a popular form called Bundelkhandi *dadara*) with this prayer: 'You are the abode of mercy! You alone can save us.'[53] Harping on British failure (or reluctance) to discipline Muslims, Pratapnarayan addressed God thus in a third poem: 'The Turks are the enemies that plague our hearts.... Salt is rubbed into our wounds as the king does not heed our cries. Rush to our help lest the ship of our existence should capsize.[54]

In these poems Pratapnarayan did not believe, as Goswami did, that the British had seen through Muslims. But even if they had, he suspected that they would tend to be indulgent towards Muslims.[55] Nonetheless, Pratapnarayan did not lag far behind Goswami in condemning the Muslims of his own day. Even more than Pratapnarayan, Harishchandra appreciated Goswami's writings on the subject. Convinced that, in their conflict with the Muslims, Hindus should turn British public opinion in their favour, he established contact with people in Britain. Among the papers he sent to impress upon British public opinion the incorrigible villainy of Muslims were the writings of Goswami quoted above.[56]

A novel by Radhakrishna Das suggests that these feelings were imbibed quite early in life, more so as the average middle-class Hindu youth was brought up on text-books like *Itihasatimirnashak*, which even *Harishchandra's Magazine* faulted for its bias against the Muslims. Radhakrishna Das was an impressionable sixteen year old when, at Harishchandra's behest, he wrote this novel, and, following the self-image of persecuted innocence, named it *Nissahaya Hindu* (The Helpless Hindu). The leading character of this novel is Madanmohan, a young patriot like Sarat in *The Lake of Palms*. He seems an idealized projection by the novelist of his own person, and one which many young male Hindus may have felt driven in those days to see as their own. On a grander scale, something similar was accomplished by Govardhanram Tripathi in *Sarasvatichandra*.

There is, in *Nissahaya Hindu*, a long account of the proceedings of a society called Bharatahitaishini Sabha. 'Bharat', in the name of this Sabha, figures in the constricted sense of the term, and, for all practical purposes, means Hindu. As the main speaker at a meeting of the Sabha, Madanmohan duly traces the decline of Bharat to the advent of Muslims in India, and then proceeds to discuss their existence within contemporary India. He uses a queer expression for the British Indian administration — *sarakari rajya* or 'government raj' — perhaps betraying thereby the belief that order returned to the country with the British. He says: 'We had hoped that the Mussalmans would be reformed in *sarakari rajya*. Instead they have become even more destructive now.' Seeking the impulse behind such wantonness, Madanmohan turns to Islam: 'The very religion of Mussalmans is cruel. Its motto is: "You obtain *bihishta* by killing the kafirs".'

The testimony of a Hindu against Muslims, the novelist realizes, may not carry enough conviction. So he introduces a young Muslim man, Abdul Aziz, who confirms (barring the attack on Islam) everything said by Madanmohan. This is managed in such a way that, despite his saying Muslim cruelty is a deviation from Islam, Abdul Aziz ends up strengthening the overall impact of Madanmohan's speech, not excluding its tirade against Islam. Abdul Aziz condemns Muslims en masse, and does not take issue explicitly with Madanmohan's attack on Islam. Coming in after Madanmohan, Abdul Aziz tells the assemblage: 'Whatever Mr. Madanmohan has said is really true. There is no doubt that the Mussalmans have been guilty of tormenting the poor Hindus, and I consider that wrong. Recently, too, the Mussalmans have created some trouble. I am with the Hindus from the bottom of my heart because they are being badly harassed.'[57] This is what sticks; not the point made by Abdul Aziz that such behaviour is un-Islamic.

The novelist clinches the issue by arranging to have a threatening letter sent to Abdul Aziz by various Muslims because, in their view, he has violated his foremost religious duty. Rebuking him for the violation, the letter says: 'The biggest religious duty for you is to finish off the kafirs. But you move in exactly the opposite direction.' This justifies the conclusion that, save for exceptions like Abdul Aziz, all Muslims are alike. It also justifies the authorial dictum with which is brought to an end this *exposé* of Muslim character: 'Undoubtedly the Muslims are extremely cruel, obstinate and sycophantic.'[58]

II

Hindu feelings against Muslims ranged, then, from an unstated and subtle assumption to straightforward abuse. This hostile feeling could often lurk in the dark crevices of consciousness. It could also become ominously explicit, overthrowing elementary norms of decency and considerations of prudence. Those who seek to understand it face a double difficulty. As something implicit and barely stated, this feeling is elusive. In its brazen and explicit form, on the other hand, one risks seeing it now as being of greater import than it may have been at the time. Given the changed nature and standards of contemporary discourse and dialogue, we are likely to hear more in the Goswami kind of outburst than was heard by his contemporaries or intended by the writer.

For one thing, the violence of these outbursts was often occasioned by some immediate issue. Such outbursts represented, at one level, a passion that passed as the issue that had aroused it subsided. Thus, both in 1883 and 1885, Goswami's rabid tirades against Muslims were written against the backdrop of fairly widespread Hindu–Muslim riots. In 1883, he wrote, 'Hindus and Mussalmans are these days at loggerheads in Agra, Vrindaban, Kashipur, Nagina, Sholapur and other places.'[59] In 1885, as reported by Goswami, the conflict had spread wider, engulfing parts of Bombay, Surat, Delhi, Sonepat, Multan, Bareilly, Farrukhabad, Aligarh, Agra, Dinapur and Rajmahal.'[60] Similarly, Pratapnarayan summoned together his choicest epithets when Hindus got the impression that the Hunter Commission favoured Urdu at the expense of Hindi. He could forget, at this point, that he and several of his contemporaries, e.g. Harishchandra and Balmukund Gupta, often wrote poetry in Urdu. He projected Urdu now as the language of Muslims, excoriating it with considerable vehemence, calling it witch, prostitute, bastard, sinner, demoness, the scum of other languages, the embodiment of all demerits, and so on.[61]

To acknowledge that some of the hostility arose out of a specific context is not to condone, for such hostility also created a context: it could not but have affected communal relations adversely. Traditionally, sectarian antagonism and religious polemics were articulated in rabidly offensive language. But this notwithstanding, it is still necessary to realize that, relative to our standards today, there was considerable mismatch between the force of this articulation and the effect intended and created. This is perhaps related to the fact, noted in the first chapter, that exaggeration and fantasy were characteristic features of the popular Indian mode of perception and articulation.

The classic text illustrating this point is *Prabodhachandrodaya*, an eleventh-century Sanskrit play by Krishna Misra which continued to inspire adaptations and translations in different Indian languages down to the present century.[62] The popularity of *Prabodhachandrodaya* for nearly a thousand years makes it a particularly relevant text. One of the greatest scholars of his time, Krishna Misra wrote this play 'to expose, ridicule, and contradict the ideas of Buddhists, Jains, Charvakas, Kapalikas and other sects which had taken hold of the public mind in his day, and to awaken in the people a spirit of inquiry into the principles of Vedantic Philosophy.'[63] In the course of this exposure an offensively vulgar portrayal is provided of rival religions or sects, with a Buddhist monk, a Jain *muni* and a Kapalika (all treated as representative characters) succumbing to base passions. Utilizing the rich Sanskrit literary tradition of the erotic, the playwright lays before us, in the third act, the moral degeneration that makes the Buddhist monk and the Jain *muni* indulge, without any sense of shame, in sexual relations with courtesans, widows and the wives of their devotees.

The Buddhist monk, for example, commands his laity: '... therefore be not displeased when mendicants desire to have your wives.' He praises 'the religion of the Saugatas' because 'it allows us to recline on soft beds, and to pass the shining moonlit nights in amorous play with young damsels who have sprinkled themselves with sweet-smelling powders, and who respectfully serve us.' He is thrilled when Kapalini, personifying false religion, embraces him 'before the audience'. Losing his defences, the monk breaks forth:

> Ah! how delightful is the embrace of this Kapalini! Often have I ardently embraced widows, and closely pressed their big swelling receptacles of milk within my arms; this by Buddha I swear a hundred times. But such rapturous emotions were never excited as by touching the rising bosom of this Kapalini.[64]

Placed in a similar situation, the Jain *muni* is no less thrilled. But because he is a Digambar, and does not wear clothes, the situation becomes particularly awkward for him. He tells himself — and us — in an aside: 'My sensitive organ is utterly ungovernable; what remedy is there? Well, this will do. I shall conceal it underneath this bunch of peacock's feathers.'[65]

This seems, now, either obscenely slanderous or hilarious. But apart from provoking a counterattack, such as *Jnanasuryodaya* by a Jain *muni* named Vadichandra Suri, *Prabodhachandrodaya* cannot be said to have aggravated the normal level of sectarian or religious tension. With all its slanderous passages, it remained a live text without a brutal edge. The only decline it suffered was that its eight Hindi translations in the eighteenth century came down to five in the following, and to three in our own times. This interest was not confined to the Hindi heartland. Malayalam was enriched with three translations of *Prabodhachandrodaya* during the nineteenth century.[66]

Of the five nineteenth-century Hindi reincarnations of *Prabodhachandrodaya*, the credit for one goes to Harishchandra. This reflects the ease with which people picked up the violent language of religious polemics. The unity of all sects within Hinduism, among which he counted Jainism and Buddhism, was for Harishchandra a prerequisite for India's revival. Nonetheless, he undertook to translate *Prabodhachandrodaya*. Equally important, he undertook the translation because he wanted to entertain people. This being the intention, Harishchandra had to limit the translation to the third act; the rest of Krishna Misra's original would not have served the purpose. Moreover, to ensure the desired effect, the translation had to retain the malicious eroticism of the original. So, humour was created by 'mocking heresy': this is what *Pakhanda Vidambana* (1872), the title of Harishchandra's text, means. As in *Prabodhachandrodaya*, the mocking tone in *Pakhanda Vidambana* may well have made many orthodox Hindus laugh; it is unlikely that Buddhists and Jains, who he counted among his Hindu brethren, would have reacted similarly.

Harishchandra was aware of the risk. In an oblique 'dedication' he categorically denies having meant to mock religion. 'Whether Hindu or Jain, who besides you here is not heresy personified.... It may be Ishvar or Brahma, Veda or Bible, all except you [i.e. an unnamed 'dear'], I think, are false'. However, the inference he wants drawn from this anarchic mysticism is unambiguous as well as self-contradictory. 'Do not, therefore, suspect me,' he says, 'of having intended to run down any religion in this translation.'[67]

As a link in an uninterrupted series of translations of *Prabodhachandrodaya*, *Pakhanda Vidambana* exemplifies the continuity of a tradition in which no quarter was given and none expected when it came to launching religious and sectarian tirades. The deadliest of these tirades, it is clear from *Pakhanda Vidambana*, were by no means reserved for Muslims. They were as enthusiastically directed against rival groups, both new and old, within Hinduism itself. The best known illustration of this is Dayananda's *Satyartha Prakash*. But judging by the religious and, especially, sectarian controversies and conflicts that raged in later-nineteenth-century India, *Satyartha Prakash* represents not a solitary peak but a large and crowded plateau. Like Dayananda's revivalism, the violence of his attack on adversary religions and sects may be seen as more or less typical of contemporary Hindu social consciousness.

When located within the perspective yielded by the traditional mode of expressing religious and sectarian differences, the viciousness of Hindu outbursts against the Muslims of the day begins to appear less ominous. A similar balancing of vision follows the realization that, over the centuries, the violence of inter-community rivalries was not always confined to trading abuses; this spilled over into vandalism and bloody persecution. This aspect of the Indian religious tradition, significantly, was not unknown during our period. In *Bharat Durdasha*, Harishchandra refers to conflict between Jains and the followers of the Vedas, and to destruction by both of each other's books.[68] Earlier, in 1875, bemoaning the decline of Indian music and commending the efforts that were beginning to be made for its revival, he bracketed Jains with Muslims as destroyers of the classical works on music.[69] Towards the turn of the century, in an essay entitled 'Archaeology' (1897), Radhakrishna Das detailed what, with typical exaggeration, he called 'daily religious strife'. Describing the process of periodic upheaval that formed the religious history of the country, he wrote:

> As one religion became ascendant at the expense of another, it transgressed all norms of right and wrong in dealing with adherents of the earlier religion. This was the chief cause of the desolation that stalked the land. When Vedic religion weakened and the Jains and Buddhists gained in strength, libraries were burnt and sacks filled with Vedic works were sunk in rivers. When the followers of Shankar became predominant, the Jains and Buddhists suffered a similar fate. Then came the Vaishnavites. These votaries of non-violence showed little compassion in obliterating the glories of the ancients.[70]

Das records his appreciation of 'learning-loving' rulers like Akbar who helped preserve some old works, but continues with added sharpness, 'And above all came the alien Mussalmans. They seem to have taken birth only to destroy the ancient glories of this country.'[71]

Despite the existence of this sharply polemical and vituperative literature, neither the fact of Hindu–Muslim antagonism nor its manner of expression appears to have been inimical to the growth of a larger national identity. Harishchandra, for instance, was unflinching in his faith in the unity of all 'Hindus', and passionately committed to its realization. This discrepancy in his position suggests that communal prejudice did not vitiate his advocacy of a larger Hindu as well as Indian national unity. As opposed to this, we have a serious problem in not seeing, in his anti-Muslim pronouncements, a bias that was inherently incompatible with his idea of a larger national identity.

Gandhi, in *Hind Swaraj*, had no such problems. With a bluntness that he maintained throughout this seminal text, he observed: 'There are Hindu iconoclasts as there are Mahomedan.' Referring to the currency of 'deadly proverbs as between the followers of Shiva and those of Vishnu', he made the point that no one saw this as a reason to suggest that 'these two do not belong to the same nation.' Again, despite their differences, the adherents of Vedic religion and Jainism did not constitute different nations.[72] Given India's history of religious strife, Gandhi was arguing, Hindu–Muslim antagonism must not lead to political confrontation, nor relations between the two communities be damaged beyond repair.

In fact, to the generations that were confronted with the problem of the political future of the country during the latter half of the nineteenth century, there was no intrinsic opposition between the emerging national consciousness and crystallized communal identities. They belonged to a society in which caste and religion were the primary units of social identification. Certain stereotyped communal attitudes — communal in the non-pejorative sense of relating to a community — had crystallized, and these were transmitted as a part of social conditioning. This did not imply, *ipso facto*, a relationship of hostility among castes and religious communities. If hostility ensued in particular cases, it was on account of an ensemble of factors, even if they were manifest along the traditional lines of social division. This was a society in which even new social unities had their members identified on the basis of caste and religion.[73] By and large, social tensions in such a society made sense in terms that corresponded to traditional social categorization. Thus, it happened that political dispensations were remembered as 'Hindu' or 'Muslim': that is the way society was perceived.

It is only natural that in this world of clearly marked socio-religious divisions, nationalism was conceived as the highest point within a constellation of loyalties. To offer a typical example, Pratapnarayan Misra talked again and again of the obligations of the individual to his own self, his family, caste, religion, and country.[74] He could, consequently, believe that the Indian National Congress and the Bharat Dharma Mahamandal were the two organizations on which depended the 'well-being and happiness' of the country.[75]

Bringing religion and language into harmony with the cause of the country, Pratapnarayan provides, in 1892, a resonant three-word formula — 'Hindi, Hindu, Hindustan' — which fired with astonishing rapidity the imagination of Hindu patriots in the Hindi-speaking regions. This became for them a veritable mantra. The slogan occurs as the refrain of each couplet in an impassioned poem consisting of eight couplets and a separately rhyming concluding stanza of six lines. Possessing the force of brevity, this poem soon acquired the near magical efficacy that flows from long-repeated incantation. The poem, of which the slogan is the very heart, comes climactically at the end of a frenzied article which was Pralapnarayan's funeral piece for his beloved journal *Brahman*. The journal had been his chief instrument of national service during its seven years of perilous existence. After these long years of perseverance, dedication and frequent strain upon his modest purse and fragile health, he was forced to succumb to the difficulties involved in carrying on the *Brahman*. After the issue carrying this article — described as his 'farewell dialogue' with readers — the journal was to cease publication. It was for Pratapnarayan a moment of deep anguish and tragic intensity that he, the *Brahman* — the identification in his mind was such that the piece reads like his own epitaph — should be silenced by the apathy of his own people. Before being silenced, he wished to leave a message which would survive in the minds of readers, and compensate for the end of a journal which had tried month after month to awaken a long slumbering people. The poem is the message. With 'Hindi, Hindu, Hindustan' it continued to reverberate long after Pratapnarayan was gone. A shadow of the original, the following literal translation of the opening couplet of the poem reads like this:

> If you truly desire your own welfare,
> Then in unison, O children of Bharat,
> Keep chanting with one voice,
> Hindi Hindu Hindustan.[76]

In the event, the *Brahman* was not silenced. Ramadin Singh, a great patron of Hindi who had earlier lent support to Pratapnarayan, was moved by the latter's 'farewell dialogue' to help him revive the *Brahman*. Unfortunately, Pratapnarayan died two years later, so did the *Brahman*, soon thereafter.

Pratapnarayan had with effortless neatness resolved the underlying tension of cherishing nationalism as a new principle of social cohesion, without feeling any the less attached to traditional groupings. With the exception of Harishchandra's celebrated line on 'the flow of wealth to foreign land', nothing written by a Hindi litterateur of the period slipped into the public mind in quite the way that 'Hindi, Hindu, Hindustan' did. With tragic intensity, Pratapnarayan hit upon a formulation that helped others move towards some clarity with regard to the problem of competing loyalties. The lucidity and brevity achieved in 'Hindi Hindu Hindustan' was new and catchy. Harishchandra had come up with something similar, though less like a slogan, when exhorting his compatriots to serve the combined cause of 'cow, *shruti* and Bharat'.[77] As symbols for Hindus there was something constricted about cow and *Shruti*. Pratapnarayan himself once came close to replicating 'Hindi Hindu Hindustan', but without creating much of an effect, when he called upon God to bring about the welfare of 'Hindi, Hindu, Hind'.[78] Perhaps the invocation to God, rather than the call to the children of Bharat, and the less perfect metrical balance, deprived this of the mystique of 'Hindi, Hindu, Hindustan'.

It may be argued that the resolution contained in Pratapnarayan's mantra was a bit too neat. It conjured away, as slogans do, the fissility that was inherent in the commitment to Hindi and Hindu simultaneously with the commitment to Hindustan. In his concern for Hindi and Hindu, as we saw, Pratapnarayan himself wrote in a way that neutralized his belief in Hindustan, insofar as Hindu–Muslim unity was essential for this. Especially after the Indian National Congress came into being, his treatment of such issues showed restraint in response to the demands of organized Indian nationalism. Yet, occasionally, his invective against Muslims cut deep.

Despite the growing sense of loyalty to Hindustan, the relationship of Hindi with Urdu and of Hindus with Muslims tended to produce conflict. But, as we shall see in the following section, this was not confined to Hindi and Hindus. The plurality of competing loyalties was more varied than could be exhausted by Hindi/Hindu. It is here that the insight offered by Gandhi in *Hind Swaraj* points to a teleology which is seen in the reality of partition. Are we not reading back into the nineteenth century the kind of communalism that emerged later, and which has grown more hideous with every passing decade in independent India? If yes, the occurrence of 'Hindu' in Pratapnarayan's formula may not have been as narrow as we would tend to read it now. This is a tricky, though vital, question.

Despite its importance, Gandhi's insight can be misleading, for there is the risk of ignoring or underestimating that elusive aspect of this feeling which operated as an assumption and was rarely articulated.

Let us recall at this stage the extra sharpness in Radhakrishna Das's account of religious antagonism in India precisely at the point where he discussed 'alien Mussalmans'. In his account, the seriousness of what happened prior to Muslim rule is not played down. If anything, the history of religious antagonism in pre-Muslim India is exaggerated, for Das writes as if religious conflicts were an everyday occurrence. Even the Hindi word *viplava*, which he uses for these daily conflicts, tends to overstate by ascribing to these conflicts the nature of a tumult. Nor is Das's an account that magnifies the violence of Muslim rule in order to exonerate, by contrast, what happened before it. The extra sharpness seems a consequence of the stereotyped image of the cruel Muslim, which Das employed almost unselfconsciously.

The image of the cruel Muslim intruded in many ways, and was not always dependent on some immediate occasion or context. A fascinating illustration of this is provided by what is often considered the first short story in Hindi. Called 'Indumati' (1900), after the name of its heroine, this story by Kishorilal Goswami (1865–1932), a prolific writer and one of the first Hindi novelists, is an adaptation of *The Tempest*. Indumati, a beautiful sixteen-year-old virgin, has been brought up by her father away from human habitation within the thick forests of Vindhyachal. She is Miranda rechristened. What is remarkable is the nature of transformation effected by Goswami with Prospero, and with his brother Antonio, the usurping Duke of Milan. Prospero appears in the story as the fugitive ruler of a Hindu kingdom named Devagarh. But he is not dethroned by his brother. Instead, he is attacked and defeated by Ibrahim Lodi, the last sultan of Delhi, because he refuses to send his wife to the sultan's harem. Antonio, the treacherous brother, thus appears as the all-too-familiar licentious Muslim ruler.

The stage is set for the theme of revenge to unfold. Indumati, who has never set her eyes upon a man other than her father, shall be married to the man who kills Ibrahim Lodi: so has vowed the Hindu king in exile. Consequently, Ferdinand is transformed into Chandrashekhar, the handsome young ruler of Ajaygarh, who is shown to have slain Ibrahim Lodi in the latter's own tent during the battle of Panipat where he was pitted against Babar. Chandrashekhar loses his way in the labyrinthine Vindhya forest and, as he must, meets Indumati. Love at first sight follows, expectedly. They are married after the necessary dramatic developments, but not because of their love. Their marriage is the fulfilment of the vow taken by Indumati's father. Love in 'Indumati' does not receive the equal status with revenge as it does in *The Tempest*. Despite the space given to the romance of Indumati and Chandrashekhar, this is primarily a story of revenge.

The stress on revenge lends added significance to the way Kishorilal Goswami transforms the relationship between Prospero and Antonio. Not that Indian literature was innocent of the theme of deadly family feud and the burning vengeful passions that keep this theme going. Rather, the revenge chosen by Goswami for his Shakespearean adaptation is one that is visited upon a wicked Muslim by a brave Hindu. That this choice should have presented itself to Goswami, and seemed to him formally inevitable, reflects the pervasive character of the anti-Muslim feeling among Hindus.[79]

The abrupt change in the tone of Radhakrishna Das's account of religious antagonism, and the turn taken by the theme of revenge in 'Indumati', may be more direct, almost brazen, in manifestation. Yet they are not unlike the unprovoked and subconscious manifestation of the deep-rooted prejudice which caused Gokhale to unwittingly separate Muslims from 'people' or Dutt to constrict the youth of India to Hindu youth. An extra edge distinguishes this animus from sectarian rivalries within Hinduism. Hindu–Muslim rivalries, being more recent, had clearer political implications too.

The Hindu ambivalence vis-à-vis Muslims was not wholly influenced by the Hindu response to colonialism. It was not invariably the case that, depending upon whether British rule was praised or damned, Muslim rule was conversely damned or praised. Resentment against Muslims was more than the reflection of a need for a dark interregnum, necessary to sustain the twin myths of divine dispensation and a glorious past. For example, the anarchy from which the British were supposed to have rescued India was initially viewed in terms of the rapaciousness of both the Muslims and the Marathas. There was, however, nothing irreversible about this characterization, and soon enough the Marathas were installed into the emerging nationalist hagiography. Among those who contributed to this positive change in the image of the Marathas was Dutt. In his *Maharashtra Jivanprabhat*, he introduced a debate between the young and ebullient Shivaji, and the sagacious and old Jaisingh, on harmonizing ends and means.[80] This was a ploy to explain away the excesses of the Maratha marauders — as they were remembered in Bengal and some other parts of the country — and to project Shivaji as a national hero. But no equivalent transformation of the stereotype of Muslim rule took place, despite periodic canonizations of Akbar, and of poets like Rahim and Rasakhan.

III

If Hindi placed a strain on the cohesive potential of Hindustan, so did the other major Indian languages. While Hindi did this by identifying Hindustan with itself, the other languages did so by becoming the source of parallel regional nationalisms. These nationalisms were not always in harmony among themselves, or in relation to a pan-Indian nationalism. Here I shall consider two kinds of language-based nationalism: one which evolved largely in reaction to the expansionist claims of a neighbouring language, and the other which developed without being thus encumbered. In the first category, we shall see how Assamese and Oriya, pitted against Bengali, developed their separate national identities. In the second category, we shall see what began as *Gujaratni asmita* (Gujarati identity) and became *Gujaratni rashtriya asmita* (Gujarat's national identity).

In the wake of the British occupation of Assam in 1836, Bengali was introduced into local schools and law courts. This was done, as the Assamese saw it, at the insistence of the East India Company's petty Bengali officials who argued that Assamese was not an independent language but merely a patois of Bengali. For about twenty years thereafter the Assamese suffered the imposition of a 'foreign' language. They had neither the leaders nor the organization to protest. It was left to the American Baptist Missionaries in Assam to criticize the injustice of this imposition.

Anandaram Dhekiyal Phukan (1829–59), one of the pioneers of modern Assamese literature, was the first native of Assam to systematically expose the disastrous 'misconceptions concerning the identity of the Bengali and Assamese languages', and to plead for 'our right to use native language, both in the education of the people and in the dispensation of justice'. Gifted with a sensitive and inquisitive mind, Anandaram prepared, during barely a decade of his working life, an irrefutable case for Assamese as an independent language. He inspired his own as well as subsequent generations to enrich Assamese, and to feel pride in it. He translated, in beautiful prose, a variety of passages from English into Assamese in order to demonstrate that 'the Bengali is not a particle more copious than the Assamese'. If anything, 'the literature of Assam was, in the year 1800, more extensive and varied than that of Bengal.' Given the opportunity, Assamese possessed the potential to develop in the way that Bengali had after 1800.[81] Anandram collected a large number of old Assamese works relating to diverse subjects — religion, history, geography, medicine, law, drama, arithmetic, and lexicography. Adding to them a survey of recent works in the language, he clinched his argument for Assamese with a rhetorical question:

> In view of the above Catalogue of Assamese Books, embracing such an extended variety, what shall we say of the statement that the Assamese is merely a provincial speech like the Yorkshire or Wiltshire patois in England, and that it is an unfit medium for communicating knowledge to the masses?[82]

This stirring and reasoned plea for Assamese was elaborated in two pamphlets entitled 'Observations on the Administration of the Province of Assam' (1853) and 'A Few Remarks on the Assamese Language and on Vernacular Education in Assam' (1855).[83]

The concern for Assamese was part of a larger concern for Assam. Anandram was well-versed in English and Bengali. Through a brief stint at the Hindu College he had been exposed to the intellectual ethos of a colonial society that was beginning to feel the springs of freedom in the midst of political subjection. He was among the first to articulate the stirrings of Assamese identity. In the concluding passage of an essay on England, which he wrote when he was just eighteen, he prayed:

> When Assam will be converted from a forest to a flower-garden, the canoes of the rivers will be converted to ships, bamboo cottages will be replaced by buildings of stones and bricks; when there will be thousands and

thousands of schools, educational gatherings, dispensaries, hospitals for the poor and destitute; and when people instead of entertaining jealousy will cherish love for one another, none will give false evidence for two tolas of opium and rather will throw aside lacs of rupees in such cases; when no one will do mischief to others, being offered bribes of crores of rupees; prostitution, opium and wine will be unknown in the country, that time, O God, the Almighty Father, bring about in no time.[84]

The sentiments attached to language were as genuine as the search for a historical basis for an Assamese identity;[85] enmeshed with these was the economic dimension. Writing a year after Anandram brought out his *Observations*, A.J. Moffatt Mills admitted that 'we made a great mistake in directing that all business should be transacted in Bengalee, and that the Assamese must acquire it.' Moffatt Mills, who had earlier served as Commissioner of Cuttack, was a judge of the Sadar Diwani and Nizamat Adalat when he was asked, in 1853, to prepare a report on the administration of Assam. Drawing upon his own experience and relying on Anandaram's testimony, he stressed the economic aspects of the problem:

> A number of Bengalees came into Assam when we took the province, and from the uneducated state of the Assamese it was necessary to give them service; but there are now in Sibsagar and Gauhatty many young men of high family and good character who have qualified themselves for employ, and it is most discouraging to them to see most of the high and even some of the inferior offices filled by foreigners.[86]

No action, however, was taken, despite official recognition of the justice of the Assamese demand for the restoration of their language. It was thus natural for more and more Assamese to take recourse to agitations. Besides this, work was carried on along the lines suggested by Anandaram, especially by Hemchandra Baruwa (1835–96) and Gunabhiram Baruwa (1837–94). These two actually demonstrated, through their creative and journalistic writings, the potential of the Assamese language that Anandaram had taken such pains to emphasize. Recalling these years of challenge and struggle, Lakshminath Bezbaruwa (c. 1868–1938, the uncrowned king of Assamese literature for nearly thirty years preceding his death) described Hemchandra's short-lived *Assam News* as the best monthly that had appeared in the province.[87]

Gunabhiram Baruwa, a near relation and first biographer of Anandaram Phukan, devoted whatever spare time he got as a government servant to research the history of Assam. In 1884, he brought out his *Assam Buranji*, a chronicle intended to inspire feelings of pride in belonging to Assam. During 1885–86, when *Assam News* had ceased to exist, Gunabhiram edited *Assam Bandhu* with the same end in view, and himself contributed a series of articles called *Assam: Atit aru Bartaman* (Assam: Past and Present). Through both his writings and the charm of his personality, as Bezbaruwa's autobiography shows, Gunabhiram furthered the cause of Assamese consciousness.[88]

This consciousness gained in strength as attempts continued to deny Assamese the status of an independent language. For example, after the publication of Miles Bronson's *Dictionary of Assamese* (1867), it was argued that of the first 688 words in the dictionary no less than 591 were Bengali. As the charge was strongly countered by the Assamese, the authorities referred the matter to R.C. Dutt, then a young ICS officer, who gave it as his opinion that Assamese was a separate language. Dutt's verdict facilitated the replacement of Bengali by Assamese in 1873.[89]

The verdict given by Dutt cannot be seen as evidence of the fact that Bengalis not domiciled in Assam had a healthy regard for the Assamese language. They may not have shared the economic motive behind the linguistic aggressiveness of their fellow Bengalis in Assam, but they were not immune to the psychological satisfaction provided by the cultural chauvinism which accompanied the expansion of their language into Assam. Lakshminath Bezbaruwa's testimony in this regard is revealing. Bezbaruwa belonged to a well-known family of Assam and married a grand-daughter of Debendranath Tagore against the wishes of his own family. Since this was not a 'love marriage', and orthodoxy then reigned supreme in such matters, the Tagore aura was perhaps a powerful factor compelling Bezbaruwa to disregard the match arranged for him by his parents. He informed them at the very last moment that he was marrying into the Tagore family. Yet when, under the leadership of Robi *Kaka* (Rabindranath Tagore) the Tagores started impressing upon him the superiority of Bengali to its 'dialect', Assamese, the young Lakshminath reacted with an independence and tenacity that sorely disappointed his famous in-laws.[90]

The sluggish implementation of the resolution of 1873, which recognized Assamese as the official language of Assam, aggravated the fear of cultural aggression. This helped continue the struggle initiated by Anandaram and intensified the search for an independent Assamese identity. This proceeded on the lines suggested by pioneers like Anandaram, Gunabhiram and Hemchandra. It involved the reconstruction of Assam's past in glowing terms; the collection and publication of old Assamese manuscripts in order to show that no other Indian language could offer, for the preceding four or five hundred years, the kinds of literary and intellectual treasure possessed by the Assamese; and the creation of a rich literature in the language. It was with these ends in view that the Assamiya Bhasha Unnatisadhini Sabha was founded in 1888 by a band of Assamese students studying in Calcutta. The launching, a year later, of a literary magazine, *Jonaki*, by the same group was another effort towards the formation of an Assamese identity. Among the moving spirits of the two ventures were Chandrakumar Aggarwala (1867–1938), Lakshminath Bezbaruwa and Hemchandra Goswami (1872–1928), a trio that was to match the fame of Anandaram, Hemchandra Baruwa and Gunabhiram Baruwa in the history of modern Assam.[91]

Assamese consciousness was not just negative and reactive, nor consisted only of resistance to the imposition of Bengali. Assamese developed a positive character as it came to be buttressed by the nostalgia for a past worthy of emulation, and by the anxiety to move out of a present so obviously wretched. The poignant elegies on Assam's misfortunes from the prolific pen of Kamalakanta Bhattacharya (1853–1936) give expression to a combination of hope and helplessness. One such poem can be paraphrased thus:

> Oh charming smile of the full-moon, do fly away. I beseech you with folded hands! Your rays do not look well in the face of Assam, so wretched! Tell me, Oh! Oblivion, how many chronicles have you devoured and put in your abdomen? I die burning within myself when I think of how many glories of the nation you have devoured.[92]

The word 'nation' in this poem denotes Assam: *Jati* occurs in the original Assamese text. This is the sense in which, during the later nineteenth century, *jati* was beginning to be used in addition to its usual sense of caste. It has several connotations when used in the sense of nation. In the context of Bhattacharya's poem, *jati* meant Assam. It could also mean, in different contexts, Hindu or India. Like *desh*, it could mean a whole range of territorial units, from one's native village to one's country. This reflected the tendency to conceive of more than one identity as national. Even if this emerging Assamese consciousness, like regional consciousness in other parts of the country, saw 'nation' as not the same as India, it was not always opposed to emerging Indian nationalism. Lakshminath Bezbaruwa, for example, who was devoted to the spread of Assamese consciousness, launched an attack on *Mau*, an Assamese periodical, because it was taking an anti-Congress course. The feeling against the editor of *Mau* was so strong that Assamese students in Calcutta took out a procession and burnt his effigy in public.[93]

Like the Assamese language, which acted as a cementing force in Assam, Oriya provided the base for the emergence of a similar consciousness in Orissa during the second half of the nineteenth century. There was, however, one difference in the pattern of confrontation between Oriya and Bengali, as compared to that between Assamese and Bengali. While the Assamese had to fight against the *fait accompli* of Bengali as being the language of their schools and offices, Oriyas had to resist the efforts of Bengali officials posted in Orissa to have Oriya replaced by Bengali. The argument, once again, was that Oriya was merely a variant of Bengali.

The language controversy in Orissa, which had been intermittently on since the 1840s, became particularly virulent during 1869–70. By this time, Oriya public opinion had begun to be organized. Following the outbreak of famine in 1866, Bichitranand Das (d. 1875) and Gourishankar Ray (1838–1917) had started *Utkal Dipika*, making it possible for matters relating to Orissa to be publicly debated. Moreover, around this time Fakir Mohan Senapati (1843–1918), who, along with Radhanath Ray (1848–1908) and Madhusudan Rao (1853–1912), was to lay the foundations of modern Oriya literature, had started taking an active interest in public affairs. The eruption of the language controversy at this stage found Oriyas more than ever determined to resist the displacement of their language.

Matters came to a head with the publication of a book entitled *Udiya Swatantra Bhasha Noy* (Oriya is Not an Independent Language), which argued for the replacement of Oriya by Bengali in all schools and government offices on the ground that Oriya was a dialect of Bengali. The account furnished by Fakir Mohan shows how, impelled by fear of cultural submersion, he exploited the threat of economic deprivation to persuade his normally pusillanimous people to take a stand on this issue. After considerable effort, he succeeded in sending a substantially signed petition to the government. The petition was forwarded with cogently argued notes in favour of Oriya by John Beames, the Collector of Balasore and a linguist, who knew Sanskrit, Bengali, Assamese, Oriya and Hindi, and by T. E. Ravenshaw, the Commissioner of Orissa division. Putting the controversy to rest, the government ordered that all possible steps be taken for the promotion of Oriya.[94]

However, even two decades after the language controversy had been settled in favour of Oriya, Fakir Mohan was led to complain in his *Utkal Bhramanam* (1892): 'The officers and the lawyers are all foreigners; not even the postal clerk is native.'[95] The 'foreigners' were Bengalis. The British, it was taken for granted, were there to stay: what was more unbearable was the presence of Bengalis in the administration, to the virtual exclusion of Oriyas. This feeling did not extend to all Bengalis, nor did it necessarily mar relations between Oriyas and Bengalis. In its actual operation, the feeling was quite restricted. Nonetheless it denoted a general Oriya perception of themselves as natives vis-à-vis foreigners.

Government orders, naturally, were not enough to enrich Oriya literature or make it an effective vehicle for education. Fakir Mohan, who had begun writing in Bengali because there were no periodicals in his own language, describes how wistful and restless the sight of a new book in Bengali would make him, inducing him to wonder when Oriya would possess similar books. Much needed to be done. Oriya had no prose literature worth the name; and its poetry was stuck in the iron laws of traditional prosody.[96]

The literature that came to be written under the stress of new material and cultural compulsions derived from the need for, and contributed to the realization of, a language-based identity. As in the case of Assamese and most other Indian languages, Oriya literature looked for, and embellished, a regional past capable of inspiring the present. In the process, the past of Orissa was recalled in all its glory and splendour, and its geography invested with sanctity. Radhanath

Ray, perhaps 'the most powerful poet of the period', gave a new orientation to the region's physical geography and imbued it 'with something hallowed in history or religion'.[97] In his *Mahayatra* (1896), he ingeniously had the Pandavas turn to Orissa in the course of their 'final journey' to heaven. They sang thus of the beauties and glories of her topography: ' If all other lands are to be compared with leaves (of a plant or tree), Utkal will be compared with the flower.'[98]

Though they put mythology to creative use, Oriya writers did not have to go very far back in time to fashion an inspiring past that would sustain their regional identity. They recalled the greatness of the medieval Orissan empire. The memory of this greatness and its popularization were facilitated by two surviving symbols of that empire: the raja of Khurda and the temple of Jagannath.[99] The lead in this respect was taken by Ramashankar Ray through his play *Kanchi Kaberi* (1880–81).[100] He was followed by Madhusudan Rao, whose *Utkal Gatha* comprised a whole series of poems with history as the source of inspiration. But it was Radhanath Ray who made the most impressive contribution to the utilization of Jagannath as a symbol of Oriya identity.[101]

The growing sense of pride in belonging to Orissa — the sense of being Oriya — and the feeling about 'foreigners', with its economic implications, gave birth to the demand of 'Orissa for Oriyas'. So, along with the complaint that not even the postal clerk was a native, appeals began to be made to the government to appoint, in Orissa, only 'natives' to the post of deputy collector, which was then the highest position to which they could normally aspire without entering the ICS.[102]

Another demand that gained momentum as a result of rising regional consciousness was for the unification of the entire Oriya-speaking region by taking away Oriya-speaking tracts from the Madras Presidency and the Central Provinces. This demand became so strong with the passage of time that it led to the establishment of an association which aimed to be 'the parliament of the people inhabiting Oriya-speaking areas notwithstanding caste, creed, language and administrative division'. This was the Utkal Sammilani — Utkal Union Conference — which had as its guiding spirit Madhusudan Das (1848–1934), the foremost contemporary leader of Orissa. A protagonist of Oriya consciousness (in spite of his conversion to

Christianity, he accepted Jagannath as a symbol of Oriya identity). Das had been a staunch supporter of the Indian National Congress. But in the year of the founding of the Utkal Sammilani he parted company with the Congress on account of the decision of its Madras session (1903) not to support 'the proposed separation of the district of Ganjam with its Agency tracts and Vizagapatnam Agency from the Madras Presidency and its amalgamation with Orissa'.[103]

Simultaneously with efforts to bring into existence a political association to promote Oriya interests, steps were being taken lo create an organization for the welfare of Oriya language and literature. It is a measure of the strength of Oriya consciousness that even when its political and cultural aspects found different organizational channels, as they should have, they operated in close co-operation. This is clear from the fact that the Utkal Samaj was founded in the same year as the Utkal Sammilani. The two organizations had their maiden sessions at the same place on successive days (Cuttack, December 1903). It is further illustration of their operational intimacy that Radhanath Ray, the first president of the Sahitya Samaj, attended the Sammilani and moved a resolution calling for the promotion of the Oriya language. The opening session of the Sammilani began with the rendering of a Sanskrit poem composed by Radhanath.[104]

Language-based regional consciousness got a fillip from the perception of external threat in Assam and Orissa. It happened differently in Gujarat. Being placed in a presidency that mainly comprised two distinct linguistic groups perhaps suggested by slow degrees the need to maintain, even sharpen, linguistic divisions as a safeguard against other groups. Also, the memory of Maratha *ghanims* — marauders — and their rapine in Gujarat could have been a supporting factor in the growth of Gujarati consciousness. But in its formative stage, during the later nineteenth century at any rate, the idea of *Gujaratni asmita* did not derive inspiration from any confrontation with an aggressive rival language. Even the bitterness of the memory of Maratha *ghanims* was beginning to be subordinated by a construction of the past within which Shivaji was apotheosized.

Although he was not its originator, the credit for the first powerful articulation of the idea of Gujarati identity is given, by common consent, to Narmad. Writing in a variety of literary forms and reflecting an awareness of the different problems that faced his country,

Narmad was no less keenly concerned about the distinctive historical–cultural identity of Gujarat and the state of Gujaratis.[105]

In a long essay, entitled 'Gujaratni Sthiti' and written in 1869, Narmad detailed the many-sided degeneration of Gujaratis over the centuries. This he did in terms that were intended to inspire his readers to reform their fallen society. He took special care to describe the resplendent grandeur of Gujarat before its conquest by the Muslims. Drawing upon both history and mythology, Narmad's lament was also a call to feel pride in being Gujarati. It ended with the exhortation that all inhabitants of Gujarat — Rajputs, Bhils, Kolis, Brahmans, Parsis and Muslims — should sink their differences and work in unison to recover its past glory.[106]

Narmad employed verse to inspire the same thought: 'We are Gujarati, we are Gujarati, we are Gujarati.'[107] In his '*Jai*! *Jai*! *Garavi Gujarat*', a lilting poem which gives Gujarati mythology, history and geography a luminous halo, Narmad gave his 'brethren' what they came to cherish as the 'national song' of Gujarat. He used for Gujaratis terms that seemed likely to be etched in the popular mind, and called upon them — the sons of Gujarat — in the name of their 'mother', to unite. Realizing his exhortations might enthuse only Hindu Gujaratis, he wrote a poem called 'Whose Gujarat?' which projected a broad-based, secular Gujarati identity.[108]

The man who made it the abiding passion of his short life to propagate the idea of *Gujarati asmita* and who gave it an organizational base, was Ranjitram Vavabhai Mehta (1882–1917). Through his essays and researches into the history and folklore of Gujarat, he sought to recover its literature and culture; and through the Gujarati Sahitya Parishad, which he was instrumental in founding in 1905, Ranjitram ensured that his mission would not remain dependent on an individual effort. The establishment of the Gujarati Sahitya Parishad was preceded, and inspired, by the Banga Sahitya Parishad, the Nagari Pracharini Sabha and the Tamil Literary Academy; these had been formed to promote the cause of Bengali, Hindi and Tamil, respectively.[109]

It was only appropriate that Govardhanram Tripathi should have been chosen the first president of the Gujarati Sahitya Parishad. The theme of his inaugural address was equally appropriate: Govardhanram charted the history of Gujarati literature over the centuries and linked it with his own day.[110] This was not a new interest he had taken up in consonance with the spirit of the founding of the Parishad. At least since the early 1890s, when his *Classical Poets of Gujarat and Their Influence on Society* (1892) appeared, he had been concerned with understanding a live Gujarati tradition.

By the time K. M. Munshi (1887–1971), a leading man of letters and prominent Congressman, emerged to carry forward what Ranjitram had taken up as a mission, *Gujaratni asmita* had become *Gujaratni rashtriya asmita*.[111] But this was a 'national identity' that existed harmoniously with a pan-Indian national identity. For Munshi, there was no question of any antagonism between regional nationalism and Indian nationalism.

In varying ways, the same thing is true of other promoters of regional consciousness. Most of them agreed on the need to harmonize the two kinds of nationalism. Radhanath Ray employed the term *Utkal Bharati*, which symbolized the fusion between region and country. Madhusudan Rao sang of the splendour of Utkal and of famed Aryan glories.[112] Kamalakanta Bhattacharya, who had implored the full moon not to shine on the unhappy land of Assam and cursed 'oblivion' for having devoured so many national glories, also prayed for the day when hundreds of patriots like Mazzini and Garibaldi would illumine *Bharat dhara* yet again.[113]

These sentiments were different from that which prompted Lakshminath Bezbaruwa and Assamese students in Calcutta to burn the effigy of the anti-Congress editor of *Mau*. This was more an upshot of political awareness, born of the realization of a colonial presence. Nationalism, regional or national, was born out of both sorts of sentiment.

Political awareness of colonialism and the idea of cultural unity both made for the existence of regional alongside pan-Indian national consciousness. But there were limits to controlling the potential tension between these two. The decision of Madhusudan Das to keep away from the Congress because of its rejection of the proposal for a united Orissa is a case in point. Likewise, the emphasis on cultural unity, with its pronounced Hindu orientation, could prove inimical to the growth of an ideologically inspired political unity that cut across sectarian and religious divisions. Regional nationalism, after all, was not immune to the unselfconscious tendency of Hindus to view themselves as the 'nation'. For example, in the very poem, 'Whose Gujarat?', in which Narmad had taken special care to include Muslims among those to whom Gujarat belonged, he also betrayed an anti-Muslim bias.[114]

Within the perspective yielded by this outline of the growth of culturally inspired, language-based identities simultaneously with the emergence of Indian nationalism, one understands a little better the implications of the consciousness and politics which gave rise to the slogan 'Hindi, Hindu, Hindustan'.

Conclusion

♠

All through the writing of this book I have worked with the fear that I might fail to maintain the necessary balance required when discussing the several elements that together constituted the structure of social consciousness. I should like to believe that I have not lapsed too often into an excess of zeal, one way or the other.[1] Nowhere has this tension been greater than in the writing of the last chapter, particularly its first two sections.

I have sought a degree of critical empathy in my understanding of our nineteenth-century forebears. Despite the rupture effected by colonialism and the triumph of an imperialist Western discourse, what I have discussed in this book remains the more-or-less unarticulated base of our own consciousness. Something basically similar has persisted beneath the surface of the diverse and dramatic changes in Indian society since the nineteenth century. This continuity, once we are aware of it, creates its own problems. We frequently wish to see angels or monsters in the past, and are accordingly grateful or malevolent towards our ancestors. This state of mind is not conducive to the exercise of critical empathy.

In the first two chapters we are unlikely to see the sorts of malevolence that are to be found described in the third chapter. Nationalism, in its violent and fundamentalist forms, alone throws up the hideous faces which create the major crisis of India's polity. The contemporary instance of *sati* infuriates, alas, only some of us: a large number of us continue to emphasize its roots in heroism and 'sacrifice'. This is the ambivalence that makes possible, down to our own day, 'rational' and philosophical justifications of *sati* as an ideal. It is impossible not to relate this to much in the second chapter on the attitudes of our forefathers in the nineteenth century. Despite having been profoundly disturbed by the recent killing, the 'sati' in Rajasthan, I have attempted to extend to our ancestors a degree of empathy which, obviously, is impossible vis-à-vis the more contemporary ambivalence on this issue.[2]

On the issue of nationalism today it is necessary to take note of the ominously rapid 'Hinduization' of the Indian polity during 1980–90, the decade I have spent writing this book. I do not feel handicapped in my perceptions by the escalation of regional movements in the country, though it has required some struggle to achieve clarity. When I first became familiar with the evidence offered in the first two sections of the last chapter, I saw a clear reflection in the nineteenth century of the kind of communalism that, in our own century, has given the term its distinctly dirty Indian shade. But within a couple of years, the unease I felt about my first article on this material, entitled 'Communal Consciousness in Late Nineteenth Century Hindi Literature' (1981), was so strong that I felt obliged to essay an auto-critique. 'Communal consciousness' was diluted to 'communal elements' in that auto-critique.

As I was writing the last chapter of this book, I saw I had said in that auto-critique that the Hindu perception of Muslims as foreigners was restrained by pragmatic considerations of Hindu–Muslim unity'.[3] This formulation overstrains the feeling that Muslims were foreigners, as against a simultaneously held and larger view of the Indian nation in which Muslims were integral. It creates the false impression that the larger view of the nation was little more than a camouflage for the view that Hindus alone constituted the nation; that the latter alone represented the Hindu position in this regard. The last chapter of the present book, however, shows that both these views were parts of a complex attitude characterized by ambiguities, contradictions and unresolved tensions. While this seems to me a fairly balanced formulation of the Hindu position on the question of the nation, I cannot discount an uneasy feeling that something of the fluidity of the phenomenon has still evaded comprehension.

This is not entirely a personal failing. The very dynamism of nationalism makes it a phenomenon within which the present constantly spills over into the past and transforms it. There are no universally acceptable criteria for defining nationalism. And yet, as the dominant principle of political cohesion in our time, the phenomenon is real, and we continue to be centrally concerned with it. It is a principle that is employed to exercise power and also to challenge established power; it is subject to fusion as well as fission. Consequently, even the apparently decisive proof of the existence of a nation-state cannot be taken as a necessarily convincing academic argument for a given nationalism; just as the absence of a state, or even territory, cannot be treated as a decisive argument against the existence of a given nationalism. In situations of conflict, the very existence of a certain nationalism can be simultaneously asserted or denied by people, depending upon how they are situated in this conflict. It is not possible to possess a fixed framework of validation with regard to a dynamic phenomenon which comprises collective self-images, with their often competing political–ideological assertions.

The Indian state, for example, would have us believe that there is only Indian nationalism in India. It negates the possibility — shall we say reality — of there being any nationalism in India other than Indian nationalism. Nationalism in the country is, thus, allowed a procrustean existence in accordance with contemporary political and constitutional requirements. Because we are to extend supreme loyalty to the nation-state, we must forget the elementary lesson of history that there is nothing sacrosanct about the boundaries of nation-states, that these are contingent units which can expand, contract and become transformed beyond recognition.

If many of us subscribe to such *ex post facto* procrusteanizations, this is not just the result of constitutional coercion. As in other nation-states, in ours a kind of teleology is at work. Taking its cue from the present, it works backwards to confirm the belief that the nation-state, as it is, marks not only an inevitable but also an inviolable stage in the 'nation's' historical evolution. It lays down how the past is to be viewed: in the light of the present requirements of the nation-state.

Fortunately, there is no unanimity about the perception of the present, except perhaps a realization that our larger society, of which the Indian nation-state happens to be the main organizing principle, faces a serious crisis. This is a realization that significantly colours our understanding of the development of nationalism in the country. In accordance with the way observers view this crisis, they project their understanding of the present onto the past. What is more, certain narrow group identities are presented as the only possible 'Indian' identity, and considerations of personal/party interests and power are rationalized as a concern for national solidarity.

In these narrowly motivated conceptions of Indian nationalism, the nation-state is cast in a monolithic mould. Despite the plurality of Indian society, the simultaneous emergence of multiple 'nationalism', and the federal spirit of the Indian constitution, the idea of a multinational Indian state finds no place in these conceptions.

This centralizing viewpoint underlies not only the communal Hindu but also certain secular conceptions of 'Indian' nationalism. The common advocacy of a strong centralized nation-state, however, represents no more than a spurious unity of view. Behind it lie varied, and often incompatible, conceptions of the nation and the state; and, consequently, different modes of ordering attachments to a variety of social unities.

There has been, it seems, a greater willingness and capacity on our part to see through the nationalist claims of those monolithic ideologies which are communal in character, while similar ideologies with a secular orientation have tended to get away with their nationalist pretensions. This is best illustrated, and partly accounted for, by the 'nationalist' historiography of the Indian national movement, particularly by its characterization of the Indian National Congress as the supreme national organization which not only led the struggle for independence but also safeguarded the interests of the poor and the oppressed against privileged groups and classes within Indian society. Some of our Marxist historiography, too, has shared this sort of position. Given the fast aggravating communal situation in the country, will we soon lose our capacity to see through even communally-oriented monolithic ideologies?

The earlier relationship of harmony between Indian nationalism and regional nationalisms has given way to varying degrees of confrontation. This has been basically a result of economic and political developments, not the inevitable outcome of any intrinsic logic within specific regional nationalisms. But such is the effect of the present on the reconstruction of the past that the changing character of the more assertive and militant of these regional nationalisms is projected back into the last century, if not earlier. Depending upon the side from which this confrontation is viewed, such anachronistic projection causes this or that regional nationalism to be abused or idealized. In either case, the strain on the polity is aggravated. The abuse unduly countenances the view that what we need is a strong centralized state, while the idealization unduly encourages the potential for polarization in the confrontations between Indian and regional nationalisms.

This happens not only in the treatment of pan-Indian and regional identities. Discussion of other identities is also usually carried on within the context of an overarching Indian nationalism. The underlying assumption is that there was, and still is, an essential opposition between them and Indian nationalism. Despite the realization that, as a new principle of cohesion, nationalism transcended (even as it derived from) traditional socio-cultural institutions, the acid test of progress seems to be the extent to which nationalism has diminished people's affection for traditional identities.

If the increasing communalization of our polity is a real threat, its polar opposite — the expectation that traditional social identities must disappear — is equally unhelpful. This expectation is not confined to the present. In its application to the past, it takes the form of the complaint that primordial loyalties hindered the emergence of a secular national outlook. The attack on Gandhi for the religious–cultural idiom he employed exemplifies the complaint. Implicit here is the assumption of an antagonistic relationship between national identity and narrower, more traditional identities. If divisions of class are not seen as necessarily inimical to the growth of nationalism, it is not clear why an antipathy should be posited between nationalism and the traditional forms of social unity. Even in the post-industrial societies of the West, religious or ethnic identities have retained their vigour, and at times their mutual bitterness, without cutting at the root of nationalism as a principle of political organization.

It is important to shake ourselves out of our cynical devaluation of tradition. As representatives of a respectable and popular position, Dutt's *The Lake of Palms* and Pratapnarayan's *sanatani maryada* cannot be wished away. If nationalism was fed by a growing realization of the basic dichotomy of interests between itself and colonialism, it was also nurtured by strong cultural factors that were inter-textured with religion. Despite differences with regard to the objectives, means, programmes and pronouncements of various organized political associations and leaders, nationalism as a phenomenon was simultaneously economic, political and cultural.

If nationalism is, indeed, a critical and constantly unfolding phenomenon — in the perception of which our ideological stance vis-a-vis its present state affects our understanding of its origins and evolution — what is my own position on the present crisis of the Indian nation-state? Here I feel lost, beyond a point. I raise the point about the ultimate impossibility of defining nationalism in order to seek a degree of freedom from the hegemonic straitjacketing of nationalism under the aegis of the state. But a gap of this kind cannot be the invitation to an anarchy wherein, depending on personal whims, nationalism is arbitrarily associated with or denied to whatever one supports or opposes; it calls, rather, for extra intellectual alertness and responsibility, a struggle to move more from the past to the present rather than the other way around.

Notes

Prologue to this Edition

1. *Acts of Literature*, London, 1991.
2. Walter Benjamin, *Illuminations*, London, 1970, pp. 4–5.
3. Sudhir Chandra, *Continuing Dilemmas: Understanding Social Consciousness*, Delhi, 2002, xiii–xxxii.
4. Gandhi to Nehru (in Hindustani), 5 October 1945. *Jawaharlal Nehru Papers*, pt. i, vol. xxvi, at the Nehru Memorial Museum & Library, New Delhi.
5. I have discussed Gandhi as an impossible possibility in my *Gandhi: Ek Asambhav Sambhavana* (in Hindi), Rajkamal Prakashan, Delhi, 2011.

Introduction

1. Realizing that Raja Radhakanta Deb carried influence with both Hindu society and the government, Vidyasagar sent him a copy of his pamphlet in favour of widow marriage. The Raja was so pleased with the pamphlet that he sent for Vidyasagar and, to help the latter in his cause, organized a meeting of the learned pundits to discuss the matter. As often happened at such public discussions, a great deal of passion was generated but no decision could be reached. However, Radhakanta Deb made no secret of his own preference when, at the end of the debate, he rewarded Vidyasagar with a pair of shawls. Soon thereafter he extended his support to organized orthodoxy; both facets together help us understand the Raja. See S. C. Mitra, *Isvar Chandra Vidyasagar: A Story of His Life and Work* (1902; rpt. Delhi: 1975, 266–7).
2. See S. K. De, *Bengali Literature in the 19th Century*, Calcutta, 1962, 507–88. When the English-educated middle classes revolted against the zamindar-dominated British Indian Association and formed, in quick succession, the Indian League and the Indian Association, K. M. Banerji was requested to be their president.
3. See *Indian Christians* (Madras, not dated); L. B. Day, *Recollections of Alexander Duff* (London, 1879); A. B. Shah, ed., *The Letters and Correspondence of Pandita Ramabai* (Bombay, 1977); Lakshmibai Tilak, *I Follow After*, translated by E. Josephine Inkster (London, 1950) [being an abridged translation of Lakshmibai Tilak's four-volume *Smriti Chitre* (1934–6)]. Particularly noticeable is the movement for an Indian National Church

that gained momentum under the aegis of the Bengal Christian Association which was founded in 1868, with K. M. Banerji as its president.
4. For the original letter in Hindustani, see *Jawaharlal Nehru Papers*, pt i, vol. xxvi (Nehru Memorial Museum and Library, New Delhi). I have used my own translation of the letter. Differently translated, the letter has been included in *The Collected Works of Mahatma Gandhi* (New Delhi, 1980), LXXXI, 319–21. The date of *Hind Swaraj* as given by Gandhi in this letter is 1908 and not 1909.
5. See S. Gopal, ed., *Selected Works of Jawaharlal Nehru* (New Delhi, 1981), xiv, 554–7. 'I do not understand', wrote Nehru — despite Gandhi's warning that he was not writing about the Indian villages as they existed — 'why a village should necessarily embody truth and non-violence. A village, normally speaking, is backward intellectually and culturally and no progress can be made from a backward environment. Narrow-minded people are much more likely to be untruthful and violent.'
6. *Jawaharlal Nehru Papers*, pt i, vol. xxvi; also *The Collected Works of Mahatma Gandhi* (New Delhi, 1980), LXXXII, 71–2.
7. 'Our educated classes', Nehru wrote further, 'have so far taken the lead in the fight for Swaraj, but in doing so they have seldom paid heed to the needs of the masses. . . . But what shall it profit the masses of India — the peasantry, the landless labourers, the artisans — if everyone of the offices held by Englishmen in India today is held by an Indian.' S. Gopal, ed., III, 371.
8. *The Collected Works of Mahatma Gandhi* (New Delhi, 1970), xxxvi, 174.
9. For Bhattacharya's discourse, see *Indian Philosophical Quarterly*, xi (4), Oct.–Dec. 1984, 383–93.
10. See G. Charbonnier, *Conversations With Claude Levi-Strauss* (London, 1970).
11. A typical example of this is provided by Partha Chatterjee, *Nationalist Thought and the Colonial World: A Derivative Discourse?* (Delhi, 1986). After going through this fine Marxist study of the making of a dominant nationalist thought pattern in colonial India, I wonder if the question mark in the title isn't really redundant. Also surprising, but in keeping with the pronounced preference for a certain western discourse, is the scrupulous omission of any reference to the kind of debate carried on by the *Indian Philosophical Quarterly* on 'Swaraj in Ideas'. This sort of ideological exclusiveness, however, is shared by 'non-progressives' as well. Even for polemical purposes, the two groups do not condescend to take note of the other.
12. Writing on the growth of Marathi literature from the mid 1860s to the late 1890s, Ranade observed:

> a very sensible contribution to the stock of our best works has been made, and the fact that Spencer, Max Muller, Sir Walter Scott,

Lord Bacon, Sir Bulwer Lytton, Buckle, Defoe, Swift, Bunyan, Smiles, and Lubbock, have furnished the models for these additions, justifies the hope that the national mind is showing signs of a great awakening.... As none of these additions have been school-books, the industry and enterprise represented by these publications have had to depend for their reward solely upon the unaided patronage of the reading public. With proper guidance and encouragement by such a body as the University, the circle of this reading public will be enlarged, and we may soon expect to have all the departments of prose literature properly represented in their due proportions, and the work of development, now indifferently attempted by stray authors, will be pushed on and completed in a systematic manner, so as to enable the national mind to digest the best thoughts of Western Europe with the same intimate appreciation that it has shown in the assimilation of the old Sanskrit learning. *The Miscellaneous Writings of the Late Hon'ble Mr. Justice M. G. Ranade* (Bombay, 1915), 31–2.

Chapter 1

1. *Amachya Deshachi Sthiti* (Nagpur, 1937) 92.
2. Ibid., 17–19.
3. Ibid., 20.
4. Ibid., 21–22.
5. Ibid., 20.
6. Ibid., 85–89.
7. Ibid., 82.
8. Ibid., 90–91.
9. Kantilal C. Pandya, Ramprasad P. Bakshi and Sanmukhlal J. Pandya, eds, *Govardhanram Madhavram Tripathi's Scrap Book 1888–1894* (Bombay, 1959), 29. *The Scrap Book* for the period 1894–1904, edited by the same editors, appeared in the same year. That for the last years, 1904–06, was edited by Kantilal C. Pandya alone and it appeared a year earlier, in 1958. Though chronology of publication militates against this arrangement, for convenience of citation these volumes, hereafter referred to as *Scrap Book*, are treated as i, ii and iii respectively.
10. Ibid., ii, 9, 69–70; iii, 1.
11. Ibid., i, 51.
12. Braj Ratna Das, ed., *Bharatendu Granthavali* (Kashi, Samvat 2010), ii, 623–24.
13. Ibid., 630–31.
14. Ibid., 633.
15. Ibid., 675–66.
16. Ibid., 699.

17. Ibid., 701–11.
18. Ibid., 761–65.
19. Ibid., 793–66.
20. Ibid., 797–809.
21. Braj Ratna Das, ed., *Bharatendu-Natakavali* (Ilahabad, Samvat 2013), ii, 208–17.
22. See Hemant Sharma, ed., *Bharatendu Samagra* (Varanasi, 1987), 460–71.
23. *Bharatendu-Natakavali*, ii, 195. The following is the text of the song:

    Paratiya paradhan dekhi na nripagan chitta chalavain.
    Gaaya dudha bahu dehin, megha subha jal barasavain.
    Hari-pada mein rati hoi, na dukha kou kahun vyapai.
    Angarejan ko raj Ees it thir kari thapai.
    Shruti-pantha chalain sajjan sabai hohin taji dushtabhaya.
    Kabibani thir rasa son rahai Bharat ki nit hoi jaya.

24. *Bharatendu Samagra*, 374.
25. *Bharatendu Granthavali*, ii, 813–17.
26. Ibid., 731–8. This lecture was serialized in the *Hindi Pradip*, at the behest of whose editor, Balkrishna Bhatt, it was delivered in June 1877. See the issues of Sep., Oct., Nov. and Dec. 1877.
27. *Bharatendu Samagra*, 482–83.
28. *Harishchandra's Magazine*, 15 Jan. 1874.
29. Sudhir Chandra, *Dependence and Disillusionment: Emergence of National Consciousness in Later 19th Century India* (New Delhi, 2011).
30. *Bharatendu Samagra*, 531.
31. *Bharatendu Granthavali*, ii, 811. See also his *mukaris* on law and titles, ibid., 812.
32. *Bharatendu-Natakavali*, ii, 218.
33. *Bharat Saubhagya* (Mirzapur, 1889) 8, 51.
34. Ibid., 35–7.
35. Ibid., 15.
36. Ibid., 68. For comparison with *Ramarajya*, see Prabhakareshwar Prasad Upadhyaya and Dineshnarayan Upadhyaya, eds, *Premghan-Sarvaswa* (Prayag, Shaka 1884), i, 286.
37. *Bharat Saubhagya*, 54.
38. *Premghan-Sarvaswa*, i, 286.
39. *Bharat Saubhagya*, 54, 62–64.
40. *Premghan-Sarvaswa*, i, 153–63; see also 363–67.
41. *Shri Radhacharan Goswami ka Jivan Charit* (Muttra, 1895), 9. This is a brief autobiographical account of Radhacharan Goswami.
42. *Yamalok ki Yatra* (Mirzapur, 1888), 15.
43. *Bharatendu*, 22 Nov. 1885, 18 Feb. 1886.

44. Ibid., June 1883. The other two questions were: why is there no separate university for the North Western Provinces and Oudh? Why is there no independent legislative council for the North Western Provinces?
45. Ibid., 29 Apr. 1885. Shiv Prasad had written:

> We could find no word for "patriotism" in the language of this land. The people here simply cannot conceive of the kind of freedom for which Englishmen removed the Stuarts from the throne. Nor can they think of the happiness that the Italians derived from becoming self-dependent, or of the national sympathy that led to the unification of Germany and made her such a big "empire." See his *Itihasatimirnashak* (1871; rpt. Ilahabad, 1889, fifth edition), 89–90.

This is a literal translation of the passage in the Hindi original, the one against which Radhacharan's attack was directed. But the English version of *Itihasatimirnashak* translated the passage differently:

> Their country has been harried by Pathans, Mugals, and Marhattas, and so demoralized by misrule that the name and idea of patriotism have departed. They cannot comprehend the liberties of the subject for which the English people overthrew the Stuart dynasty, the joy of Italian independence, or the national sentiment which has brought about the unification of the great German Empire. *Itihas Timirnashak History of India in Three Parts* by Raja Siva Prasad (Lucknow, 1889, eighth edition), 82.

46. *Bharatendu*, 29 Apr. 1885.
47. Ibid., 19 Oct. 1883.
48. Narayan Prasad Arora and Satybhakta, eds, *Pratap Lahari* (Kanpur, 1949), 40. The word used in the couplet is 'Hindu', but it is intended to mean Indian.
49. Vijayshankar Mall, ed., *Pratapnarayan-Granthavali* (Kashi, Samvat 2010), i, 65–66.
50. *Pratap Lahari*, 189; *Pratapnarayan-Granthavali*, 69.
51. *Pratap Lahari*, 49.
52. Ibid., 30, 141, 250.
53. Ibid., 49.
54. Ibid., 250.
55. Ibid., 117, 140; *Pratapnarayan-Granthavali*, 367, 408.
56. *Pratap Lahari*, 35, 113; *Pratapnarayan-Granthavali*, 272, 311, 371.
57. *Pratap Lahari*, 22, 26, 29, 45, 53, 57, 98.
58. *Pratapnarayan-Granthavali*, 265–67, 270–78. See also p. 407 for the contention that poverty — and not social customs, as the official view would insist — caused decline in the health of Indians. Reformers like Keshab Chandra Sen, Dr Mahendra Lal Sarkar and B. M. Malabari shared the

view that customs such as child marriage adversely affected the average health of Indians.
59. Ibid., 272–77, *Pratap Lahari*, 26.
60. *Bharatendu-Natakavali*, ii, 206; *Pratap Lahari*, 27, 58, 62; *Pratapnarayan-Granthavali*, 671–78, for the relevant passages in *Suchal-Shiksha*. While dealing with the comprehensive nature of the British hold over India, Chiplunkar observed in *Amachya Deshachi Sthiti* that this hold threatened the very cultural survival of the ruled, and deprived them of their basic traits. See pp. 90–93.
61. *Pratap Lahari*, 97.
62. Ibid., 141.
63. *Pratapnarayan-Granthavali*, 66–67.
64. Ibid., 265.
65. Ibid., 278.
66. *Pratap Lahari*, 115–16, 207, 246–53.
67. Ibid., 212.
68. Judging by the second issue of the *Hindi Pradip*, the immediate impulse to start the paper in spite of financial and domestic difficulties seems to have been provided by the North Western Provinces government order No. 1494 of 18 July 1877, saying that only those English-speaking Indians would be entitled to government service who also knew either Persian or Urdu. See *Hindi Pradip*, Oct. 1877.
69. Pratapnarayan wrote a blistering attack on the government while reacting to this incident. See *Pratapnarayan-Granthavali*, 76–77.
70. Madhukar Bhatt, *Pandit Balkrishna Bhatt: Vyaktitva aur Krititva* (Varanasi, 1972), 54–57.
71. *Hindi Pradip*, Sep. 1877.
72. Ibid., Feb. 1878. Without saying so in such unmistakable terms — perhaps struggling towards the kind of correlation Bhatt had seen between Indian poverty and British prosperity — Premghan made pointed reference to the fact that, during the sixty years of Victoria's reign, England had moved from virtual poverty to become a mighty and prosperous nation; as against this, during the same period, India had sunk into squalor. *Premghan-Sarvaswa*, i, 288.
73. *Hindi Pradip*, Mar. 1878.
74. Ibid., Aug. 1878.
75. Ibid., Sep. 1878.
76. Ibid., Dec. 1877.
77. *Nutan Brahmachari Upanyas* (Prayag, Samvat 1968) 3.
78. *Hindi Pradip*, Feb. 1878.
79. Ibid., Sep., Dec. 1878.
80. *Harishchandra's Magazine*, 15 Feb. 1874. The review is in English; ii, 55–56, 77–85.

81. Kavi Dalpatram Dahyabhai, *Dalpat Kavya* (Mumbai, 1878). In a poem on the British Indian legal system, for example, Dalpat described the harassment it caused the Indian people, and yet prayed to God: 'Let there always be such rule which provides happiness to the people.' Ibid., 65.
82. See *Narmakavita* (1887; rpt. Mumbai, 1914), 80–94, 790–93, 815–22, 829, 870–71. For the reference to *swaraj*, see his essay 'Aryotkarsha' (1882) in *Dharmavichar* (Mumbai, 1914), 97–105. Narmad wrote loyal poems on the death of Prince Albert, the betrothal of the Prince of Wales, the visit of the Prince of Wales to India, and the assumption of the title of Empress, Qaiser-i-Hind, by Queen Victoria. He even composed a loyal poem in the English language.
83. *Dalpat Kavya*, 59.
84. *Narmakavita*, 81.
85. *Bharat Saubhagya*, 72.
86. Shyamsundar Das, ed., *Radhakrishna-Granthavali* (Prayag, 1930), i, 10.
87. *Hindi Pradip*, Feb. 1878.
88. *Chitthe aur Khat* (Calcutta, Samvat 1981), 10.
89. *Radhakrishna-Granthavali*, 144.
90. *Bharatendu Samagra*, 461. The fact that even Dadabhai Naoroji (1825–1917) named his book *Poverty and Un-British Rule in India* would suggest the spread of faith in a norm associated with the British.
91. *Bharatendu-Natakavali*, 208.
92. *Pratap Lahari*, 58.
93. *Pratapnarayan-Granthavali*, 277.
94. *Pratap Lahari*, 123; *Pratapnarayan-Granthavali*, 272, 412.
95. *Premghan-Sarvaswa*, i, 287.
96. Quoted in H. M. Das Gupta, *Studies in Western Influence on Nineteenth Century Bengali Poetry 1857–1887* (Calcutta, 1935), 45, note 1. But Hemchandra also wrote: 'Know it as gospel truth that the enlightened policy of the English nation is the *sine qua non* of the emancipation of India.' And: 'for the future of India there is no other course open to the destiny of her life. With them [the English nation] she must rise or fall.' Ibid., 50, note I.
97. *Bharatendu Granthavali*, ii, 721.
98. Harishchandra made a direct reference to this in *Bharat Durdasha*, while contending that local officials were in the habit of disregarding laws and punishing what they capriciously regarded as disloyalty. *Bharatendu Samagra*, 467–68. See also *Bharatendu-Natakavali*, ii, 215, for a similar observation in *Bharat-Janani*.
99. *Pratap Lahari*, 246–51.
100. Premghan's younger brother, then studying at the Muir Central College, Allahabad, and very keen on staging the play at the time of

the Congress session, reported this reaction of Rampal Singh in a letter to the playwright. See the preface to *Bharat Saubhagya*, 8.
101. *Scrap Book*, i, 149–50. For the expression of similar sentiments, but with a different stress, see *Bankim Rachanabali* (Calcutta, 1390 B.S.), ii, 237–38, 244. In a remarkably hard-hitting statement, Bankim questioned the view that oppression could be distinguished in terms of whether the oppressors belonged to your own nation or were foreigners. He wrote: 'To this I feel like replying that to one who is oppressed, the oppression of his/her own people or that of the foreigner are alike. It does not seem that the pain inflicted by one's own people is somewhat sweet while that perpetrated by the foreigner is bitter. But I will not offer this reply.' (244)
102. See *Sarasvatichandra* (Mumbai, 1985), in, 176 ff.
103. *Scrap Book*, ii, 158–59.
104. Ibid., 159.
105. Ibid., 15–52. See also the entry for 29 Mar. 1891; Ibid., i, 24–25.
106. *Dharmavichar*, 97–105; Ramesh Shukla, *Narmad: Ek Samalochana* (Mumbai, 1979), 207.
107. *Pratap Lahari*, 250–52.
108. *Radhakrishna-Granthavali*, 8–9.
109. In *Vishasya Vishamaushadham* Harishchandra uses this very axiom. *Bharatendu-Natakavali*, ii, 194. About simulation, O. Manoni makes the following interesting observation about colonials as opposed to the colonized: 'Colonials live in a less real social world, and this diminished reality is less able to wake the dreamer . . .'. *Prospero and Caliban: The Psychology of Colonization* (New York, 1964), 107. In fact, this diminution of reality seems necessary for both the colonizer and the colonized, and myth-making contributes to this diminution.
110. *Dharmavichar*, 102–3.
111. *Bharatendu-Natakavali*, ii, 170ff.
112. Ibid., 194.
113. The rulers' view of this is graphically described in the reminiscences of an Anglo-Indian civilian:

> Our life in India, our very work more or less, rests on illusion. I had the illusion, wherever I was, that I was infallible and invulnerable in my dealing with Indians. How else could I have dealt with angry mobs, with cholera-stricken masses, and with processions of religious fanatics? It was not conceit. Heaven knows! It was not the prestige of the British Raj, but it was the illusion which is in the very air of India. They expressed something of the idea when they called us the "Heaven born," and the idea is really make-believe — mutual make-believe. They, the millions, made us believe we had a divine

mission. We made them believe that they were right. Unconsciously, perhaps, I may have had at the back of my mind that there was a British Battalion and a Battery of Artillery at the Cantonment near Ajmere; but I never thought of this, and I do not think that many of the primitive and simple Mers had ever heard of or seen English soldiers. But they saw the head of the Queen-Empress on the rupee, and worshipped it. They had a vague conception of the Raj, which they looked on as a power, omnipotent, all-pervading, benevolent for the most part, but capricious, a deity of many shapes and many mood.... Walter Lawrence, *The India We Served* (Boston, 1929), 42–43.

114. How Muslims related to British rule is not discussed here.
115. The need to inspire the recipients of English education with implicit faith in the superiority of British rule is articulated in the following observations by Alexander Grant (1826–84):

> When it is reflected that the native University students furnish, or will ere long furnish, the school teachers, the pleaders, the practitioners of European medicine, the subordinate revenue and judicial officers, the overseers of public works, and above all, the newspaper writers, who are constantly disseminating, wise or foolish, disaffected or loyal, criticisms of the acts of Government, it cannot but be felt that it is of the utmost importance that the fountainhead of all this stream of influence, namely the professors and principals of colleges, should be as high and as pure as possible. Without solid and special learning in the professors there is no saying what subversive sentiments may become associated with European learning. Quoted in B. G. McCully, *English Education and the Origins of Indian Nationalism* (New York, 1940), 158n.

The care with which Grant himself discharged this historic pedagogic role is reflected in the alacrity with which he discerned and quashed the subversiveness of Mahadev Govind Ranade's mind when Ranade was a student at the Elphinstone Institute. Ranade had, in an essay, made a disparaging comparison between British rule and Maratha rule. Grant took prompt action:

> He temporarily suspended Ranade's scholarship and referred in his annual report to the 'foolish and impertinent expressions' of the young man on 'the Government which is educating him.' The whole tenor of Ranade's life and public work is a measure of the effectiveness of both Grant as an individual and of the hegemonic function for which the educational system had been devised. See James Kellock, *Mahadev Govind Ranade: Patriot and Social Servant*

(Calcutta, 1926), 11; Richard P. Tucker, *Ranade* and the *Roots of Indian Nationalism* (Bombay, 1972), 35–8. It is significant that Balshastri Jambhekar (1812–46), the first Indian to become a teacher at the Elphinstone Institution and the pioneer of many a public activity in the Bombay presidency, wrote in Marathi a history of Hindustan which was read by generations of school students. His history described the organized oppression and loot carried on under the aegis of rulers, until the British came and checked this rapacity. See *Amachaya Deshachi Sihili*, 82. Chiplunkar, it may be noted, criticized Jambhekar for saying this. But, as we have seen, he himself praised the British for the peace they had established in India, even though he also saw the havoc wrought by this peace.

Harishchandra's generation was reacting to British rule at a point when this rule was a *fait accompli*. A literary reconstruction of early reactions to the British is found in *Sarasvatichandra*, iii, 176 ff. In his 'Aryotkarsha', Namrad too visualizes such an early reaction. See *Dharmavichar*, 100–1.

116. *History of Hindustan, Being an English Translation of Raja Siva Prasad's Itihasatimirnashak*, part i (Lucknow, 1890, third edition), 34–5.
117. Ibid., 87. Sec also Shiv Prasad's *Strictures upon Strictures of Sayyad Ahmad Khan Bahadur, C.S.I.* (Benares, 1870, for private circulation only), 7.
118. *Itihas Timirnashak History of India in Three Parts*, 86–7; *Itihasatimirnashak* (in Hindi), part ii, 96. In his *Travels of a Hindoo* (London, 1869), i, 228–9, Bholanauth Chunder wrote: 'The advent of the Anglo-Saxon race was not merely fortuitous, but had been fore-ordained in the wisdom of providence.... Nothing short of Hindoostan ought to be given away to the English in grateful reward for their introducing the art of printing, which is emancipating thousands of minds from the yoke of a superstition that held us as brutes for centuries.'
119. *Itihasatimirnashak*, 70–1.
120. H. M. Trivedi, ed., *B. K. Thakore: A Diary Part I: Year 1888* (Baroda, 1969), 30.
121. Ibid.
122. Ibid., 30–1.
123. Ibid., 31–2.
124. *Radhakrishna-Granthavali*, 157.
125. *The Vicissitudes of Aryan Civilization in India* (Bombay, 1880), ix–x.
126. *Radhakrishna-Granthavali*, 272.
127. 'Literary fame' — as is clear from his letters to his elder brother — being his 'first love', Dutt's ambition was to belong:

> to that band of noble-hearted patriots and gifted men who have taught us to regard our past religion and history and literature

with legitimate and manly admiration. For our first and greatest indebtedness for the progress of this half-century is to those who have brought us to have faith in ourselves.

He wrote similarly about religion:

'Religion is a sentiment more than a doctrine or creed, and 1 often feel regret that this sentiment, ingrained in the Indian heart, is not fostered by the modern system of education.' And of himself in this respect: '1 never had any regular and systematic religious instruction at home. My mother, who was a pious Hindu, and deeply religious by nature and instinct, told us, when I scarcely knew my alphabet, those sacred legends in which religious lessons are conveyed in the East.... I felt impelled to make this ancient storehouse accessible lo my countrymen generally.' J. N. Gupta, *Life and Work of Romesh Chunder Dutt, C.I.E.* (London, 1911), 52, 388–9. The descriptions, in *The Lake of Palms*, of Saral's visit to Banaras and Bhubaneswar, or of the working of the Christian missionary and the schoolmaster, which have been discussed in the text, further document Dutt's progressive conservatism.

128. Romesh Dutt, *The Lake of Palms: A Story of Indian Domestic Life* (London, 1902), 57.
129. Ibid., 60.
130. Ibid., 187–8.
131. Ibid., 188.
132. Ibid.
133. Ibid., 58.
134. Ibid.
135. Ibid., 58–9.
136. *B. K. Thakore: A Diary Part II.* Year 1889–1890, 9. *Swayambhu*: existing by oneself; not created.
137. Ibid.
138. Ibid., 42–3.
139. *Bharat Bharati* (Jhansi, 1935).
140. *Bharatendu Samagra*, 483.
141. *Bharatendu Granthavali*, iii, 316.
142. *Pratap Lahari*, 36.
143. *Hindi Pradip*, Dec. 1877.
144. *Bharat Saubhagya*, 86.
145. *Dalpat Kavya*, n, 56.
146. *Bharatendu-Natakavali*, ii, 217.
147. *Bharatendu Samagra*, 484.

148. S. C. Srinivas Chariar, ed., *Political Opinions of Sir T. Madava Rao, K.C.S.I.* (Madras, 1890), 1–2.
149. Ibid., 7, 10.
150. Speaking in the House of Commons on 10 July 1833, Macaulay said:

    It may be that the public mind of India may expand under our system till it has outgrown that system; that by good government we may educate our subjects into a capacity for better government; that, having become instructed in European knowledge, they may, in some future age, demand European institutions. Whether such a day will ever come I know not. But never will I attempt to avert or retard it. Whenever it comes, it will be the proudest day in English history. To have found a great people sunk in the lowest depths of slavery and superstition, to have so ruled them as to have made them desirous and capable of all the privileges of citizens, would indeed he a title to glory all our own. The sceptre may pass away from us. Unforeseen accidents may derange our most profound schemes of policy. Victory may be inconstant to our arms. But there are triumphs which are followed by no reverses. There is an empire exempt from all natural causes of decay. Those triumphs are the pacific triumphs of reason over barbarism; that empire is the imperishable empire of our arts and our morals, our literature and our laws. A. B. Keith, ed.. *Speeches and Documents on Indian Policy 1750–1921* (London, 1922), i, 265.

151. *Scrap Book*, ii, 61–2.
152. Ibid., 72.
153. Ibid., i, 16, 24.
154. Ibid., 99.
155. G. M. Tripathi, *The Classical Poets of Gujarat and Their Influence on Society and Morals* (1894; rpt. Bombay, 1958), 32.
156. See *Bharatendu Samagra*, 555–79.
157. See *Scrap Book*, ii, 244–5; iii, 9, 14–15, 45, 59.

    During 1902–3 Govardhanram undertook to write an ambitious essay, entitled 'Adhyatmajivan athava Amarjivan no Shrutibodh', in which he sought to understand the basic assumptions and findings of western physics, chemistry, physiology and psychology in order to test the veracity of ancient Indian knowledge with regard to such issues as God, human volition, man's immortality and states of consciousness. For the essay, see Vishnuprasad Trivedi and others, eds., *Shri Govardhanram Shatabdi Smarakagrantha* (Nadiad, 1955), 3–67.

158. See Sisir Kumar Das, *The Artist in Chains: The Life of Bankimchandra Chatterji* (New Delhi, 1984), 158–61.

159. Jogeshchandra Bagal, ed., *Bankim Rachanabali* (Kolikata, 1390 Bangabda), ii, 186–8.
160. Ibid., 217–21.
161. Ibid., 225, 228–9.
162. The *Lake of Palms*, 149–54. Later in the novel Dutt writes:

> All the wonderful feats of faith and endurance, all the rigid submission to vows and penances, which were witnessed in Europe in the Middle Ages, are seen in India at this present day. Sufferers from long and chronic ailments, people bereaved by the death of dear or near relations, weary and aged men in the last stages of life, delicate girls and young wives with fond desires hidden in their bosoms, flock to this distant shrine in hope of relief from pain, or for the fulfilment of long-cherished objects. Philosophy smiles at the simple faith of the unreasoning, but it is faith and not philosophy which has held together large populations through centuries of distress of disaster, and has often enabled them to combine and work for those results which form the brightest chapters in the records of the past.

> Also: 'Travel and change and the seeing of new places and new sights — all of which are secularized in modern Europe — still wear the mantle of religious and of pious duty in India.' These authorial observations apart, Sarat thinks as he approaches Jagannath Puri and sees thousands of pilgrims shouting in chorus, 'Jagannath Ji ki Jai — 'Glory to the Lord of the earth': 'The temples and shrines of India ... had not been reared in vain, if they had kept untold millions together as one nation with one faith; if they had sent into their hearts obscure glimpses of that Immortal Light, which all living beings grope'. Ibid., 177–8, 189–90.

Chapter 2

1. *Ranade: His Wife's Reminiscences*, English translation by Kusumavati Deshpande (New Delhi, 1969), 32–3. The original work in Marathi first appeared in 1910.
2. See Wamanrao Madhav Kolhatkar, 'Widow Re-marriage', in C. Y. Chintamani, ed., *Indian Social Reform* (Madras, 1901), 300–6; and G. R. Havaldar, *Ravsaheb Vishwanath Narayan Mandlik Yanche Charita* (in Marathi) (Bombay, 1927), i, 302–13. For an admiring pen-portrait of Deshmukh, see N. R. Phatak and others, *Rationalists of Maharashtra* (Calcutta, 1962), 3–11.
3. Part of this letter was published in the 20 May 1870 issue of *Indu Prakash*, an Anglo-Marathi weekly of reformist persuasion.

4. *Ranade: His Wife's Reminiscences*, 32. Mrs Ranade's assessment of her husband's action was:

   Even today, so many feel that if there is any black spot in his life, it is the traditional character of his second marriage. But I for one feel that if there is any aspect of his life of self-sacrifice and large-heartedness which is nobler than others, it is this one. Whatever anyone might say, I have tremendous respect for the decision he took in this particular regard, and I am sure whoever thinks of his life with true understanding, will feel likewise. (Ibid.)

5. Ibid., 40–2.
6. Subal Chandra Mitra, *Isvar Chandra Vidyasagar*, 264–6.
7. Quoted in K. C. Pandya, *Shriyut Govardhanram* (1910; rpt. Mumbai, 1965), 49.
8. See *Scrap Book*, i, 31–2, 35–6, 70–3. In the entry that made him feel 'frozen', Govardhanram had written:

   That wonderful woman, my wife, is equally cool, and asks me to fulfil father's wishes; . . . my old parents do not show a corresponding sublimity of heart. Father is cool the other way, and never has an idea of the burden he places! However, I cannot take his contradictions into consideration in performing my duty to him, which . . . is to fulfil his aspirations, whether I like them or not. But I have duties to others, and the position into which he reduces me makes me come short in these duties.

9. Ibid., i, 173, 186; n, 45–6, iii, 1.
10. Ibid., i, 120.
11. Ibid., 123.
12. Ibid.
13. Ibid., 237; also 128–31, 165.
14. Ibid., 186, 233, 237–8.
15. Ibid., 234, 262.
16. Ibid., 120, 128.
17. Ibid., 37,186. 'To allow otherwise', he wrote, 'would be to encourage family tyranny and check individual growth.'
18. Ibid., 181.
19. Ibid., 263.
20. Ibid.
21. Ibid., 260–8.
22. On 16 May 1895, for instance, he wrote: 'Father, mother, wife and all, including uncle: these are only human beings with affection for me, based on raw materials that are brittle. They can be unsettled by any

whiff adverse to their interests, beliefs, tastes, pursuits, habits, virtues, vices, and what not.' He admitted with deep sadness:

> Everybody in my largest circle has been tested, the beliefs have changed, the affections have been deprived of their family character, and I see my people as being only part of a larger mankind, no longer distinguishable from the world of mankind by any special affection in my heart, except by the accident of nearness and by the duties that arise from there. (Ibid., ii, 64).

Earlier, on 19 January the same year, he wrote: 'Nobody — not even uncle — can sacrifice more to Duty than myself . . . .' Ibid., 49. See also 22, 32, 209–10. The inclusion, by Govardhanram, of his wife in the 16 May 1895 entry was only an aberration. A victim of 'hysteria and bronchitis and a kind of monomania or delusion that every-body is against her', she and their children (including the married daughters) were seen by Govardhanram as distinct from the rest of the family. I have dealt with this aspect at greater length in 'A Nineteenth Century View of the Hindu Joint Family: Notes from Govardhanram Tripathi's *Scrap Book*', in Sudhir Chandra, *Continuing Dilemmas: Understanding Social Consciousness* (Delhi, 2002), pp. 191–215.

23. *Scrap Book*, ii, 224.
24. Ibid., i, 115.
25. 'Almost the worst' because, as we learn from his *Scrap Book*, Govardhanram also maintained, in Gujarati, a diary in which he permitted himself even greater abandon in the expression of his feelings.
26. *East and West*, Jul.–Sep., Oct.–Nov. 1902.
27. *Sarasvatichandra*, iv, 164.
28. Ibid.
29. *Bharatendu Samagra*, 462–3.
30. *Bharatendu Granthavali*, iii, 937.
31. Ibid., 901.
32. *Bharatendu Samagra*, 531.
33. *Bharatendu Granthavali*, iii, 819–22, 825, 853.
34. Ibid., 836, 900–1.
35. Ibid., 900.
36. Ibid., 583.
37. Ibid., 900–1.
38. Ibid., 856. For Bankim's 'Ingrej Stotra', see *Bankim Rachanabali*, ii, 9–10. Harishchandra has added a few passages to his otherwise literal translation of Bankim's Stotra.
39. *Bharatendu Granthavali*, iii, 868–73.
40. Pratapnarayan Misra, for example, makes fun of English-educated reformers for considering it a sign of advancement to urinate shamelessly

while standing. *Pratap Lahari*, 242. Balakrishna Bhalt, similarly, wrote sarcastically: 'Only he can save the country who stands erect as he urinates'. Quoted in Jitram Pathak, *Adhunik Kavya Mein Rashtriya Chetana ka Vikas* (Ilahabad, 1971), 96.

41. See *Bharatendu-Natakavali*, ii, 110. See also *Haris Chandra's Magazine*, 15 Nov. 1873, for an unrestrained attack on the Bramhos.
42. *Harishchandra's Magazine*, 15 Feb. 1874.
43. *Bharatendu Granthavali*, iii, 841. For 'Sabai Jati Gopal Ki', see ibid., 819–22.
44. The hemistich reads: *'Nari nar sama honhi'*.
45. The following four couplets appeared as the logos of *Bala-bodhini*:

> Jo Hari soi Radhika jo Shiva soi Shakti,
> Jo nari soi purush yamein kachhu na vibhakti.
> Sita Anusuya sati Arundhati anuhari,
> Sheel laj vidyadi guna lahau sakal jag nari,
> Pitu pati sut karatal kamal laalit lalana log,
> Padhein gunain seekhain sunain naasein sab jag sog.
> Veer prasavini budh badhu hoi heenata khoy,
> Nari nar ardhanga ki saanchehi swamini hoy.

46. *Bharatendu Samagra*, 479.
47. *Bharatendu Granthavali*, iii, 845–7, 877–9; *Bankim Rachanabali*, ii, 13–20.
48. Cf. *Dalpat Kavya*, 75–7, 91, 356–420; *Priyamvada*, Dec. 1888, and *Sudarshan*, Jul. 1886. *Priyamvada* and *Sudarshan* were edited by Manilal Nabhubhai Dwivedi (1858–98). Classified among the leading exponents of new Hinduism in Gujarat, Manilal reveals an ambivalence towards both orthodoxy and reformism that militates against such a classification. See Dhirubhai Premshankar Thakar; *Manilalni Vichardhara* (Amdavad, 1948). For the underlying conservatism of social reformers and organized attempts to bring about social reform, e.g. the Indian National Social Conference, see C. Y. Chintamani, ed., *Indian Social Reform*.
49. *Hindi Pradip*, May 1878.
50. Ibid., Sep. 1896.
51. Ibid.
52. Ibid.
53. 'Jaisa Kaam Vaisa Parinaam', *Hindi Pradip*, Oct. and Nov. 1878.
54. 'Naya Abhidhan *Oudh Punch* ke Dhang Par', ibid., Dec. 1878.
55. The words used are: *'Vyabhichar ki vriddhi, Angarejon ki sabhyata ka saar'*. Ibid.
56. Ibid., May 1878.
57. *Harishchandra's Magazine*, 15 Nov. 1873.
58. *Bharatendu*, Nov. 1883. Radhacharan even proposed legislation in order to make purdah illegal. Ibid., Aug. 1883.

59. Ibid., Mar. 1885.
60. Ibid., Dec. 1883. The compromise suggested by Radhacharan bears clear evidence of Arya Samaj influence. He was at this stage favourably disposed towards the Arya Samaj. His advice to the Arya Samajists was to treat Dayananda's incomplete enunciation of the Vedas not as the last word but as a possible method of interpretation. But he also insisted that the Samaj was not a separate sect but part of Sanatan Dharma. Ibid. Less than two years later, however, Radhacharan was condemning Dayananda as the destroyer of the Vedas. Ibid., Jul. 1885. A month later, in the August 1885 issue of *Bharatendu*, he criticized not only Dayananda but also other religious reformers like Munshi Kanhaiyalal Alakhdhari and Keshab Chandra Sen for wielding the sword of religious disputation and initiating sectarian disruption. Writing in the *Brahman* of December 1884, Pratapnarayan, too, employed such expressions as 'old fools' and 'enlightened gentlemen'.
61. *Yamalok ki Yatra*, 3, 11–2, 21–5, 27–8. Radhacharan deals with this theme in Napit Stotra as well (Patna, 1882), where he follows the example of Harishchandra's 'Sabai Jati Gopal Ki' and 'Jati Vivekini Sabha'.
62. *Yamalok ki Yatra* is in this respect different from Radhacharan's ostensibly humorous pieces, which are unequivocally critical of social reform. As an example may be cited his 'Kaliyug Raj ka Circular'. Reminiscent of the commandments of Harishchandra's spurious prophet, the 'Circular' makes use of exaggeration to revile social reformers. *Bharatendu*, May 1883.
63. *Pratapnarayan-Granthavali*, 106.
64. I have used the term 'conservative', as distinct from reaction or resistance to change per se. This is not simply out of regard for semantic fidelity: it corresponds to the actual historical usage of the term, as can be seen from the authoritative anthology provided by C. Y. Chintamani in *Indian Social Reform*.
65. *Suchal-Shiksha* (Patna, 1911), i, 59.
66. Ibid., 60–1; see also *Pratap Lahari*, 62.
67. *Pratapnarayan-Granthavali*, 171.
68. *Kali Kautuk Rupak* (1885; rpt. Patna, 1913).
69. *Bidhava Vivah Vivaran or A Treatise on widow marriage in accordance with the authorities of Reason, Shastras and Law* (this is how the title is given in English, though the booklet is in Hindi) (Mathura, 1923, second edition) 1–3.
70. *Bharatendu*, Aug. 1883.
71. See 'Bal Vidhava Upanyasa', ibid.; and 'Bidhava Bilap (Lavani)', ibid., Aug. 1885.
72. Ibid., Dec. 1883.

73. Ibid., May 1883.
74. I read this unknown work by Pratapnarayan at the Hindi Sahitya Sammelan Library, Allahabad. This work is different from Harishchandra's *Bharat Durdasha*, which does not carry the suffix *Rupak*. The work discussed here is also different from the one by Pratapnarayan which bears the same title. The latter, like Harishchandra's play of the same name, deals with the political situation of the country. It has been discussed by scholars like Ram Vilas Sharma, *Bharatendu Yuga aur Hindi Bhasha ki Vikas Parampara* (Nai Dilli, 1975), and Sureshchandra Shukla 'Chandra', *Pratapnarayan Misra: Jivan aur Sahitya* (Kanpur, Samvat 2021). The *Bharat Durdasha Rupak* which I have discussed here is not even mentioned by Sharma and Shukla. There is no ready answer to the obvious question of why Pratapnarayan should have given the same title, with Rupak as the only distinguishing word, to two of his own plays. That he should have used the same title as the one chosen by Harishchandra, and created an avoidable confusion, is only slightly less intriguing than the choice of one title for two of his own plays. In fact, the use of the same title by more than one author was common practice at that time. Since the title page is missing from the copy available at the Sahitya Sammelan Library, it is not possible to provide the complete reference.
75. *Bharat Durdasha Rupak*, 103–5. Cf. Premghan's long article, 'Vidhava Vipatti Varsha' (1882), *Premghan-Sarvaswa*, ii, 185–203; Kashinath Khatri, *Bal-Vidhava-Santap*; see Braj Ratna Das, *Bharatendu-Mandal* (Kashi, Samvat 2006), 30. *Sarasvatichandra*, which is discussed below, further shows the wide prevalence of Vidyasagar's arguments.
76. *Brahman*, 15 Nov. 1883.
77. *Pratap Lahari*, 119.
78. *Bharatendu*, 25 Aug. 1885.
79. *Pratapnarayan-Granthavali*, 319–22.
80. The use of anxiety in this context is not without the influence of Harold Bloom, *The Anxiety of Influence: A Theory of Poetry* (New York, 1973).
81. Jogeshchandra Bagal, ed., *Bankim Rachanabali* (Kolikata, 1398 Bangabda), i, 275.
82. Ibid., 543. Bankim himself rated *Krishnakanter Will* his best novel. He began writing it in 1875 for his *Bangadarshan*, which ceased to exist soon thereafter. In 1877, when the journal was revived, Bankim resumed the novel and completed its serialization. In 1878 it appeared as a book.
83. See Isvarchandra Vidyasagar, *Marriage of Hindu Widow* (Calcutta, 1976). This contains the two tracts Vidyasagar wrote in January and October 1855.
84. Cf. the wild charges levelled at widows by the roguish royal priest in *Vaidiki Himsa Himsa Na Bhavati*, and the enthusiastic approval he is shown eliciting from his audience. *Bharatendu-Natakavali*, ii, 94.

85. *Bankim Rachanabali*, II, 93.
86. Ibid., 346.
87. Ibid., 257.
88. Ibid., 363–7. Bankim did not complete this essay. But even the incomplete text clearly outlines his basic argument. His essay on polygamy may also be seen for the development of the same argument. Ibid., 294–8.
89. Quoted in Subal Chandra Mitra, *Isvar Chandra Vidyasagar*, 280–1. The argument of numbers, it may be noted, was pretty commonly employed in the battle between the 'reformist' minority and the 'orthodox' majority. For example, when the battle lines between the two opposing camps were drawn during the Rukhmabai case — involving the restitution of conjugal rights — it was used in letters to the *Mahratta*: 'Is the happiness and peace of the whole society to be disturbed in order to do sentimental justice to a single individual?' *Mahratta*, 10 Apr. 1887. For the public controversy generated by the case, which parallels in many ways the discussion on widow marriage, see Sudhir Chandra, *Enslaved Daughters: Colonialism, Law and Women's Rights* (Delhi, 1998).
90. Subal Chandra Mitra, 280.
91. *Sarasvatichandra*, i, 7–8. The same point is elaborated in the Gujarati preface that follows the one in English. Ibid., 9–12. Govardhanram did not regret his choice of form. Even when only the first volume had appeared he could see that the novel 'works without doubt, and people feel the book'. *Scrap Book*, i, 31.
92. Govardhanram had a sense of his own significance and 'duties in regard to the country'.
93. See ibid., 26, 89–90, 93, 199.
94. Ibid., 93.
95. *Sarasvatichandra*, iv, 816–17. Sarasvatichandra, too, had earlier discussed with Kumud the adverse effect their marriage would have on his patriotic mission. Ibid., 755.
96. Ibid., iv, 773–82.
97. Ibid., 808.
98. Ibid., 777.
99. *Scrap Book*, iii, 67. Shivalal was Govardhanram's uncle's grandson.
100. *Bankim Rachanabali*, ii, 73.
101. *Bharatendu Samagra*, 479.
102. *Sarasvatichandra*, i, 291.
103. *Bankim Rachanabali*, i, 290.
104. See *Marriage of Hindu Widows*, The discussion about the particular validity of the *Parashar Samhita* recurs through both the tracts that Vidyasagar wrote on the subject of widow marriage.

105. *Bharatendu-Natakavali*, ii, 94.
106. Not that marriage with the man a widow loves is necessarily a test of her victory. In Pratapnarayan's *Bharat Durdasha Rupak*, the widow marries her former lover. So also in *The Lake of Palms*. But in these cases the reader cannot get over the feeling that a good deal of authorial manipulation has gone into what looks like a contrived turn of events. As against this, Tagore's Binodini leaves a lasting impression as a person in spite of her tragic destiny.
107. For a different reading of *Chokher Bali* — different from the one I have suggested — see S. N. Ray, 'Individual and Society in the Works of Rabindranath Tagore', in Wang Gungwu, ed., *Self and Biography* (Sydney, 1975), 71.

Chapter 3

1. *Bharatendu Granthavali*, iii, 901–2.
2. Ibid., 391–419, 765–74.
3. The famous line is: 'In Musalman harijanan pai kotin Hindu variye'. See *Bharatendu Granthavali*, ii, 263–4.
4. *Harishchandra's Magazine*, 15 Feb. 1874.
5. *Hindi Pradip*, Feb. 1878.
6. Ibid., Balmukund Gupta elaborated the same point in *Bharatmitra*, 25 Nov. 1905 and 9 Mar. 1907. See *Chitthe aur Khat*, 48–63.
7. In fact, this play is an adaptation of Michael Madhusudan Dutt's Bengali farce entitled, *Budo Shaliker Bade Roam*, which was first published in 1859.
8. *Pratapnarayan-Granthavali*, 181. See also *Pratap Lahari*, 25–6, 34–8.
9. *Pratapnarayan-Granthavali*, 178–83, 262–3, 332, 413, 521–2.
10. Harishchandra wrote: 'Masjid lakhi Bisunath dhig pare hiye jo ghav'. *Bharatendu Granthavali*, ii, 699. He also wrote: 'Jahan Bisesar Somnath Madhav ke mandir, Tahan mahajid bani gayin hot ab Alla Akbar.' Ibid., 684.
11. *Travels of a Hindoo*, i, 261.
12. *Bharatendu Granthavali*, ii, 723.
13. He wrote: 'Jin Javanan tav dharam nari dhan tinahun leeno'. Ibid., 764.
14. Ibid., iii, 315–6.
15. Ibid., 120.
16. *Rajasihan-Keshari athava Maharana Pratapsinha* (Kashi, Samvat 1996 9th edition). This is also included in *Radhakrishna-Granthavali*, 645–785.
17. *Bharatendu Granthavali*, ii, 699.
18. *Hindi Pradip*, 18 Mar. 1879.

19. As for details, Harishchandra too talks of 'our idols' having been broken 'in front of our eyes'; 'our women having been forcibly taken away'; Hindu heads having been 'chopped off like grass'; and Hindus having been forced to become Muslim by 'being spat into their mouths'. *Bharatendu Granthavali*, iii. 316. He freely employs epithets like perverse, cruel, lascivious, cow-killer, temple-destroyer, etc., for Muslim rulers. Ibid., 318–20.
20. Many Hindi writers of the period knew Bengali, and there was a regular flow of translations, adaptations and wholesale plagiarization of Bengali works into Hindi. But the same cannot be said about contact between Hindi and Gujarati, even though a Harishchandra could occasionally compose a poem in Gujarati and a Dalpat could try his hand at verse in Brijbhasha. Nor was the influence of Bengali so pronounced on Gujarati, in the way it was on Hindi. Still, the kind of sentiments that we find expressed in Hindi and Bengali were not confined to literature in these two languages alone. For example, in a long essay that he wrote in 1868–9 on 'Gujarationi Sthiti' — the state of Gujaratis — Narmad could not possibly have been influenced by Bankim or other Bengali writers whose influence on Harishchandra and his contemporary Hindi writers is so marked. And yet this essay offers a reconstruction of the oppressive Muslim rule which, in its general pattern and thrust, resembles most others elsewhere. Narmadashankar L. Dave, *Narmagadya*, Vadodara, 1975 (first published Bombay, 1874), 100 ff. Chiplunkar also refers savagely to the violence, rapine, heartless expansionism and sexual excesses of Muslims; these supposedly conformed to the teachings of their Prophet. G. T. Ashtekar, *Bharatendu Harishchandra evam Vishnushastri Chiplunkar* (Jaipur, 1978), 368.
21. Premghan's line is: 'Tiya dhan dharam haran man than'. *Premghan-Sarvaswa*, i, 148.
22. *Brahman*, 15 Mar. 1883.
23. *Premghan-Sarvaswa*, i, 124.
24. The lines are:

> Jahan rajkanyan ke dola Turkan ke ghar janya,
> Tahan dusari kaun baat he jeha man log lajanya,
> Bhala in hijaran te kuchh hona hai.
> *Brahman*, 15 Mar. 1883.

25. *Pratapnarayan-Granthavali*, 57–60. Considering that in this article Pratapnarayan's angry sarcasm is directed against the British in India — exposing in no uncertain terms the hollowness of their sense of justice and much wonted rule of law — the free-wheeling between Hindu, Hindustani and Bharatiya *bhratrigan* is particularly indicative

of the unconscious hold of equation between 'Hindu' and 'India'. The attack on Muslims, in an article like this, could not but have adversely affected the prospect of a united Indian stand vis-a-vis the tyrannous league between non-official Europeans in India and the British Indian government. This is the league Pratapnarayan is lashing out against in this article. Obviously, the feeling against Muslims was strong enough to spontaneously surface, even in situations where the best course would have been restraint.

26. *Hindi Pradip*, Mar. 1879.
27. Ibid., Feb. 1885, emphases added.
28. Ibid., May 1879. See also issues of *Pradip* for Feb. 1878, Sep. 1879, Aug. 1881, Sep. 1882, and Dec. 1905.
29. *Pratapnarayan-Granthavali*, 387–91. Balmukund Gupta was equally categorical when he wrote: 'Bharatvarsha is the land of the Hindus....' Quoted in Jhabarmall Sharma and Banarasidas Chaturvedi, eds., *Balmukund Gupta-Smarak Grantha* (Calcutta, Samvat 2007), 231.
30. *Bharatendu Granthavali*, iii, 796–302. Hemchandra Banerji, whose influence on Harishchandra 1 have noted before, used Hindu and Arya in the same sense. In his *Birbahu Kabya* he wrote: 'Once more shall I found the Hindu Empire .... Again shall I beat in joy the trumpet of victory and declare to the world that *India* is up.' And: 'It seemed *Mother India* once more sat upon her throne.... Around her thronged the new race of the Aryans ... who brushed off the stain of her old infamy ...' (Emphases added.) Quoted in H. M. Das Gupta, 46–7, notes.
31. The term used by Harishchandra is *mahaghor kaal*. Ibid., 801.
32. Ibid., 902.
33. *Bharatendu Samagra*, 462.
34. Quoted with a note of approval in *Bharatoddharaka*, vol. i, no, 2 (Shravan Krishna 1, Samvat 1941). Emphasis added.
35. D. G. Karve and D. V. Ambekar, eds., *Speeches and Writings of Gopal Krishna Gokhale* (Bombay, 1966), u, 35–6. About the tendency to equate 'Hindu' and 'Indian', J. E. Sanjana, a non-conformist Parsi scholar of Gujarati literature, had the foresight to observe in the course of a series of lectures at the Bombay University: 'this purely Hindu outlook has been and is a constant and important, though often not consciously realized, factor in the mental outfit of all Gujarati writers, from Dalpat and Narmad down to Govardhanram and Gandhi, Mashruwala and Munshi.' *Studies in Gujarati Literature* (Bombay, 1950), 144. Sanjana further remarks that the editor of Gopalrao Hari Deshmukh's famous *Hundred Letters* emphasized that though Deshmukh consistently used the term 'Hindu', what he meant was 'Indian'. Ibid., 75–6. In *Amachya Deshachi Sthiti* Chiplunkar often equates Hindu with Indian. In a series of

lectures on the early phase of modern Hindi literature, delivered as late as 1972, Shrinarayan Chaturvedi, a veteran and erudite scholar, would have us believe that the term 'Hindu' has been used for 'Indian' in Hindi literature since the days of Bharatendu Harishchandra. Chaturvedi also maintains that from the point of view of the Hindus, subjection to the British was 'much better' than subjection to the Muslims. *Adhunik Hindi ka Aadikaal* (1857–1908) (Ilahabad, 1973), 51, 91.
36. See Jogeshchandra Bagal, ed., *Romesh Rachanabali* (Kolikata, 1982), 1–82, 151–249. For the dialogue between Jaisingh and Shivaji, see 184–88. An English translation of *Bang Vijeta* by Ajoy Dutt is available as *Todar Mull: The Conqueror of Bengal* (Allahabad, n.d.). The translator's preface is dated 1947.
37. *The Lake of Palms*, 57.
38. *Bharatendu Samagra*, 461.
39. *Narmagadya*, 35ff.
40. *Bharat Durdasha Rupak*, 104. 'Niyoga' means a 'practice prevalent in ancient times which permitted a childless widow to have intercourse with the brother or any near kinsman of her deceased husband to raise up issue to him, the son so born being called *kshetraj*. See Vaman Shivram Apte, *The Practical Sanskrit-English Dictionary* (Bombay, 1924), 551. In actual practice, as is clear from the example of Kunti and Madari, *niyoga* was not confined to widows.
41. The argument about the deliberate attempt to construct a Hindu ideology has been suggested to me by Alok Bhalla.
42. Balkrishna Bhatt, *Nutan Brahmachari Upanyas*, 6.
43. See *Bhagyavati* (1878), a novel by Shraddharam Phillauri (1838–82), in Sarandas Bhanot, ed., *Shraddharam Granthavali* (Kurukshetra, 1966), 191.
44. Quoted in J. T. F. Jordens, *Swami Shraddhananda: His Life and Causes* (Delhi, 1981), 38.
45. Durgaprasad Misra, *Shribharat Dharmma* (Calcutta, Samvat 1957), 47–8.
46. Ibid., 81–2.
47. Quoted in G. T. Ashtekar, 357.
48. *Amachya Deshachi Sthiti*, 21–2.
49. *Bharatendu*, 19 Oct. 1883.
50. Ibid., 23 Oct. 1885.
51. Ibid.
52. Nareshchandra Chaturvedi, ed., *Pratapnarayan Misra Kavitavali* (Ilahabad, 1987), 19.
53. Ibid., 7.
54. Ibid., 19.

55. In one poem Pratapnarayan said that while the Hindus were eunuchs, the British rulers were afraid of the Muslims. Ibid., 5. In another poem he expressed the fear that as both the English and the Muslims were the children of Adam, the former would treat the latter as brothers and, consequently, disregard the Hindus. Ibid., 29.
56. Harishchandra, who had written to friends in England about the riots in Agra, asked for copies of *Bharatendu*, which he meant to despatch to them by way of evidence. See Harishchandra's undated letter to Radhacharan in *Bharatendu Granthavali*, iii, 970. The December 1883 issue of *Bharatendu* carried a pro-Hindu account of the trouble in Agra.
57. *Nissahaya Hindu* (Banaras, 1890), 4–22, 30–45. *Bihishta* means paradise.
58. Ibid., 46, 64.
59. *Bharatendu*, 19 Oct. 1883.
60. Ibid., 23 Oct. 1885.
61. *Pratapnarayan-Granthavali*, 49–50. See also 58, 68, 116, 133–4; and *Pratap Lahari*, 18, 109, 254, 255.
62. I have used the English translation by J. Taylor, *Prabodha Chandrodaya or Rise of the Moon of Intellect* (Bombay, 1886). For an account of the history of this major text down the centuries, see Saroj Agrawal, *Prabodhachandrodaya aur Usaki Hindi Parampara* (Prayag, 1883 Shaka).
63. J. Taylor, 4.
64. Ibid., 35–41.
65. Ibid., 42.
66. Saroj Agrawal, 198.
67. *Bharatendu Samagra*, 38, 303.
68. Ibid., 461
69. *Bharatendu Granthavali*, III, 917.
70. *Radhakrishna-Granthavali*, 144–5.
71. Ibid., 145.
72. *The Collected Works of Mahatma Gandhi* (Ahmedabad, 1963), x, 29–30.
73. Even now it is common practice in small towns and villages to ask a stranger his name and, almost immediately thereafter, his caste.
74. *Pratapnarayan-Granthavali*, 97, 149, 162, 300, 309.
75. Ibid., 313.
76. Ibid., 725–8. The opening couplet in Hindi reads:

> Chahahu ju sanchahu nij kalyan.
> Tau sab mili Bharat santan,
> Japau nirantar ek jaban,
> Hindi Hindu Hindustan.

77. *Bharatendu Samagra*, 529. *Shruti* means Vedic or sacred text.
78. He wrote: 'Hindi Hindu Hind kar, Karahu Nath Kalyan.' *Pratapnarayan-Granthavali*, 728.

79. Shrinarayan Chaturvedi, ed., *Saraswati Heerak Jayanti Ank* (Ilahabad, 1961), 141–6.
80. *Romesh Rachanabali*, 185–7.
81. Anandaram Dhekiyal Phukan, 'A Few Remarks on Assamese Language and Vernacular Education in Assam', quoted in Maheswar Neog, *Anandaram Dhekiyal Phukan* (New Delhi, 1980), 38–41.
82. Ibid., 41.
83. For these pamphlets, see Maheswar Neog, *Anandaram Dhekiyal Phukan: Plea for Assam and Assamese* (Jorhat, 1977).
84. The essay, entitled 'Inglandar Bibaran', was published in the April 1847 issue of *Orunodoi*, a monthly founded by the Baptist missionaries. In the evolution of modern Assamese and the spread of Assamese consciousness, *Orunodoi* played an important role. For the passage quoted here see Dimbeswar Neog, *Modern Assamese Literature* (Jorhat, 1955), 126–7.
85. In 1884, even before Anandaram took up the cause of Assam and Assamese, Kashiram Tamuli Phukan brought out his *History of Assam*, in which he strung together old Ahom chronicles.
86. Quoted in Dimbeswar Neog, 100–2.
87. Lakshminath Bezbaruwa, *Meri Jivan-Smritiyan* (Hindi translation of his autobiography, *Mor Jivan Sowaran*), (New Delhi, 1977), 64.
88. Ibid., 64, 122–3; see also Dimbeswar Neog, 134–42.
89. Dimbeswar Neog, 99–100.
90. Bezbaruwa, 110–11. Relations between Assamese and Bengalis at the inter-personal level were not necessarily embittered by the language conflict. Apart from Bezbaruwa's marriage into the Tagore family, we have the example of Gunabhiram marrying his daughter to a Bengali. Dimbeswar Neog, whose work betrays a pronounced and continuing anger against the Bengalis, writes about R. C. Dutt's verdict in grateful terms and approvingly quotes P. C. Ray's comment about the 'patriotism and national conceit of the Bengalis living in Assam'. Dimbeshwar Neog, 99.
91. Bezbaruwa, 79–80; Dimbeswar Neog, 160, 181–201; Surya Kumar Bhuyan, *Studies in the Literature of Assam* (Gauhati, 1956), 64–85.
92. The original couplets and their English translation are given in Dimbeswar Neog, 172.
93. Bezbaruwa, 75.
94. Mayadhar Mansinha, *Phakirmohan Senapati* (Hindi translation, New Delhi, 1979), 25–7. At the time of this controversy Senapati had good personal relations with Beames, as the latter was getting valuable assistance for his *Comparative Grammar of the Aryan Indian Languages* from the former.

95. G. N. Dash, 'Jagannath and Oriya Nationalism', in Anncharlott Eschmann and others, eds., *The Cult of Jagannath and the Regional Tradition of Orissa* (New Delhi, 1978), 365, note 30.
96. Mansinha, 22–3.
97. Priyaranjan Sen, *Modern Oriya Literature* (Calcutta, 1947), 65–6.
98. Quoted in Dash, 369–70.
99. See H. Kulke, '"Juggernaut" under British Supremacy and the Resurgence of the Khurda Rajas as "Rajas of Puri"', in Eschmann and others, eds., 345–57.
100. Dash, 368 including note 45. In the introduction to his first dramatic composition, written in 1880 when he was about twenty, Ramashankar wrote that 'sick with the performance of Bengali plays in Orissa, his mind revolted and he wanted to produce plays in Oriya depicting the glories of the historic Oriya people'. Mayadhar Mansinha, *History of Oriya Literature* (New Delhi, 1962), 220.
101. Sen, 89; Dash, 369.
102. Dash, 365, note 30.
103. Ibid., 371–2. Dash says that the immediate cause of the establishment of Utkal Sammilani was the refusal of the Indian National Congress, at its Madras session in 1903, to support the proposed unification of the Oriya-speaking region at the expense of the Madras Presidency. He misses the simple point that the first session of the Sammilani at Cuttack and the Madras session of the Congress were held almost simultaneously in the last week of December.
104. Gopinath Mohanty, *Radhanath Ray* (New Delhi, 1978), 22, 24.
105. See *Narmagadya*, 100–61; Narmadashankar Lalshankar, *Junun Narmagadya* (Mumbai, 1912, second edition), 346–48, 451–90; Vishwanath Maganlal Bhatt, *Narmadnun Mandir: Gadya Vibhag* (Amdavad, 1937), 214–32.
106. *Narmagadya*, 100–61.
107. Vishwanath Maganlal Bhatt, ed., *Narmadnun Mandir: Padya Vibhag* (Amdavad, 1965), 76–7.
108. Ibid., 74–6.
109. For a first-hand account of the circumstances and motivation that led Ranjitram to found the Gujarati Sahitya Parishad, see Ranjitram Vavabhai Mehta, *Ranjitram Nibandho* (Mumbai, 1923), i, 1–30. See also Hiralal Tribhuvandas Parekh, *Arvachin Gujaratnun Rekha Darshan* (Amdavad, 1979), 460; and Mansukhlal Jhaveri, *History of Gujarati Literature* (New Delhi, 1978), 143.
110. *Parishad Pramukhona Bhashano* (Amdavad, 1974), i, 1–30.
111. Parekh, 460.
112. Sen, 90.
113. Dimbeswar Neog, 173.

114. After listing rather rhetorically the categories to which Gujarat does not belong, Narmad comes to those to which it does. The first, and really substantial, category is those whose ancestors lived in Gujarat, and who had 'somehow' preserved Arya dharma. Invoking the calm courage and sacrifice of those who had preserved this dharma, the word 'somehow', at this point in the poem, betrays Narmad's underlying bias and vitiates the effect of the earlier lines. The two lines that follow only confirm the suspicion that, more likely than not, it is as a grudging concession to pragmatic considerations that the poet agrees to have Gujarat belong even to those who, *in spite* of being the adherents of an alien faith, have the interest of Gujarat at heart.

Conclusion

1. I say this without the illusion that, by weighing my words, I can wholly control my reader's construction of what I write.
2. Cf. Sudhir Chandra, '*Sati: The Dharmic Fallacy*', New Quest, Mar.–Apr. 1988, 111–14.
3. See 'Communal Consciousness in Late Nineteenth Century Hindi Literature', in Mushirul Hasan, ed., *Communal and Pan-Islamic Trends in Colonial India* (New Delhi, 1981), 170–85; and 'Communal Elements in Late Nineteenth-Century Hindi Literature', *Journal of Arts and Ideas*, Jan.–Mar. 1984, 5–18.

About the Author

Sudhir Chandra is currently Associate Fellow, Nantes Institute of Advanced Studies, France. He has authored *Enslaved Daughters: Colonialism, Law and Women's Rights* (1998) and *Dependence and Disillusionment: Emergence of National Consciousness in Later 19th Century India* (1975), and edited *Social Transformation and Creative Imagination* (1984). His authored volumes in Hindi are *Gandhi: Ek Asambhav Sambhavana* (2011), *Gandhi ke Desh Mein* (2009) and *Hindu Hindutva Hindustan* (2003).

Index

Age of Consent Bill, 110
Aggarwala, Chandrakumar, 165
Akbar, Mughal emperor, 134–35, 142, 155, 161
'Amachya Deshachi Sthiti', 19–22, 147, 181, 184, 200, 201
Ananda Kadambini, 37
Andher Nagari Chaupatta Raja, 35, 93
'Angrez Stotra', 94–97, 102
apunapau, 45, 80
'Archaeology', 155
Aryan Witness, The, 6
Arya Samaj, 65
'Aryotkarsha', 59
Assam: Atit aru Bartaman, 164
Assam Bandhu, 164
Assamese nationalism, 166–67
Assamiya Bhasha Unnatisadhini Sabha, 165
Assam News, 163–64
'A Wonderful Dream Ek Adbhut Apurva Swapna', 95

Babar, 60–61, 160
Badashahadarpan, 134
Bala-bodhini, 97, 194
Ballia, Bharatendu Harishchandra's lecture in, 96, 130, 139
Banerji, Hemchandra, 30, 56, 200
Banerji, K. C., 6
Banerji, Rev. Krishna Mohan, 6, 179, 180
Banerji, Surendranath, 28
Bangadarshan, 117–18, 196
Banga Vijeta, 141–42
Baruwa, Gunabhiram, 163–64, 165
Baruwa Hemchandra, 163, 165
Beames, John, 167
Bengali confronted, 161–62, 164, 166–67
Bezbaruwa, Lakshminath, 163–66, 171, 203

Bhagvad Gita, 6
Bharat-Bharati, 71
Bharat Durdasha, 32, 34, 37, 47, 54, 96, 106, 154, 185
Bharat Durdasha Rupak, 109–10, 113, 143–44, 196
Bharatendu, 40–41, 43, 108, 182, 183, 195, 196, 201, 202
Bharatendu *mandal*, 27
Bharat-Janani, 30–32, 37, 73, 185
Bharat Mein Yavan Raj, 135–37
Bharatmitra, 53, 140, 145, 198
Bharat Saubhagya, 38–39, 53, 55
Bhattacharya, Kamalakanta, 165–66, 171, 180
Bhattacharya, Krishna Chandra, 12–14
Bhatt, Balkrishna, 43, 47–50;
and British rule, 47–49, 73
Caste, 100
Muslims, 132–33, 137–38
social reform, 99–102
women, 101–2
Brahman, 37, 43, 47, 157, 195, 196, 199
British rule, and Muslim 'anarchy', 71, 154–55, 160; as viewed by
Balkrishna Bhatt, 47–49, 73
Balmukund Gupta, 53
Bankimchandra Chatterji, 58
Bharatendu Harishchandra, 28–37, 59, 73–74, 149
Dalpatram Dahyabhai, 52
Govardhanram Tripathi, 23–25, 55–57, 74–77
Hemchandra Banerji, 30, 56, 200
Indians, 18–78
Narmad, 52–53, 58–59
Pratapnarayan Misra, 43–47, 49, 53–55, 58
Radhacharan Goswami, 40–43
Shiv Prasad, 60–61

T. Madhav Rao, 74
Vishnu Krishna Chiplunkar, 20–23; loyalty to, 46–47, 51–52; *see also* colonialism
Bronson, Miles, 164
Buddhists, 129, 142, 152, 154–55
Budhe Munha Munhase, 132

caste, 101, 123–24, 139–40; and Balkrishna Bhatt, 99
Bharatendu Harishchandra, 92
Chandra, Bholanath, 133, 143
Charbonnier, 13
Chatterji, Bankimchandra, 58, 111; and views on British rule, 77
widow marriage, 111
women, 111
Chiplunkar, Vishnu Krishna, 19–23, 27, 147, 184, 188, 199–200
Chitthe aur Khat, 53, 185, 198
Chokher Bali, 112, 127, 198
Christians, patriotic Indian, 6
Classical Poets of Gujarat and their Influence on Society, The, 171, 190
colonialism, 7, 9, 11, 16, 19, 22; and Indian subjects, 19–21, 26, 28, 32, 35, 41–42, 51, 61, 63
nationalism, 166
revivalism, 68, 71
tradition, 10–12, 128; *see also* British rule
Congress Socialist Party, 12
'Communal Consciousness in Late Nineteenth Century Hindi Literature', 174, 205
Curzon, viceroy, 75, 146

Dahyabhai, Dalpatram, 52, 185
Das, Bichitranand, 166
Das, Madhusudan, 166, 168, 171
Das, Radhakrishna, 53, 63–64, 135, 160; and views
on British rule, 149
Muslims, 149–50, 155, 159
Dave, Narmadashankar Lalshankar, 52–53, 58–59, 143, 169–70, 172, 185, 199–200; and

British rule, 52–53, 58–59
Muslims, 143, 170, 172
Day, Rev. Lal Bihari, 6
Dayananda, Swami, 100, 145, 154, 195, 195
Deb, Raja Radhakanta, 6, 179
Derozians, 6
Deshmukh, Gopalrao Hari, 80–81, 90, 191; and views on widow marriage, 80
Dharma shastras, 94
Dictionary of Assamese, 164
Dutt, R. C., 65–71, 79, 141–43, 160–61, 164, 177, 188; and views on Muslims, 141–43

East India Company, 61, 161
Economic History of India, The, 65
Elliot, 131
'English poetry', 18–78

Gandhi, 12–14, 33, 78, 155–56, 158, 177; and
Nehru, 7–10
social reconstruction, 7, 9
Gokhale, Gopal Krishna, 140, 143, 160
and Muslims, 141
Goswami, Hemchandra, 165
Goswami, Kishorilal, 159–60
Goswami, Radhacharan, 40–43, 71, 102–3, 105–6, 108–9, 111, 132–33, 135–37, 148; and views
on British rule, 41–43
Muslims, 132–33, 135–36
social reform, 102–6
widow marriage, 108–9, 111
Gujarati nationalism, 169–70
Gujarati Sahitya Parishad, 170, 204
'Gujaratni Sthiti', 170, 199
Gupta, Balmukund, 146, 152; and British rule, 53
Gupta, Maithilisharan, 70–71

Harishchandra, Bharatendu, 15–16, 27–37, 40–41, 43–47, 49, 52–53, 55, 59, 72–73, 77, 80, 92–98, 101, 103–5, 116, 125–26, 130–36, 138–39, 140, 143,

149–50, 152–55, 157–58, 201; and Ballia lecture, 96, 130, 139
British rule, 29, 31–35, 37, 72, 149–50
caste, 92–93
Indian women, 97–98, 134
mukari, 35–36, 43
Muslims, 131–35, 139, 143
social reform, 92–99
Harishchandra Chandrika, 28
Harishchandra's Magazine, 28, 33, 35, 52, 101, 131, 149, 182, 184, 194, 198
Hastie, William, 76
Hindi, 15, 27–29, 30, 33, 41, 53, 101, 105, 108, 111, 130, 137, 143, 151, 153, 157–59, 161, 167, 170
Hindi Pradip, 37, 48, 53, 100, 102, 182, 184, 185, 189, 194, 198, 200
Hind Swaraj, 7–8, 10, 14, 78, 155, 158, 180
Hinduization, 174
Hindu–Muslim riots, 151
Hindus, and Muslims, 132, 139–40
  decline of, 143, 147
  identity, 136–37, 139, 141–42, 155
Historians of India, 131
History of Civilization in Ancient India, 65, 69–71
Hit Prabodh, 108
Hume, 75

Ilbert Bill, 44
Iliad, The, 6
imagery in Indian writing, 53
Indian Association, 28
Indian National Congress, 28, 38, 40–41, 50, 75, 133, 148, 156, 158, 169, 176, 204
Indian National Social Conference, 40
'Indumati', 159–60
'Ingrej Stotra', 94, 97, 101
Itihasatimirnashak, 52, 60–61, 131, 149, 183, 188

Jagannath temple, 168
'Jai! Jai! Garavi Gujarat', 170
Jainism, 153, 156
jati, 146, 165, 166

Jayachand, 129
Jnanasuryodaya, 153
joint family, 48, 83–92, 123, 127; and
  Gopalrao Hari Deshmukh, 90
  Govardhanram Tripathi, 83–92
  Ishvarchandra Vidyasagar, 90
  Mahadev Govind Ranade, 80

Kalidasa, 75–76
Kali Kautuk Rupak, 106, 195
'Kaliraj ki Sabha', 101–2
'Kaliyug Raj Ka Circular', 109, 195
Kamalakanter Patra, 116
Kanchi Kaberi, 168
Kankan, Madhavi, 141
Kavivachansudha, 28, 33, 55, 97
Kayasthas, 104, 108
Kempson, M., 60
Koran, 130'
Krishnakanter Will, 111, 114–17, 124–27, 196
Kunte, M. M., 63

Lake of Palms, The, 66–69, 77, 79, 142, 150, 177, 189, 191, 198, 201
Levi-Strauss, C., 13
loyalty to British rule, 21, 29–30, 36, 46, 51–55, 72

Macaulay, 70, 74, 190n150
Madhav Rao, Raja Sir T., 74
Mahabharata, 15, 64–65, 144
Maharashtra Jivanprabhat, 69, 71, 141, 161
Mahayatra, 168
Mahmud, Syed, 138
Mahratta, 62, 133, 197
Mau, 166, 171
Mehta, Ranjitram Vavabhai, 170, 204
'Methods for the Improvement of the Hindus', 99, 101–2
Mill, 75, 77
Misra, Krishna, 152–53
Misra, Pandit Durgaprasad, 145
Misra, Pratapnarayan, 43–47, 49, 53–55, 58, 72–73, 105–11, 113, 132–33, 136–39, 144, 149, 151, 156–58, 177, 193,

195, 196; and
British rule, 43–44
Muslims, 132, 136
slogan, 156–58
widow marriage, 107–11
modernity, and tradition, 2–6, 14–15, 77
Moffat Mills, A. J., 163
Mudrarakshas, 32
Munshi, K. M., 171
Munshiram (Swami Shraddhananda), 145
Muslim rule, 41, 47, 52; and
British rule, 71–72, 129, 132–36, 141–47, 159–61
consequences ascribed to, 134–36, 143–46, 129, 130–6; *see also* Muslims
Muslims, 31, 34, 41, 45, 47, 52, 63, 65–66, 71–72, 128–39, 141–43; and
Balkrishna Bhatt, 132–33, 138
Bharatendu Harishchandra, 72, 130–36, 139
Bholanath Chandra, 133
Gopal Krishna Gokhale, 140
Hindus, 132, 139–40
Narmad, 143
Pratapnarayan Misra, 132, 136
Radhacharan Goswami, 132–33, 135–37, 148
Radhakrishna Das, 149–50, 155, 159–60
R. C. Dutt, 141
Sanatanists, 146
Vaishnava saints, 130

'Natak', 76
nationalism, 7, 36, 58, 65, 69, 140, 156–58;
Assamese, 161–6
Gujarati, 161
Oriya, 161, 166–69
regional, 130, 161, 171–72, 176–77
National Social Conference, 40, 110
Nehru, Jawaharlal, 7–9; and Gandhi, 7–9, 179, 180
Nibandhamala, 19, 22, 147
Nil Devi, 34, 72, 98, 125
Nissahaya Hindu, 150, 202
Nutan Brahmachari, 50, 184, 201

'Observations on the Administration of the Province of Assam', 162
Oriya nationalism, 161, 166–69

Padmanji, Baba, 107
Pakhanda Vidambana, 154
'Panchave Paighambar', 94–97
Parashar Samhita, 126–27, 197
patriotism, 42, 46, 55, 60, 63, 65, 68, 90–91, 183
Phukan, Anandaram Dhekiyal, 161, 164, 203
Prabodhachandrodaya, 152–64, 202
Prasad, Raja Shiv, 42, 52, 60–61, 131
'Premghan' (Chaudhari Pandit Badari Narayan Upadhyaya), 37–40, 43, 53–54, 73, 136, 182, 184, 185, 199
Prithviraj Chauhan, 129, 132, 134
Puranas, 64, 100, 103

'Qanoon Tazirat Shohar', 98

Rajasthan-Keshari Athava Pratapsinha, 135
Rajput Jivansandhya, 141–42
Ramadin Singh, 157
Ramayana, 15, 64–65
Rampal Singh, Raja, 38, 55, 186
ramarajya, 39, 47, 52–53
Ranade, Mahadev Govind, 15, 80, 187
Rao, Madhusudan, 166, 168, 171
rationalism, 13
Ravenshaw, T. E., 167
Ray, Gourishankar, 166
Ray, Radhanath, 166–69, 171
Ray, Ramashankar, 168
reform, social, 24, 41, 80–81, 83, 92–99, 102–3, 105–6, 109, 116, 123
and caste system, 92
education, 102–3
joint family, 83–92
widow marriage, 93–95, 103, 116–17, 119–28
women, 97–8, 100–2
revivalism ('glorious past'), 64–65, 71, 92, 147, 160
Ripon, 33, 35, 39, 47
'Riponashtaka', 33

Roy, Raja Rammohan, 6, 15

Sahitya Samaj, 169
Samaj, 141
sanatan dharma, 100, 195
sanatani maryada, 106, 109–10, 177
Sanatanists, 145–46
Sankhya, 77
Sansar, 65–6, 141
Sarasudhanidhi, 41
Sarasvatichandra, 56, 90–91, 118–23, 125–27, 150, 186, 188, 193, 196, 197,
Sarasvati, Pandita Ramabai, 6
sati, 97, 107, 110, 124–26, 143–45, 147, 173
Satyartha Prakash, 154
Scrap Book, 24, 26, 56–57, 74–75, 84–91, 121, 123–24, 126, 181, 186, 190, 192, 193, 197
Seditious Meetings Bill, 140
Senapati, Fakir Mohan, 166, 203
Shastri, Hannukund, 140
Shastri, Pandit Vishnu, 81–82
Shiv Prasad, Raja, 42, 52, 60–61, 131, 183
Shraddhananda, Swami, *see* Munshiram
Shri Bharat Dharma Mahamandala, 138
Shribharat Dharmma, 146, 201
social consciousness, Indian, 1–2, 5, 7, 10, 17;
 and the West, 14
 tradition, 5, 7, 9–10, 14, 17–18
social reconstruction, 7–9; *see also* reform
Stotra Pancharatna, 96
'Stree Seva Paddhati', 98
Suchal-Shiksha, 46, 184
Sumanonjali, 29
swaraj, 7, 12–13, 53, 59

Tagore, Debendranath, 164
Tagore, G. M., 6
Tagore, Rabindranath, 112, 127, 164, 198, 203
Tempest, The, 159–60
Thakore, B. K., 62–63, 69–70
Tilak, 48
Tilak, Rev. Narayan Vaman, 6

Townsend, 62
tradition, and colonialism, 10–12, 128
 modernity, 2–14
Tripathi, Govardhanram Madhavram, 23–27, 55–58, 74–77, 83–92, 111, 118–21, 123–27, 150, 170–71, 190, 193;
 and views
 on British rule, 55–56
 joint family, 84–92
 widow marriage, 111, 124
 women, 119; *see also* reform, revivalism
Tulsidas, 58
Twadiya Samaj, 34

Udiya Swatantra Bhasha Noy, 166–67
Upadhyaya, Chaudhari Pandit Badari Narayan, *see* 'Premghan'
Upanishads, 69, 75
Urdu, 137–38, 151–52, 158
Utilitarianism, 76, 86, 92
Utkal Bhramanam, 167
Utkal Dipika, 166
Utkal Gatha, 168
Utkal Samaj, 169
Utkal Sammilani, 168, 169, 204

Vaidiki Himsa Himsa Na Bhavati, 95, 116, 196
varna, *see* caste
Vaishnava saints, Muslim, 130–31
Vaishnavism, 138
'Vaishnavism and India', 138
Vedas, 6, 103, 154, 195
'vernacular mind', 13
Vicissitudes of Aryan Civilization in India, The, 63, 188
Victoria, Queen, 28, 32–33, 38, 53–55, 61
Vidyasagar, Ishvarchandra, 6, 81–83, 90, 107, 109, 116–18, 126, 179, 192, 196, 197; and views on
 joint family, 90
 widow marriage, 6, 81–83, 109, 126
Vijay Singh, 64–65
Vishabriksha, 111–16, 118, 126–27
Vishasya Vishamaushadham, 32, 59–60, 186

Wedderburn, 75
western influences, *see* 'English poetry'
Westernization, *see* modernity
'Whose Gujarat?', 170, 172
Widow Marriage Act, 107–8, 111

widow marriage, 6, 40, 93–96, 103, 107–11, 116–17, 119–28, 143; and
Bankimchandra Chatterjee, 111, 116–17
Gopalrao Hari Deshmukh, 80
Govardhanram Tripathi, 111, 124
Ishvarchandra Vidyasagar, 6, 81–83, 109, 126
Mahadev Govind Ranade, 80–82
Pratapnarayan Misra, 107–11

Radhacharan Goswami, 103, 108–9, 111
Widow Remarriage Association, 80
women, Indian, 98, 100–4, 124–25; and views of
Balkrishna Bhatt, 99, 101
Bankimchandra Chatterjee, 111
Bharatendu Harishchandra, 95, 97–98, 125
Govardhanram Tripathi, 118–19
Rabindranath Tagore, 127; *see also* widow marriage

Yamalok Ki Yatra, 41, 102–3, 106, 182, 195
Yamuna Paryatan, 107
Young Bengal, 6

For Product Safety Concerns and Information please contact our EU representative GPSR@taylorandfrancis.com
Taylor & Francis Verlag GmbH, Kaufingerstraße 24, 80331 München, Germany

www.ingramcontent.com/pod-product-compliance
Lightning Source LLC
Chambersburg PA
CBHW071352290426
44108CB00014B/1519